The Actual Art of Governing

The Actual Art of Governing

Justice Robert H. Jackson's Concurring Opinion in the Steel Seizure Case

GERARD N. MAGLIOCCA

OXFORD
UNIVERSITY PRESS

OXFORD
UNIVERSITY PRESS

Oxford University Press is a department of the University of Oxford.
It furthers the University's objective of excellence in research, scholarship,
and education by publishing worldwide. Oxford is a registered trade mark of
Oxford University Press in the UK and in certain other countries.

Published in the United States of America by Oxford University Press
198 Madison Avenue, New York, NY 10016, United States of America.

Library of Congress Cataloging-in-Publication Data
Names: Magliocca, Gerard N. author
Title: The actual art of governing : Justice Robert H. Jackson's concurring opinion
in the steel seizure case / Gerard N. Magliocca.
Description: New York, NY : Oxford University Press, 2025. |
Includes bibliographical references and index.
Identifiers: LCCN 2025019925 (print) | LCCN 2025019926 (ebook) |
ISBN 9780197768532 hardback | ISBN 9780197768556 epub | ISBN 9780197768563
Subjects: LCSH: Jackson, Robert H., 1892-1954 | Judicial opinions–United States | Concurring opinions–United States | Executive-legislative relations–United States | Truman, Harry S., 1884-1972 | War and emergency powers–United States | Steel industry and trade–Law and legislation–United States | Strikes and lockouts–Law and legislation–United States | Korean War, 1950-1953 | Youngstown Sheet and Tube Company–Trials, litigation, etc. |
Sawyer, Charles, 1887-1979–Trials, litigation, etc.
Classification: LCC KF213.J3 M34 2025 (print) | LCC KF213.J3 (ebook) |
DDC 342.73/044–dc23/eng/20250424
LC record available at https://lccn.loc.gov/2025019925
LC ebook record available at https://lccn.loc.gov/2025019926

DOI: 10.1093/9780197768563.001.0001

The manufacturer's authorized representative in the EU for product safety is
Oxford University Press España S.A., Parque Empresarial San Fernando de Henares,
Avenida de Castilla, 2 – 28830 Madrid (www.oup.es/en or product.safety@oup.com).
OUP España S.A. also acts as importer into Spain of products made by the manufacturer.

For Bruce Ackerman

All we have of freedom, all we use or know–
This our fathers bought for us long and long ago.
Ancient Right unnoticed as the breath we draw–
Leave to live by no man's leave, underneath the Law.
Lance and torch and tumult, steel and grey-goose wing
Wrenched it, inch and ell and all, slowly from the king.
Till our fathers 'stablished, after bloody years,
How our King is one with us, first among his peers.
So they bought us freedom–not at little cost–
Wherefore must we watch the King, lest our gain be lost.

Rudyard Kipling, "The Old Issue"

Contents

PART 3: RESULTS

Acknowledgments

More than two decades ago, I was in an old bookstore in Washington, DC and stumbled upon a first edition of Robert H. Jackson's book on *The Struggle for Judicial Supremacy.* When I opened the book, I saw to my surprise Justice Jackson's signature on the inside page, with an inscription written to James G. Wilson "with pleasant recollection of our association in the Department of Justice and with high regards and good wishes." This autographed copy is now the jewel of my library. The thought of writing my own book about Jackson proved irresistible. But instead of attempting a biography, I decided to examine one of his greatest opinions in a constitutional case that every law student reads.

Let me begin by thanking the Library of Congress, the Harvard Law Library, the Hoover Institution, the Robert H. Jackson Center, the Truman Presidential Library, and Columbia University for assisting me with remote and in-person research into their archives. I was keen to include some political cartoons in this book, but that would not have been possible without the assistance of Roberta Newman and copyright permissions from the Library of Congress, the Herb Block Foundation, Getty Images, and the *Albany Times-Union.* I am grateful to the *Green Bag 2d* journal for permission to reprint much of my essay on "Robert Jackson's Non-Delegation Doctrine" from its March 2022 issue. The same appreciation goes to the *Journal of Supreme Court History* for letting me reprint much of my article on "The Untold Story of Robert H. Jackson's *Youngstown* Concurrence," from its March 2025 issue. John Q. Barrett and Adam White provided insights from their own copious Jackson research that proved invaluable. And I received thoughtful and challenging comments on the first draft of the book from Bruce Ackerman, Carlo Andreani, Richard Primus, and Brad Snyder.

My most important debts, as always, are to the Indiana University Robert H. McKinney School of Law and to my family. Normally I pay tribute to my faculty colleagues in my books, but this time I want to salute my students who patiently sat through a Robert H. Jackson seminar and helped me work through some of these ideas. My wife Preeti and my daughter Avika know what they mean to me. Words fail me only when I try to express just how much joy they bring to me.

Introduction
A Dazzling Solo

In a speech at the University of North Carolina in 1937, Assistant Attorney General Robert H. Jackson said, "We may well remind ourselves that there is not only a past and a present—there is also a future. And we are among its founders."[1] Justice Jackson's 1952 concurrence in *Youngstown Sheet and Tube Company v. Sawyer*, also known as the *Steel Seizure Case*, is the founding constitutional text for the separation of powers between Congress and the President.[2]

In *Youngstown*, the Supreme Court held that President Harry S. Truman violated the law when he seized and operated the nation's steel mills to prevent a strike during the Korean War.[3] Chief Justice William H. Rehnquist, who was clerking for Jackson on the Court when the concurrence was written, would later call his Justice's opinion "[a] 'state paper' of the same order as the best of the Federalist Papers, or of John Marshall's opinions for the Court."[4] Professor Sanford Levinson describes the *Youngstown* concurrence as "the greatest opinion in our 215-year history of constitutional opinions."[5] Though written by one Justice speaking only for himself, Jackson's opinion is now required reading in every constitutional law class and a pillar of landmark Supreme Court rulings such as *United States v. Nixon* and *Trump v. United States*.[6] But icons attract skeptics. Some scholars contend that the *Youngstown* concurrence is an "empty vessel" that "solves practically nothing."[7] Another critic calls the opinion "elegant, but ultimately unhelpful and misleading" and "a prime reason modern separation-of-powers jurisprudence is in such disarray."[8] One point is undeniable: Justice Jackson's *Youngstown* concurrence is inescapable.

Jackson's opinion captures the fundamental truth that the President is bound by law but always seeking to escape.[9] Frustration with congressional gridlock on major problems tempts presidents to act first and seek permission later, or not at all. International crises may make presidents believe that they cannot follow the law without jeopardizing national security. Domestic emergencies, real or imagined, lead to calls for exceptions to settled rules. The prospect of partisan advantage may lead legal guardians in all three

The Actual Art of Governing. Gerard N. Magliocca, Oxford University Press. © Oxford University Press (2025).
DOI: 10.1093/9780197768563.003.0001

branches to look the other way when a president of their party acts alone. And sometimes there are unprecedented situations where no law exists and the cry for executive action becomes irresistible.

To help resolve these recurring dilemmas, Jackson crafted a legal framework built on what he called "the actual art of governing." He learned that art through his personal experience as a presidential adviser in tumultuous times, by observing long-standing practices between Congress and the White House, and by learning from the traditions of other successful and unsuccessful constitutional democracies. Jackson understood that there is a substantial difference between a written Constitution and the way that government works. His *Youngstown* concurrence was an ambitious attempt to update our Constitution for a new age of active government and global leadership. Jackson was a creative force behind many parts of the New Deal before he joined the Court and was the architect of the Nazi war-crimes trial held immediately following World War II.[10] He brought that same imagination to bear on how a presidential office designed by the Framers with drastically different assumptions about the federal government should be understood in a world of mass communications and atomic weapons. Though he never served in Congress, Jackson's opinion was also sensitive to Congress's role in regulating the President, even on matters of war and peace. His guiding light was the rule of law as established by legislative deliberations, which he described in the concurrence as the essence of free government, even with "all its defects, delays and inconveniences."

While the concurrence is now famous, lawyers often misunderstand or ignore what Jackson said. Some think that, once he joined the Supreme Court, he changed his view on whether presidents could seize private property in the interests of national security. But he did not. Some assume that the opinion says that courts must decide the legality of executive action taken in what the Justice called the "zone of twilight" where there are no relevant statutes. But the opinion does not say that. Some emphasize the limits that the concurrence placed on presidential authority. But they miss the vital point that Jackson effectively eliminated the need for Congress to declare war in order for the President to take military action overseas. Some believe that the opinion supports the legality of any legislative grant of emergency power to the executive. But the concurrence's analysis of that issue was actually far more sophisticated and rested on a constitutional premise that is no longer valid. Finally, Jackson summed up his opinion by stating that the

President's informal powers were so great that the Supreme Court should not rule against Congress in doubtful cases. But the Court has never cited the *Youngstown* concurrence for this central lesson.

Turning from substance to style, the influence of Jackson's solo is remarkable because his opinion breaks all the rules for judicial writing in the United States. Judges almost never inject their personal experience into their rulings, because doing so might undermine the principle that law should be neutral and objective. Jackson's concurrence instead drew openly on his insights as President Franklin D. Roosevelt's solicitor general and attorney general. Judges almost always rely on text, history, and court doctrine to interpret the Constitution. Jackson's opinion dismissed those tools and instead relied mainly on structural and practical considerations. Judges rarely look at foreign constitutions or discuss political partisanship in their decisions. The *Youngstown* concurrence did both. Judges do not usually talk about Hitler and quote Napoleon in their opinions. Jackson did. What was behind this extraordinary method and rhetoric? Is Jackson's *Youngstown* opinion great because of or despite these unusual choices?

The Actual Art of Governing is the first comprehensive account of Justice Jackson's concurring opinion. The book begins with a discussion of the Justice and the professional experience that informed his thinking about executive power, including some surprising episodes that arose during his tenure as solicitor general and attorney general. The story then turns to the details of the *Youngstown* case and a behind-the-scenes look at how Jackson drafted his opinion, including the revelation that some portions were taken without attribution from a 1937 Justice Department memo written by another lawyer. The second part of the book consists of several stand-alone essays on the opinion's leading themes, such as Jackson's pragmatism, the role of the commander in chief, and emergency powers. These chapters track the order in which the themes appear in the concurrence. The third and final part turns to the opinion's impact. In the 1970s, the concurrence became the gold standard for judges, academics, and Congress because of President Nixon's Watergate abuses. After that, the concurrence was implemented by Justice (later Chief Justice) Rehnquist, elevating an opinion that, in a remarkable coincidence, had been written during his clerkship by his Justice. And Rehnquist's own law clerk John Roberts would take up that torch when he became Chief Justice of the United States, but this time by reimagining Jackson's opinion as a shield against the criminal prosecution of Donald Trump. There is much to explain and explore.

The Actual Art of Governing can be read differently depending on the reader's familiarity with *Youngstown*. Many law students, lawyers, and constitutional experts know the concurrence by heart. They should feel free to skim or skip chapter 3, which simply reproduces the entire text of the opinion. Those who do not know much about the case should probably read the book from beginning to end, as the first two chapters provide useful background information. But jumping ahead to chapter 3 and reading the opinion first is also fine. Jackson's writing remains fresh long after he last put pen to paper.

The concurring opinion's most powerful idea is that the Constitution must be read with a practical eye. The same is true for Jackson's concurrence. This generation of founders must examine his work anew and think about whether and how his vision is suited to our times.

PART 1
ELEMENTS

1
The Justice

Robert Jackson learned the law from the ground up. Born in 1892 on a Pennsylvania farm, he was raised in Jamestown, a small town in western New York.[1] He did not attend college and spent only one year at Albany Law School. Jackson became a lawyer by serving as an apprentice to two local attorneys. Apprenticeship was the standard training method for lawyers until the twentieth century, but Jackson would be the last Supreme Court Justice without a law degree.[2] After completing the apprenticeship, he built a successful general practice in New York State.

Jackson became active in state politics, and he first met Franklin D. Roosevelt when FDR was a state legislator. In 1934, President Roosevelt persuaded Jackson to join the New Deal as counsel to the Bureau of Internal Revenue. He quickly took on a high-profile case as the lead attorney in the civil tax trial of Andrew Mellon, the former treasury secretary and one of the richest men in America.[3] By 1937, Jackson was a trusted presidential adviser and the head of the Antitrust Division in the Justice Department. He won acclaim for his testimony before the Senate Judiciary Committee on behalf of Roosevelt's court-packing plan, which one journalist called "one of the ablest and most eloquent" presentations by the Administration.[4] In February 1938, Jackson was confirmed as solicitor general, the lawyer who represents the United States before the Supreme Court. He is considered one the greatest advocates to hold that office.[5] Justice Louis Brandeis allegedly said that Jackson should be solicitor general for life.[6]

Like many leaders who lacked a formal education, Jackson was a well-read man. He is often described as the best writer ever to sit on the Supreme Court, in part because he rejected jargon in favor of a plain style that drew on poetry, literary sources, and popular culture.[7] He was also a master of condensing complex ideas into memorable quotes. His opinion in *West Virginia State School Board of Education v. Barnette*, holding that children in public schools could not be required to salute the flag, is an excellent example.[8] In *Barnette* Jackson conceded that the "task of translating the majestic generalities of the Bill of Rights, conceived as part of the pattern

The Actual Art of Governing. Gerard N. Magliocca, Oxford University Press. © Oxford University Press (2025).
DOI: 10.1093/9780197768563.003.0002

of liberal government in the eighteenth century, into concrete restraints on officials dealing with the problems of the twentieth century, is one to disturb self-confidence."[9] But "[i]f there is any fixed star in our constitutional constellation, it is that no official, high or petty, can prescribe what shall be orthodox in politics, nationalism, religion, or other matters of opinion or force citizens to confess by word or act their faith therein."[10] "Those who begin coercive elimination of dissent," he warned, "soon find themselves exterminating dissenters. Compulsory unification of opinion achieves only the unanimity of the graveyard."[11] Jackson would bring that eloquence to bear in *Youngstown*, translating the majestic generalities of Article II—what he called "an Eighteenth-Century sketch of a government hoped for"—for the Cold War.

Jackson's education in the school of life also probably led him to trust experience more than theory. Starting in 1938, as Roosevelt's solicitor general and then attorney general, he found himself at the center of many contentious debates within the executive branch about the scope of presidential power. After he was named to the Court in 1941, he was called upon to judge controversial actions by the Roosevelt administration taken to wage the Second World War. Then in 1945, President Truman appointed Justice Jackson as the chief US prosecutor for the first Nuremberg Trial of the Nazi leadership. These experiences taught Jackson many lessons in the actual art of governing that he contemplated while writing the *Youngstown* concurrence.

Washington National Airport

Jackson's first brush with the indefinite nature of executive authority came when the President wanted to build a new national airport. The old airport (named after Herbert Hoover) was described by Jackson as "a pasture intersected by a highway. When a plane came in, they had to close the road to traffic and open it again after the plane had landed. It was dangerous and inadequate, and everyone regarded it as long behind the times."[12] But Congress could not agree on where a new airport should be located. Frustrated with this deadlock, Roosevelt told Jackson at a cabinet meeting to find the money and break ground "a week from Monday."[13] Jackson somehow scrounged up the money from untapped sources, and the airport (now Reagan National) was built, as he later said, "without congressional authorization or appropriation."[14]

Figure 1.1 Attorney General Robert H. Jackson. Library of Congress, Prints & Photographs Division, photograph by Harris & Ewing, [LC-DIG-hec-28932].

Reflecting on this affair, Jackson was ambivalent about its legality. He wrote that "[t]he President's action in this matter was an instance in which, although the President acts beyond the Constitution, he invades no private right and therefore is probably not subject to an injunction by a court. Here was a case where he took nobody's property. He spent some public money, but the Supreme Court long ago held that that could not be enjoined." Jackson went on: "There was no basis on which anyone could stop him, even though he was perhaps exceeding the powers of his office. But I do not say that he was exceeding the powers of his office—I would certainly go a very long way to find authority to sustain that kind of an exercise of power where the congressional process seemed stalled." Was the National Airport unconstitutional? The fact that flights still land there says that the answer is no. But Jackson was never sure, and he would reconsider the airport example in *Youngstown* when thinking about what lay within the "zone of twilight."

Wiretapping for National Security

After Jackson was named attorney general in 1940, he was presented with a sensitive problem about federal eavesdropping authority. In 1939, the Supreme Court held in *Nardone v. United States* that the executive branch was not authorized by Congress to tap phones.[15] Jackson complied with this decision and sought congressional authorization for wiretapping, but President Roosevelt was unhappy. The attorney general recalled that Roosevelt "said he could not believe that the Supreme Court could mean that the enemies of this country could use its communication system and not be detected."[16] When the Administration's lobbying efforts on Capitol Hill failed to get immediate results, the President sent Jackson a secret memo authorizing him to conduct surveillance "of persons suspected of subversive activities against the Government of the United States, including suspected spies."[17] Though Jackson would later say that he "had not liked this approach," he implemented Roosevelt's directive and was confident that FBI Director J. Edgar Hoover "was careful to remain within those bounds" set by the President.[18] But the story was more complex. Jackson spent the next year pressing Congress for wiretapping legislation without revealing that wiretapping was ongoing or that he was fighting with Hoover over the proper scope of electronic surveillance.[19]

Nardone forced Jackson to consider whether national-security concerns give the President authority to act on his own. He explained that this was "[t]he only case that I recall in which [Roosevelt] declined to abide by a decision of the Supreme Court."[20] In other words, Jackson knew that FDR was either stretching or breaking the law. Worse still, this executive authority was exercised without any outside scrutiny. With war underway in Europe, however, blindness to foreign threats posed a serious risk. In Jackson's view, Congress was to blame for refusing to respond to *Nardone* with a new wiretapping statute: "They closed their eyes entirely to the fact that without

Figure 1.2 President Franklin D. Roosevelt signing the Lend-Lease Act in 1941. FDR and Attorney General Jackson disagreed about the constitutionality of the Act's legislative veto provision. Library of Congress. Associated Press, 1941.

the authorization they would have wire-tapping without responsibility, and with the authorization they would have wire-tapping with responsibility."[21] Jackson's insight that congressional inaction to a serious problem would lead to more executive power in practice would also find its way into the *Youngstown* concurrence.

The Destroyer Deal

A public contest over unilateral presidential power ensued when Roosevelt decided on his own to trade American warships to Great Britain for long-term lease options on British military bases in the Western Hemisphere.[22] In the summer of 1940, Britain was in dire straits. Shipping losses from Nazi submarine attacks and the disaster at Dunkirk compelled Prime Minister Winston Churchill to plead with FDR to send Britain fifty or sixty old destroyers.[23] Since the President could not give or sell vessels without congressional authorization, the Administration hit on the idea of "exchanging" the ships for something of military value: namely, options for long-term leases on naval bases in Canada and in the Caribbean. Attorney General Jackson was asked to provide a legal opinion explaining why the White House could make this trade.[24] His answer was that Congress gave the President the power to dispose of the destroyers if "the consummation of the transaction does not impair or weaken the total defense of the United States."[25] The "destroyers-for-bases agreement," or "destroyer deal," is an example of how statutes can supplement or restrict executive power, and this was the proposition for which Jackson would cite that precedent in *Youngstown*.

The Destroyer Deal also shows that statutes must be construed and that those who construe them enjoy considerable discretion. The attorney general's opinion found the statutory authority for the President in an 1883 Act of Congress that regulated the disposal of vessels that were unfit for further use.[26] But the destroyers were obviously *not* unfit for further use, as the British fleet was desperate to use them. How, then, did the statute authorize the transfer of these vessels? Jackson's answer was that the final clause of the relevant section gave the President the right to dispose of any vessel, by saying, "[N]o vessel of the Navy shall hereafter be sold in any other manner than herein provided, or for less than such appraised value, unless the President of the United States direct in writing." According to Jackson, this clause meant that the President could dispose of any vessel, even one still fit for use. A better interpretation was that the clause gave the President discretion only to sell vessels unfit for service.[27] Nevertheless, the deal proved popular and was not challenged in court, in part because most people thought that Roosevelt received much more from Britain than he gave away.

The North American Aviation Seizure

Jackson's practical schooling continued with the President's decision to take over North American Aviation's airplane factory in California, which produced planes for the military.[28] In June 1941 the factory's union went on strike seeking higher wages. There were claims that the strike was driven by communist activists, though this was a common criticism of strikes in this era. Four days into the strike, Roosevelt issued an executive order stating that this was "a situation seriously detrimental to the defense of the United States. Because of this situation, as President and Commander in Chief of the armed forces of the United States, I have determined that this plant must be reopened at once. I have therefore directed that the Secretary of War shall immediately take charge of the plant."

Attorney General Jackson issued a "statement" (rather than an opinion) defending the President's authority.[29] He said that the seizure was justified by "the aggregate of the Presidential powers derived from the Constitution itself and from statutes enacted by the Congress," though he did not cite any statutes. Jackson argued that, by protecting government property in the factory and by supplying the needs of the Army, the Navy, and some foreign nations, the President was carrying out the mandate of Congress. In doing this, Roosevelt could draw on "that wide discretion as to method vested in him by the Constitution for the purpose of executing the laws." The attorney general also cited the Constitution's Commander-in-Chief Clause, stating that "These weapons for the protection of the continued existence of the Nation are placed in his sole command and the implication is clear that he should not allow them to become paralyzed by failure to obtain supplies for which Congress has appropriated the money." Finally, Jackson claimed that "[t]he situation at the North American plant more nearly resembles an insurrection than a labor strike. . . . The distinction between loyal labor leaders and those who are following the Communist Party line is easy to observe." "There can be no doubt," he said, "that the duty constitutionally and inherently rested upon the President to exert his civil and military, as well as his moral, authority to keep the defense effort of the United States a going concern."

In 1952, the Truman Administration cited the North American Aviation seizure as precedent for its authority to seize the nation's steel mills to support the Korean War.[30] Justice Jackson would disagree, stating in his

Youngstown concurrence that "I do not regard [North American Aviation] as a precedent for this, but, even if I did, I should not bind present judicial judgment by earlier partisan advocacy." Jackson's opinion drafts explained why he was right to advise FDR that the seizure of private property for military production was lawful, and why he was right to conclude that Truman's seizure of private property for the same reason was unlawful. In the concurrence he also depicted his tenure as attorney general as "partisan"; however, the adjective was somewhat misleading, as Jackson did not always carry out his President's requests.

The Lend-Lease Act and Legislative Vetoes

The final executive experience that shaped Jackson's thinking in *Youngstown* was his private debate with Roosevelt over the constitutionality of the legislative veto.[31] In 1941, Congress passed the Lend-Lease Act, which gave FDR sweeping authority to provide Britain with military aid.[32] The Act stated that this extraordinary power would end after two years, or sooner if a concurrent resolution was passed by a majority in each house of Congress.[33] A concurrent resolution, unlike a bill, cannot be vetoed by the president. Though Roosevelt told Jackson that a provision "which seeks to repeal legislation by concurrent resolution" was "clearly unconstitutional,"[34] he signed the Lend-Lease Act anyway, because the Act was vital for national security and could not be passed without the concurrent-resolution clause.[35] Nonetheless, he asked Jackson to write an opinion explaining why such a "legislative veto" unlawfully bypassed the ordinary process for repealing a statute and should not become a standard clause in legislation.

Jackson agreed with FDR that the legislative veto strengthened Congress (at least in theory), but he was not convinced by Roosevelt's legal claim. "[W]as it unconstitutional? That was a different question, which we discussed over and over. The question on which my doubts were not fully satisfied never bothered the President in the least. It seemed to me to depend on whether the provision was to be considered as a reservation or limitation by which the granted power would expire to terminate on the contingency of a concurrent resolution or was to be regarded as authorizing a repeal by concurrent resolution."[36] In other words, if Congress could limit a grant of executive authority to two years or through substantive criteria, why could a grant not also be limited through a procedure like a concurrent resolution? The alternative might be that Congress would refuse to delegate critical authority to the President or to his officials. Moreover, the legislative veto was now a fixed, if irregular, practice in major legislation.

Since the attorney general would not write the opinion that FDR wanted, Roosevelt wrote one himself. Jackson recalled: "The document probably is the only one of its kind in our history—it is extraordinary for the President to render a legal opinion to the Attorney General."[37] In this opinion, FDR said: "The Constitution contains no provision whereby the Congress may legislate by concurrent resolution without the approval of the President. The only instance in which a bill may become law without the approval of the President is when the President vetoes a bill and it is then repassed by two-thirds vote in each House. It is too clear for argument that action repealing an existing Act itself constitutes an Act of Congress and, therefore, is subject to the foregoing requirements."[38] The President asked Jackson to keep the opinion under wraps, but requested that this "should be published some day as an official document, and I leave the method thereof to your discretion."[39] This was unusual in that Roosevelt made his opinion an unofficial secret document rather than an official classified document.[40] When the *Youngstown* case came to the Court, Justice Jackson would consider whether that was the appropriate occasion to reveal the President's covert opinion.

Military Detentions

After Jackson was appointed to the Supreme Court in 1941, he began considering presidential power from a more detached perspective. America's entry into the Second World War led to another round of broad executive actions, most famously the military orders requiring the exclusion of Japanese-American citizens from the West Coast, and then their detention.[41] After struggling with these questions for two years, Justice Jackson dissented in *Korematsu v. United States*, saying that the exclusion policy was unconstitutional but that the courts should not get involved.[42] This ambivalence on presidential power and the role of courts in difficult cases would appear again in Jackson's *Youngstown* opinion.

The Supreme Court's first encounter with President Roosevelt in wartime came in Ex Parte *Quirin*.[43] In 1942, a German U-boat landed eight Nazi agents in the United States to sabotage civilian installations. The saboteurs were arrested and put on trial before a military commission established by the President. They petitioned for a writ of habeas corpus and the Justices agreed to hear their case. Through a back channel, Roosevelt allegedly made it known that he would not obey a judicial order to turn the saboteurs over to a civil court.[44] After oral argument, the Court issued a brief order upholding the President's authority and denying the petition. A few days later, the military commission declared the saboteurs guilty and sentenced them to death. Six were executed, while two received long prison sentences. Three months later, the Court issued a unanimous opinion explaining why these proceedings were lawful.

As became his habit in significant cases, Jackson wrote a draft opinion in *Quirin* to test his reasoning. There was a settled practice for presidents to use military commissions for captured enemies, and "I see no indication that Congress has intended to confine the President's discretion in dealing with captured invaders or intended to confer any rights on them." He also said that "[t]he seizure and trial of these prisoners is not in pursuit of the functions of internal government of the country," which would pose a different issue. More important, the Justice was not convinced that the courts should review military decisions at all. "I press this view," he said, "because in the long run it seems to me that we have no more important duty than to keep clear and separate the lines of responsibility and duty of the judicial and of the executive/military arms of government. Merger of the two is the end of liberty as we in this country have known it. If we are uncompromisingly to discountenance military intervention in civil justice, we would do well to refuse to meddle with military measures dealing with captured unlawful enemy belligerents." Jackson did not publish this opinion but would refer to military commissions in *Youngstown*.[45]

Soon the Court heard the first case challenging the President's policy about Japanese-Americans. In *Hirabayashi v. United States*, a citizen was convicted in a civil court of violating a military curfew established for people of Japanese ancestry.[46] The Court upheld the conviction on the ground that the curfew was authorized by an act of Congress and did not violate the Constitution.[47] Once again, Jackson wrote a draft opinion that he did not publish. This time he began with: "The Court is sustaining a novel exercise of the war power, which I regard as the Achilles Heel of our constitutional system." He said that since the war power is "[g]rounded in necessity, the power must be measured chiefly by necessity." While he did not rule out judicial review, "the consequences of a clash between judicial power and the war power, particularly in the midst of a foreign war, would be so grave that so far as is consistent with our duty we should minimize occasions upon which it might happen." As in *Quirin*, Jackson's solution was that the Court "should refrain altogether from considering the validity of these military orders." This was "a case where courts are asked to become auxiliary to the military power by using criminal procedure to sanction military orders." "But if we review and approve" military orders, "we accept what were otherwise an incident into the body of law as a principle." In other words, Jackson thought that a "construction of the due process clause which will make it approve this order was ultimately a more dangerous thing than the promulgation of this order." Thus, "I would leave the political departments of government to face the accountability without embarrassing their lawful acts by litigation or rationalizing their questionable ones by judicial decision." *Hirabayashi*, like the *Quirin* decision, would make an appearance in Jackson's *Youngstown* concurrence.

Korematsu upheld the criminal conviction of a Japanese-American who violated the military exclusion policy.[48] This time Jackson did dissent. As in his *Hirabayashi* draft, Jackson reasoned that the exclusion was unconstitutional but that the Court should not have reviewed the case.[49] "A military order is not apt to last longer than the military emergency," he explained.[50] "But once a judicial order rationalizes such an order to show that it conforms to the Constitution, or rather rationalizes the Constitution to show that the Constitution sanctions such an order, the Court for all time has validated the principle of racial discrimination in criminal procedure and of transplanting American citizens. The principle then lies about like a loaded weapon ready for the hand of any authority that can bring forward a plausible claim of urgent need." "I should hold," he wrote, "that a civil court cannot be made to enforce an order which violates constitutional limitations even if it is a reasonable exercise of military authority."[51] He concluded with this ominous note: "If the people ever let command of the war power fall into irresponsible and unscrupulous hands, the courts wield no power equal to its restraint."[52] Jackson would revisit *Korematsu* in his *Youngstown* deliberations and use his concurring opinion to expand on his thought that the courts could not always be relied upon to protect the constitutional balance.

Nuremberg Prosecutor

Jackson's final searing experience with executive authority came at Nuremberg. In 1945, Jackson took a sabbatical from the Supreme Court to lead the American prosecution of the surviving Nazi leadership.[53] He found himself in the position of designing the proceeding and then presenting the case against the accused. In undertaking these unprecedented tasks, Jackson demonstrated his ability to think panoramically about legal principles. He relied almost entirely on functional judgments about issues such as how to marry Anglo-American criminal law and procedure with the civil-law traditions of continental Europe represented by France, Germany, and the Soviet Union. In an early progress report to President Truman, he stated, "I am not disturbed by the lack of precedent for the inquiry we propose to conduct."[54] Though many other lawyers were deeply disturbed by the lack of precedent (Chief Justice Harlan Fiske Stone privately called the trial "a high-grade lynching"),[55] that difference of opinion just highlights the freedom from formalism that would be a hallmark of Jackson's *Youngstown* concurrence.

Jackson's opening address to what he called a "novel and experimental" tribunal is now hailed as a rhetorical masterpiece. The speech closed with a line from Rudyard Kipling stating that all people should have "leave to live by no man's leave, underneath the law,"[56] which would reappear near the end of the *Youngstown* concurrence. During the trial, Jackson cross-examined leading defendants and proved beyond doubt the scale of Hitler's horrors. Late in the trial, Jackson wrote an essay in *The New York Times* in which he observed that "Friends of liberty will find grim instruction in the rise of the Nazi Party, its methods of seizure of power, and its establishment of dictatorial control over the German people. Jurists will find admonition in the way the rule of law was set aside, an independent judiciary destroyed and party and class use of the courts as instruments of political policy was established."[57] Nuremberg also gave Jackson a front-row seat to America's new role as a global leader and as the Soviet Union's chief rival. The tensions between the Soviets and the other Allied powers during the trial were chalked up at the time to differences between their respective legal systems.[58] But in a 1951 speech Jackson would warn that "[w]e can no longer take either security or liberty for granted. The best that we can now hope for seems to be a prolonged period of international tension and rumors of war, with war itself as the ever-threatening alternative."[59]

Jackson's colleagues thought that he was a changed man after Nuremberg.[60] The crimes of the Holocaust that he was forced to confront for a year made him more wary of free expression and executive authority. In a 1947 speech, he explained: "It should be known to all Americans what the early symptoms of totalitarianism are, for only in its early stages can such a movement be stopped by peaceful means."[61] His subsequent opinions dwelled more often on the lessons of fascism.[62] For instance, in one dissent he quoted *Mein Kampf* to highlight the dangers of radical speech.[63] Concurring in the conspiracy convictions of American communists in 1950, he warned that "[t]otalitarian groups here and abroad [have] perfected the technique of creating private paramilitary organizations to coerce both the public government and its citizens."[64] When the Truman Administration invoked emergency power to justify its action in *Youngstown*, Jackson could not avoid thinking about the rise of Nazi Germany.

In sum, Robert Jackson's view of executive power (like the rest of his philosophy) was a work in progress. His unusually broad experience put him on every side of the issue at one point or another. Jackson would not be forced to reconcile the many versions of himself until *Youngstown*.

2
The Case

In April 1952, both the Korean War and the talks between the nation's steel companies and their unions were at a stalemate.[1] President Truman faced the prospect of a strike that would halt steel production and put American troops at risk. When mediation failed to produce a settlement, the President issued an executive order directing Secretary of Commerce Charles Sawyer to take over the steel mills and keep them running while the labor negotiations continued.[2] The steel companies sued seeking an injunction. Within a month, *Youngstown* was heard by the Supreme Court. Justice Jackson joined the Court's majority in holding that the President could not seize and operate the steel mills on his own authority. Understanding why requires careful consideration of Truman's other options, the District Court proceedings, the Supreme Court arguments, and the opinions of the other Justices.

The President's Unpalatable Choices

President Truman was very unpopular when he seized the steel mills. At the end of March, he announced that he would not run for reelection.[3] He made that decision in part because his approval rating was under 30 percent and he had lost the New Hampshire primary.[4] The quagmire in Korea was a factor in Truman's poor standing in the polls, but people were also unhappy about inflation and corruption scandals involving Administration officials.[5] In addition, the Democrats had held the White House for nearly twenty years, and this run of success, unprecedented for a political party since Reconstruction, inevitably led to voter fatigue.[6] In considering why the Court decided *Youngstown* against him, Truman's unpopularity cannot be ignored. Popular presidents tend to get their way at the Court; unpopular ones often do not.[7]

One of *Youngstown*'s lessons is that constitutional law often limits power by requiring officials to pursue their goals through less popular or more

The Actual Art of Governing. Gerard N. Magliocca, Oxford University Press. © Oxford University Press (2025).
DOI: 10.1093/9780197768563.003.0003

time-consuming means. There were options for the President to address the strike under acts of Congress, but all of them were deemed practically or politically unacceptable by the Truman Administration. First, the Labor Management Relations Act of 1947, better known as the Taft-Hartley Act, gave the President the power to seek a court injunction that would impose a cooling-off period for a strike that could "imperil the national health or safety."[8] But using the Taft-Hartley Act was a political nonstarter, because the law was enacted over President Truman's veto and its restrictions on labor organizing were poison to the unions that supported the Democratic Party.[9] Second, the Selective Service Act of 1948 allowed the President to place factory orders for the military and to take over those factories if the orders were not filled in a timely fashion.[10] The difficulties here were practical. Placing steel orders and waiting for them not to be filled would take time.[11] Moreover, the military needed finished steel products, not the steel itself, which made using the Selective Service Act nearly impossible.[12] Third, the Defense Production Act of 1950 gave the President power to exercise eminent domain through a court order to produce supplies "needed for the national defense."[13] But the Administration gave this option little consideration because of the complex procedures required to trigger the authority.[14] Finally, Truman could have asked Congress for new legislation authorizing a seizure, but there was no reason to think such legislation would pass in time, or indeed at all.

Instead, the President chose unilateral executive action, which solved his political problem and promised a swift resolution.[15] To emphasize the gravity of the situation, Truman gave a prime-time radio and television address on April 8 to explain his decision. "Tonight our country faces a grave danger. We are faced by the possibility that at midnight tonight the steel industry will be shut down. This must not happen."[16] "These are not normal times," he said. "These are times of crisis. We have been working and fighting to prevent the outbreak of world war. So far we have succeeded. The most important element in this successful struggle has been our defense program. If that is stopped, that situation can change overnight." Furthermore, "[w]ith American troops facing the enemy on the field of battle, I would not be living up to my oath of office if I failed to do whatever is required to provide them with the weapons and ammunition they need for their survival." Truman did not say exactly why he could order the seizure and operation of the steel mills. But in the executive order, he cited "the authority vested in me by the Constitution and laws of the United States, and as President of the United

Figure 2.1 President Harry S. Truman. Library of Congress. Edmonston Studio, 1945.

States and Commander in Chief of the armed forces of the United States."[17] The President then sent a message to Congress stating that new legislation to resolve the crisis was not "essential" but "might be very desirable."[18] At a press conference a week later, Truman was asked if he could seize newspapers and radio stations on his own in the interests of national security.[19] He replied: "Under similar circumstances, the President has to act for whatever is best for the country. That's the answer to your question."[20]

Figure 2.2 "Iron-Fisted Breach." Jerry Costello, *Knickerbocker News*, April 23, 1952. Times Union.

The Lawsuit in the District Court

Right after the President's speech, the steel firms brought a federal lawsuit in the District of Columbia to block Truman's action.[21] The case was ultimately assigned to Judge David A. Pine, who held a hearing on April 24.[22] Under questioning from Judge Pine, Assistant Attorney General Holmes

Baldridge made one gaffe after another. For instance, when Judge Pine asked if "the Executive has unlimited power in time of an emergency,"[23] Baldridge replied, "He has the power to take such action as is necessary to meet the emergency." Judge Pine followed up: "If the emergency is great, it is unlimited, is it?" Baldridge responded: "I suppose if you carry it to its logical conclusion, that is true. But I do want to point out that there are two limitations on the Executive power. One is the ballot box and the other is impeachment." Judge Pine then wanted to know if "the Executive determines the emergencies and the courts cannot even review whether it is an emergency." "That is correct," was the reply. *The Washington Post* led with a dramatic front-page headline: "U.S. Argues President Is Above Courts."[24]

Things went downhill from there. The next day Judge Pine asked Baldridge if the President could declare an emergency and seize Baldridge's house without any judicial review. He replied, "I would rather, Your Honor, not answer a case in that extremity." After more back-and-forth, Judge Pine posed the following question: "[W]hen the sovereign people adopted the Constitution, it enumerated the powers set up in the Constitution, limited the powers of the Congress and limited the powers of the judiciary, but it did not limit the powers of the Executive. Is that what you say?" "That is that way that we read Article II of the Constitution," was the reply. This time *The New York Times* led with "President's Power Is Not Restricted, Says U.S. Lawyer."[25] The Administration recognized that the hearing had been a debacle and issued a "clarification" stating that the President's powers are "limited, of course, by the provisions of the Constitution, particularly those that protect the rights of individuals."[26]

But the damage was done. Judge Pine granted an injunction on April 29 and declared the President's action unlawful.[27] He held that Article II did not give Truman the authority to seize the steel mills and that past examples of executive property seizures could not justify this one.[28] "I believe," Judge Pine wrote, "that the contemplated strike, if it came, with all its awful results, would be less injurious to the public than the injury which would flow from a timorous judicial recognition that there is some basis for this claim to unlimited and unrestrained Executive power."[29] Justice Jackson's senior law clerk, George Niebank, wrote in his *Youngstown* bench memo that "Pine went too far, but I am inclined to excuse him as being pushed into doing so by the extremes of [the Government's] arguments."[30] The D.C. Circuit stayed Judge Pine's injunction pending appeal, but the Supreme Court granted certiorari on May 3 rather than waiting for the appellate court to rule on the merits of the case.[31] Just nine days later, the briefs were filed and the Court heard oral argument.

The Supreme Court Argument

Anticipation was high when the Justices took the bench. Justice Felix Frankfurter told a friend that the courtroom looked like "the crowd waiting for the World Series."[32] The steel firms were represented by John W. Davis, a former solicitor general and a legendary advocate who had argued over 100 cases in the Supreme Court.[33] Making his presentation with few interruptions, Davis went out of his way to quote Judge Pine's exchanges with Assistant Attorney General Baldridge in the District Court, and twisted the knife by praising Baldridge's "commendable candor" in describing the President's claim of unlimited authority for emergencies,[34] stating that Truman was claiming "kingly prerogatives."[35] The actual solicitor general, Philip B. Perlman, received no such deference, and was instead peppered with questions by nearly all the Justices. Jackson complained afterward that the solicitor general had treated the Court like a jury.[36]

The United States relied on the North American Aviation seizure and Attorney General Jackson's justification of that action as precedent for Truman's action. "Turning to the record," Jackson recalled, "it was a shock to realize that of those who participated in the conference at which that decision was made, I am the only survivor."[37] When Perlman brought up this example, Jackson asked him, "Are you not taking a good deal for granted when you take that as a precedent here? Looking back at the matter, if I remember rightly, North American was under a direct contract with the United States, and they were subject to control, to that extent, by the United States."[38] After Perlman conceded that steel mills did not have a similar relationship with the government, Jackson raised more objections. The owners of North American Aviation, unlike the steel companies, acquiesced in Roosevelt's seizure. Jackson also claimed that the 1941 strike was "in essence a strike against the Government" and involved communist subversion. He added that "I looked it up because I wondered how much of this was laid at my door."[39] Perlman replied, "Your Honor, we lay a lot of it at your door." Jackson answered, "I claimed everything, of course, like every other Attorney General does. It was a custom that didn't leave the [Justice] Department when I did."[40] Of course, he had not in fact claimed everything when he was attorney general, but his views on executive authority had evolved since 1941. Writing to his son after the argument, Jackson said that presidential power "is a subject I have struggled with in several capacities."[41]

Toward the end of the second day's argument, Jackson suggested that the Korean War was distinguishable from World War II. In response to the solicitor general's claim that the President's action must be upheld because "this is wartime," the Justice asked, "Has not Congress categorically disclaimed this as a war, but denominates it rather as a police action? It looks like a war to me, but Congress has specifically disclaimed this as a war. I do not know what you invite us to do. Can we say it is a war when the President says, 'No, it is not'?"[42] One implication of Jackson's query was that a formal declaration of war, which was never made in Korea, would have authorized the seizure. Another was that a communist victory over South Korea simply was not a national emergency comparable to Hitler's aggression.

The Justices held their private conference for *Youngstown* on May 16. Chief Justice Vinson argued that the North American Aviation seizure justified Truman's action, and he cited Jackson's supporting statement as authority.[43] Jackson's main comment during the conference was that the President "can throw the Constitution overboard but we can't."[44] When Jackson returned to his chambers, where his law clerks were itching to hear the news, he said "Well, boys, the President got licked."[45] Six Justices voted to affirm the District Court's injunction, and this tally did not change as the opinions were written.[46] Jackson's only note in his tally sheet was that he "would affirm doing [as] little damage as possible."

The Decision and the Other Opinions

Youngstown is one of the rare modern Supreme Court cases in which nearly every Justice wrote an opinion. Justice Hugo L. Black wrote for the Court.[47] Justice Black's opinion was terse because time was of the essence and, as Justice Frankfurter noted in a separate statement, in such an important and complex case the views of the Justices "can hardly be reflected by a single opinion for the Court. Individual expression of views in reaching a common result is therefore important."[48] Going through these individual views adds context to Justice Jackson's opinion.

Justice Black began by saying that "[t]he mill owners argue that the President's order amounts to lawmaking, a legislative function which the Constitution has expressly confided to the Congress and not to the President.

The Government's position is that the order was made on findings of the President that his action was necessary to avert a national catastrophe which would inevitably result from a stoppage of steel production, and that in meeting this grave emergency the President was acting within the aggregate of his constitutional powers as the Nation's Chief Executive and the Commander in Chief of the Armed Forces of the United States."[49] After summarizing the facts and proceedings below, Black wrote that "[t]he President's power, if any, to issue the order must stem either from an Act of Congress or from the Constitution itself."[50] But "we do not understand the Government to rely on statutory authorization for the seizure" because the Administration considered the statutory provisions "much too cumbersome, involved, and time-consuming for the crisis which was at hand."[51] He also noted that in the Taft-Hartley Act debate Congress "rejected an amendment which would have authorized such governmental seizures in times of emergency."

Black therefore said that, "if the President had authority to issue the order that he did, it must be found in some provision of the Constitution."[52] He concluded that there was no such authority. First, the "order cannot properly be sustained as an exercise of the President's military power as Commander-in-Chief of the Armed Forces. . . . [W]e cannot with faithfulness to our constitutional system hold that the Commander in Chief of the Armed Forces has the ultimate power as such to take possession of private property in order to keep labor disputes from stopping production. This is a job for the Nation's lawmakers, not for our military authorities." Black did not explain why this was a job for the nation's lawmakers. "Nor can the seizure order be sustained because of the several constitutional provisions that grant executive power to the President," he continued. "In the framework of our Constitution, the President's power to see that laws are faithfully executed refutes the idea that he is to be a lawmaker."[53] But what is the difference between faithfully executing the law and being a lawmaker? Black did not explain that either, although as a former senator he might have thought that the answer was obvious.[54] Finally, he dismissed the argument that prior executive property seizures justified Truman's: "It is said that other Presidents without congressional authority have taken possession of private business enterprises to settle labor disputes. But even if this be true, Congress has not thereby lost its exclusive authority to make laws necessary and proper to carry out the powers vested by the Constitution."[55] In other words, while not declaring the past seizures unlawful, he implied that presidential practice alone could not create presidential authority. Black summed up this way: "The Founders of this Nation entrusted the lawmaking power to the Congress alone in both good and bad times. It would do no good to recall the historical events, the fears of power and the hopes for freedom that lay behind their choice. Such a review would but confirm our holding that this seizure order cannot stand."[56]

Figure 2.3 "The Girl (Statue of Liberty)." C. D. Batchelor, *The New York Daily News*, June 3, 1952. Getty Images.

Justice Frankfurter wrote a concurring opinion that was anything but terse. He prefaced his ruling by saying that "the considerations relevant to the legal enforcement of the principle of separation of powers seem to me more complicated and flexible than may appear from what Mr. Justice BLACK has written." In keeping with that perspective, he wrote a meandering essay on separation of powers before coming to the point:[57] that is, that past legislation shows "that Congress deemed seizure so drastic a power as to require that it be carefully circumscribed whenever the President was vested with this extraordinary authority."[58] Like Black, he discussed Congress's rejection of executive seizure authority in the Taft-Hartley Act debate.[59] But Frankfurter went further than Black by saying that this rejection was tantamount to a prohibition on property seizures by the President.[60] While the Korean War might mean that new legislation should be enacted, "[a]bsence of authority in the President to deal with a crisis does not imply want of power in the Government. Conversely the fact that power exists in the Government does not vest it in the President."[61] Turning to the Constitution, Frankfurter disagreed with Black's rigid division between lawmaking and executive power. Echoing what Jackson would say more eloquently in his concurrence, Frankfurter said that the authority of the three branches could not "be derived from an abstract analysis. The areas are partly interacting, not wholly disjointed. The Constitution is a framework for government. Therefore the way the framework has consistently operated fairly establishes that it has operated according to its true nature."[62] "It is an inadmissibly narrow conception of American constitutional law," he explained, "to confine it to the words of the Constitution and to disregard the gloss which life has written upon them. In short, a systemic, unbroken, executive practice, long pursued to the knowledge of Congress and never before questioned, engaged in by Presidents who have also sworn to uphold the Constitution, making as it were such exercise of power part of the structure of our government, may be treated as a gloss on 'executive Power' vested in the President."[63] But the practice of executive property seizures was nothing like this. There were only three examples—all from President Roosevelt—and "these three isolated instances do not add up, either in number, scope, or contemporaneous legal justification" to a systemic executive practice and were not "sanctioned by long-continued acquiescence of Congress giving decisive weight to a construction by the Executive of its powers."[64]

Justice William O. Douglas also concurred but stressed the relationship between the seizure's illegality and the Fifth Amendment's Takings Clause.[65]

Douglas wrote that the "legislative nature of the action taken by the President seems to me to be clear. When the United States takes over an industrial plant to settle a labor controversy, it is condemning property. The seizure of the plant is a taking in the constitutional sense."[66] Just compensation must then be paid to the property owner. But Douglas noted that '[t]he President has no power to raise revenues";[67] only Congress does. What followed was that "[t]he branch of government that has the power to pay compensation for a seizure is the only one able to authorize one or make lawful one that the President had effected."[68] Individual rights, on this reading, could help judges apply separation of powers. "We pay a price for our system of checks and balances," Douglas summed up. "It is a price that today may seem exorbitant to many. Today a kindly President uses the seizure power to effect a wage increase and to keep the steel furnaces in production. Yet tomorrow another President might use the same power to prevent a wage increase, to curb trade unionists, to regiment labor as oppressively as industry thinks it has been regimented by this seizure."[69]

Justice Harold Burton, a former senator who was appointed to the Court by Truman, concurred on more specific grounds.[70] He reviewed the President's statutory options and emphasized "the clarity of the congressional reservation of seizure for its own consideration."[71] Burton said that the reservation distinguished this "emergency from one in which Congress takes no action and outlines no governmental policy."[72] In other words, the President might have been free to act unilaterally if Congress had said nothing about property seizures. Burton also left the door open for executive action despite congressional disapproval about "an imminent invasion or threatened attack. We do not face the issue of what might be the President's constitutional power to meet such catastrophic situations. Nor is it claimed that the current seizure is in the nature of a military command addressed by the President, as Commander-in-Chief, to a mobilized nation waging, or imminently threatened with, total war."[73] "The controlling fact here," he concluded, "is that Congress, within its constitutionally delegated power, has prescribed for the President specific procedures, exclusive of seizure, for his use in meeting the present type of emergency. Congress has reserved to itself the right to determine where and when to authorize the seizure of property in meeting such an emergency. Under these circumstances, the President's order of April 8 invaded the jurisdiction of Congress."[74]

Justice Tom Clark, who was Truman's attorney general before joining the Court, largely agreed with Justice Burton but concurred only in the result.[75]

In part, that was because he thought that "the Constitution does grant to the President extensive authority in times of grave and imperative national emergency. In fact, to my thinking, such a grant may well be necessary to the very existence of the Constitution itself."[76] But "where Congress has laid down specific procedures to deal with the type of crisis confronting the President," Clark wrote, "he must follow those procedures in meeting the crisis, but that in the absence of such action by Congress, the President's independent power to act depends upon the gravity of the situation confronting the nation." Clark's bottom line was that the Administration did not follow the procedures laid out by Congress, and thus the steel seizure was unlawful.[77]

Chief Justice Fred Vinson, joined by Justices Stanley F. Reed and Sherman Minton, dissented.[78] "Those who suggest that this is a case involving extraordinary powers should be mindful that these are extraordinary times," Vinson explained.[79] "A world not yet recovered from the devastation of World War II has been forced to face the threat of another and more terrifying conflict."[80] The Chief Justice argued that by seizing the steel mills the President was carrying out Congress's programs and appropriations in support of the Korean War.[81] But he relied mostly on past unilateral executive practice "to save [legislative] programs until Congress could act."[82] This historical practice "amply demonstrates that Presidents have taken prompt action to enforce the laws and protect the country whether or not Congress happened to provide in advance for the particular method of execution."[83] A temporary seizure gave Congress time to approve or reject the President's action, and the Chief Justice observed that "[t]here is no statute prohibiting seizure as a method of enforcing legislative programs."[84] "Certainly there is no basis for fear of dictatorship," he said, "when the Executive acts, as he did in this case, only to save the situation until Congress could act."[85] Vinson concluded by rejecting the majority's "messenger-boy concept" of the presidency that could only plead rather than act in a crisis.[86]

The President was unhappy with the *Youngstown* decision but immediately complied.[87] He then addressed a joint session of Congress and asked for new authority to operate the mills, quoting from Justice Jackson's concurrence about "the ease, the expedition, and the safety with which Congress can grant" emergency powers.[88] Congress did nothing. The ensuing strike at the steel mills lasted seven weeks, though there was no notable impact on the Korean War or on world peace.[89] Public reaction to the Court's ruling was positive.[90] Governor Earl Warren of California, who would succeed Chief Justice Vinson, said in *The Los Angeles Times* that he considered "this to be a red-letter day in the history of our country. The decision of the Supreme Court holding that everyone in the nation, including the President, is subject to the written provisions of law removes the challenge to the basic American principle that we have three equal and coordinate branches of government, all of which must live within the framework of the Constitution."[91] Justice Jackson's concurring opinion gave this basic American principle its most memorable expression.[92]

3
The Opinion

(634) MR. JUSTICE JACKSON concurring in the judgment and opinion of the Court.*

That comprehensive and undefined presidential powers hold both practical advantages and grave dangers for the country will impress anyone who has served as legal adviser to a President in time of transition and public anxiety. While an interval of detached reflection may temper teachings of that experience, they probably are a more realistic influence on my views than the conventional materials of judicial decision which seem unduly to accentuate doctrine and legal fiction. But as we approach the question of presidential power, we half overcome mental hazards by recognizing them. The opinions of judges, no less than executives and publicists, often suffer the infirmity of confusing the issue of a power's validity with the cause it is invoked to promote, of confounding the permanent executive office with its temporary occupant. The tendency is strong to emphasize transient results upon policies–such as wages or stabilization–and lose sight of enduring consequences upon the balanced power structure of our Republic. A judge, like an executive adviser, may be surprised at the poverty of really useful and unambiguous authority applicable to concrete problems of executive power as they actually present themselves. Just what our forefathers did envision, or would have envisioned had they foreseen modern conditions, must be divined from materials almost as enigmatic as the dreams Joseph was called upon to interpret for Pharaoh. A century and a half of partisan debate and scholarly speculation yields no net result but only supplies more or less apt quotations from (635) respected sources on each side of any question. They largely cancel each other.[1] And court decisions are indecisive because of the judicial practice of dealing with the largest questions in the most narrow way.

* The corresponding page numbers for the opinion in the official volume of the United States Reports are inserted at the appropriate points in the text.

[1] A Hamilton may be matched against a Madison. 7 The Works of Alexander Hamilton, 76–117; 1 Madison, Letters and Other Writings, 611–654. Professor Taft is counterbalanced by Theodore

The Actual Art of Governing. Gerard N. Magliocca, Oxford University Press. © Oxford University Press (2025).
DOI: 10.1093/9780197768563.003.0004

The actual art of governing under our Constitution does not and cannot conform to judicial definitions of the power of any of its branches based on isolated clauses or even single Articles torn from context. While the Constitution diffuses power the better to secure liberty, it also contemplates that practice will integrate the dispersed powers into a workable government. It enjoins upon its branches separateness but interdependence, autonomy but reciprocity. Presidential powers are not fixed but fluctuate, depending upon their disjunction or conjunction with those of Congress. We may well begin by a somewhat over-simplified grouping of practical situations in which a President may doubt, or others may challenge, his powers, and by distinguishing roughly the legal consequences of this factor of relativity.

1. When the President acts pursuant to an express or implied authorization of Congress, his authority is at its maximum, for it includes all that he possesses in his own right plus all that Congress can delegate.[2]

Roosevelt. Taft, Our Chief Magistrate and His Powers, 139–140; Theodore Roosevelt, Autobiography, 388–389. It even seems that President Taft cancels out Professor Taft. Compare his "Temporary Petroleum Withdrawal No. 5" of September 27, 1909, United States v. Midwest Oil Co., 236 U.S. 459, 467, 468, with his appraisal of executive power in "Our Chief Magistrate and His Powers" 139–140.

[2] It is in this class of cases that we find the broadest recent statements of presidential power, including those relied on here. United States v. Curtiss-Wright Corp., 299 U.S. 304, involved, not the question of the President's power to act without congressional authority, but the question of his right to act under and in accord with an Act of Congress. The constitutionality of the Act under which the President had proceeded was assailed on the ground that it delegated legislative powers to the President. Much of the Court's opinion is dictum, but the ratio decidendi is contained in the following language:

> "When the President is to be authorized by legislation to act in respect of a matter intended to affect a situation in foreign territory, the legislator properly bears in mind the important consideration that the form of the President's action—or, indeed, whether he shall act at all—may well depend, among other things, upon the nature of the confidential information which he has or may thereafter receive, or upon the effect which his action may have upon our foreign relations. This consideration, in connection with what we have already said on the subject, discloses the unwisdom of requiring Congress in this field of governmental power to lay down narrowly definite standards by which the President is to be governed. As this court said in Mackenzie v. Hare, 239 U.S. 299, 311, 'As a government, the United States is invested with all the attributes of sovereignty. As it has the character of nationality it has the powers of nationality, especially those which concern its relations and intercourse with other countries. We should hesitate long before limiting or embarrassing such powers.' (Italics supplied.)" Id., at 321–322.

That case does not solve the present controversy. It recognized internal and external affairs as being in separate categories, and held that the strict limitation upon congressional delegations of power to the President over internal affairs does not apply with respect to delegations of power in external affairs. It was intimated that the President might act in external affairs without congressional authority, but not that he might act contrary to an Act of Congress. Other examples of wide definition of presidential powers under statutory authorization are Chicago & Southern Air Lines, Inc. v. Waterman Steamship Corp., 333 U.S. 103, and Hirabayashi v. United States, 320 U.S. 81. But see, Jecker v. Montgomery, 13 How. 498, 515; United States v. Western Union Telegraph Co., 272 F. 311; aff'd, 272 F. 893; rev'd on consent of the parties, 260 U.S. 754; United States Harness Co. v. Graham, 288 F. 929.

In these circumstances, (636) and in these only, may he be said (for what it may be worth) to personify the federal sovereignty. If his act is held unconstitutional under these circumstances, it usually means that the Federal Government (637) as an undivided whole lacks power. A seizure executed by the President pursuant to an Act of Congress would be supported by the strongest of presumptions and the widest latitude of judicial interpretation, and the burden of persuasion would rest heavily upon any who might attack it.

2. When the President acts in absence of either a congressional grant or denial of authority, he can only rely upon his own independent powers, but there is a zone of twilight in which he and Congress may have concurrent authority, or in which its distribution is uncertain. Therefore, congressional inertia, indifference or quiescence may sometimes, at least as a practical matter, enable, if not invite, measures on independent presidential responsibility. In this area, any actual test of power is likely to depend on the imperatives of events and contemporary imponderables rather than on abstract theories of law.[3]
3. When the President takes measures incompatible with the expressed or implied will of Congress, his power is at its lowest ebb, for then he can rely only upon his own constitutional powers minus any constitutional powers of Congress over the matter. Courts can sustain exclusive presidential control in such a case only by disabling (638) the Congress from acting upon the subject.[4] Presidential claim to a power at once so conclusive and preclusive must be scrutinized with caution, for what is at stake is the equilibrium established by our constitutional system.

[3] Since the Constitution implies that the writ of habeas corpus may be suspended in certain circumstances but does not say by whom, President Lincoln asserted and maintained it as an executive function in the face of judicial challenge and doubt. Ex parte Merryman, 17 Fed. Cas. 144; Ex parte Milligan, 4 Wall. 2, 125; see Ex parte Bollman, 4 Cranch 75, 101. Congress eventually ratified his action. Habeas Corpus Act of March 3, 1863, 12 Stat. 755. See Hall, Free Speech in War Time, 21 Col. L. Rev. 526. Compare Myers v. United States, 272 U.S. 52, with Humphrey's Executor v. United States, 295 U.S. 602; and Hirabayashi v. United States, 320 U.S. 81, with the case at bar. Also compare Ex parte Vallandigham, 1 Wall. 243, with Ex parte Milligan, supra.

[4] President Roosevelt's effort to remove a Federal Trade Commissioner was found to be contrary to the policy of Congress and impinging upon an area of congressional control, and so his removal power was cut down accordingly. Humphrey's Executor v. United States, 295 U.S. 602. However, his exclusive power of removal in executive agencies, affirmed in Myers v. United States, 272 U.S. 52, continued to be asserted and maintained. Morgan v. Tennessee Valley Authority, 115 F.2d 990, cert. denied, 312 U.S. 701; In re Power to Remove Members of the Tennessee Valley Authority, 39 Op. Atty. Gen. 145; President Roosevelt's Message to Congress of March 23, 1938, The Public Papers and Addresses of Franklin D. Roosevelt, 1938 (Rosenman), 151.

Into which of these classifications does this executive seizure of the steel industry fit? It is eliminated from the first by admission, for it is conceded that no congressional authorization exists for this seizure. That takes away also the support of the many precedents and declarations which were made in relation, and must be confined, to this category.[5]

(639) Can it then be defended under flexible tests available to the second category? It seems clearly eliminated from that class because Congress has not left seizure of private property an open field but has covered it by three statutory policies inconsistent with this seizure. In cases where the purpose is to supply needs of the Government itself, two courses are provided: one, seizure of a plant which fails to comply with obligatory orders placed by the Government;[6] another, condemnation of facilities, including temporary use under the power of eminent domain.[7] The third is applicable where it is the general economy of the country that is to be protected rather than exclusive governmental interests.[8] None of these were invoked. In choosing a different and inconsistent way of his own, the President cannot claim that it is necessitated or invited by failure of Congress to legislate upon the occasions, grounds and methods for seizure of industrial properties.

(640) This leaves the current seizure to be justified only by the severe tests under the third grouping, where it can be supported only by any remainder of executive power after subtraction of such powers as Congress may have over the subject. In short, we can sustain the President only by

[5] The oft-cited Louisiana Purchase had nothing to do with the separation of powers as between the President and Congress, but only with state and federal power. The Louisiana Purchase was subject to rather academic criticism, not upon the ground that Mr. Jefferson acted without authority from Congress, but that neither had express authority to expand the boundaries of the United States by purchase or annexation. Mr. Jefferson himself had strongly opposed the doctrine that the States' delegation of powers to the Federal Government could be enlarged by resort to implied powers. Afterwards in a letter to John Breckenridge, dated August 12, 1803, he declared:

"The Constitution has made no provision for our holding foreign territory, still less for incorporating foreign nations into our Union. The executive in seizing the fugitive occurrence which so much advances the good of their country, have done an act beyond the Constitution. The Legislature in casting behind them metaphysical subtleties, and risking themselves like faithful servants, must ratify and pay for it, and throw themselves on their country for doing for them unauthorized, what we know they would have done for themselves had they been in a situation to do it." 10 The Writings of Thomas Jefferson 407, 411.

[6] Selective Service Act of 1948, 18, 62 Stat. 625, 50 U.S.C. App. (Supp. IV) 468 (c).

[7] Defense Production Act of 1950, 201, 64 Stat. 799, amended, 65 Stat. 132, 50 U.S.C. App. (Supp. IV) 2081. For the latitude of the condemnation power which underlies this Act, see United States v. Westinghouse Co., 339 U.S. 261, and cases therein cited.

[8] Labor Management Relations Act, 1947, 206–210, 61 Stat. 136, 155, 156, 29 U.S.C. (Supp. IV) 141, 176–180. The analysis, history and application of this Act are fully covered by the opinion of the Court, supplemented by that of MR. JUSTICE FRANKFURTER and of MR. JUSTICE BURTON, in which I concur.

holding that seizure of such strike-bound industries is within his domain and beyond control by Congress. Thus, this Court's first review of such seizures occurs under circumstances which leave presidential power most vulnerable to attack and in the least favorable of possible constitutional postures.

I did not suppose, and I am not persuaded, that history leaves it open to question, at least in the courts, that the executive branch, like the Federal Government as a whole, possesses only delegated powers. The purpose of the Constitution was not only to grant power, but to keep it from getting out of hand. However, because the President does not enjoy unmentioned powers does not mean that the mentioned ones should be narrowed by a niggardly construction. Some clauses could be made almost unworkable, as well as immutable, by refusal to indulge some latitude of interpretation for changing times. I have heretofore, and do now, give to the enumerated powers the scope and elasticity afforded by what seem to be reasonable, practical implications instead of the rigidity dictated by a doctrinaire textualism.*

The Solicitor General seeks the power of seizure in three clauses of the Executive Article, the first reading, "The executive Power shall be vested in a President of the United States of America." Lest I be thought to exaggerate, I quote the interpretation which his brief puts upon it: "In our view, this clause constitutes a grant of all the executive powers of which the Government is capable." If that be true, it is difficult to see why the (641) forefathers bothered to add several specific items, including some trifling ones.[9]

The example of such unlimited executive power that must have most impressed the forefathers was the prerogative exercised by George III, and the description of its evils in the Declaration of Independence leads me to doubt that they were creating their new Executive in his image. Continental European examples were no more appealing. And if we seek instruction from our own times, we can match it only from the executive powers in those governments we disparagingly describe as totalitarian. I cannot accept the view that this clause is a grant in bulk of all conceivable executive power

* [Author's Note] After the opinion was issued, an eagle-eyed reader spotted a typo in the concurrence. See Letter from Jarrell Gardnzik to Mr. Justice Jackson (June 19, 1952), in Jackson Papers, Box 176 (pointing out that there was a comma missing between the words "reasonable" and "practical"). A covering note to the letter says that the comma was then added.

[9] ". . . he may require the Opinion, in writing, of the principal Officer in each of the executive Departments, upon any Subject relating to the Duties of their respective Offices . . . ." U.S. Const., Art. II, 2. He ". . . shall Commission all the Officers of the United States." U.S. Const., Art. II, 3. Matters such as those would seem to be inherent in the Executive if anything is.

but regard it as an allocation to the presidential office of the generic powers thereafter stated.

The clause on which the Government next relies is that "The President shall be Commander in Chief of the Army and Navy of the United States ...." These cryptic words have given rise to some of the most persistent controversies in our constitutional history. Of course, they imply something more than an empty title. But just what authority goes with the name has plagued presidential advisers who would not waive or narrow it by nonassertion yet cannot say where it begins or ends. It undoubtedly puts the Nation's armed forces under presidential command. Hence, this loose appellation is sometimes advanced as support for any presidential action, internal or external, involving use of force, the (642) idea being that it vests power to do anything, anywhere, that can be done with an army or navy.

That seems to be the logic of an argument tendered at our bar—that the President having, on his own responsibility, sent American troops abroad derives from that act "affirmative power" to seize the means of producing a supply of steel for them. To quote, "Perhaps the most forceful illustration of the scope of Presidential power in this connection is the fact that American troops in Korea, whose safety and effectiveness are so directly involved here, were sent to the field by an exercise of the President's constitutional powers." Thus, it is said, he has invested himself with "war powers."

I cannot foresee all that it might entail if the Court should indorse this argument. Nothing in our Constitution is plainer than that declaration of a war is entrusted only to Congress. Of course, a state of war may in fact exist without a formal declaration. But no doctrine that the Court could promulgate would seem to me more sinister and alarming than that a President whose conduct of foreign affairs is so largely uncontrolled, and often even is unknown, can vastly enlarge his mastery over the internal affairs of the country by his own commitment of the Nation's armed forces to some foreign venture.[10] (643) I do not, however, find it necessary or appropriate

[10] How widely this doctrine espoused by the President's counsel departs from the early view of presidential power is shown by a comparison. President Jefferson, without authority from Congress, sent the American fleet into the Mediterranean, where it engaged in a naval battle with the Tripolitan fleet. He sent a message to Congress on December 8, 1801, in which he said:

> "Tripoli, the least considerable of the Barbary States, had come forward with demands unfounded either in right or in compact, and had permitted itself to denounce war on our failure to comply before a given day. The style of the demand admitted but one answer. I sent a small squadron of frigates into the Mediterranean . . . with orders to protect our commerce against the threatened attack. . . . Our commerce in the Mediterranean was blockaded and that of the Atlantic in peril. . . . One of the Tripolitan cruisers

to consider the legal status of the Korean enterprise to discountenance argument based on it.

Assuming that we are in a war de facto, whether it is or is not a war de jure, does that empower the Commander in Chief to seize industries he thinks necessary to supply our army? The Constitution expressly places in Congress power "to raise and support Armies" and "to provide and maintain a Navy." (Emphasis supplied.) This certainly lays upon Congress primary responsibility for supplying the armed forces. Congress alone controls the raising of revenues and their appropriation and may determine in what manner and by what means they shall be spent for military and naval procurement. I suppose no one would doubt that Congress can take over war supply as a Government enterprise. On the other hand, if Congress sees fit to rely on free private enterprise collectively bargaining with free labor for support and maintenance of our armed forces, can the Executive, because of lawful disagreements incidental to that process, seize the facility for operation upon Government-imposed terms?

There are indications that the Constitution did not contemplate that the title Commander in Chief of the (644) Army and Navy will constitute him also Commander in Chief of the country, its industries and its inhabitants. He has no monopoly of "war powers," whatever they are. While Congress cannot deprive the President of the command of the army and navy, only Congress can provide him an army or navy to command. It is also empowered to make rules for the "Government and Regulation of land and naval Forces," by which it may to some unknown extent impinge upon even command functions.

That military powers of the Commander in Chief were not to supersede representative government of internal affairs seems obvious from the Constitution and from elementary American history. Time out of mind, and even now in many parts of the world, a military commander can seize private

having fallen in with and engaged the small schooner Enterprise, . . . was captured, after a heavy slaughter of her men . . . . Unauthorized by the Constitution, without the sanction of Congress, to go beyond the line of defense, the vessel, being disabled from committing further hostilities, was liberated with its crew. The Legislature will doubtless consider whether, by authorizing measures of offense also, they will place our force on an equal footing with that of its adversaries. I communicate all material information on this subject, that in the exercise of this important function confided by the Constitution to the Legislature exclusively their judgment may form itself on a knowledge and consideration of every circumstance of weight." I Richardson, Messages and Papers of the Presidents, 314.

housing to shelter his troops. Not so, however, in the United States, for the Third Amendment says, "No Soldier shall, in time of peace be quartered in any house, without the consent of the Owner, nor in time of war, but in a manner to be prescribed by law." Thus, even in war time, his seizure of needed military housing must be authorized by Congress. It also was expressly left to Congress to "provide for calling forth the Militia to execute the Laws of the Union, suppress Insurrections and repel Invasions ...."[11] Such a limitation on the command power, written at a time when the militia rather than a standing army was contemplated as the military weapon of the Republic, underscores the Constitution's policy that Congress, not the Executive, should control utilization of the war power as an instrument of domestic policy. Congress, fulfilling that function, has authorized the President to use the army to enforce certain civil rights.[12] On the other hand. Congress has forbidden him to use the army for the purpose (645) of executing general laws except when expressly authorized by the Constitution or by Act of Congress.[13] While broad claims under this rubric often have been made, advice to the President in specific matters usually has carried overtones that powers, even under this head, are measured by the command functions usual to the topmost officer of the army and navy. Even then, heed has been taken of any efforts of Congress to negative his authority.[14]

We should not use this occasion to circumscribe, much less to contract, the lawful role of the President as Commander in Chief. I should indulge the widest latitude of interpretation to sustain his exclusive function to command the instruments of national force, at least when turned against the outside world for the security of our society. But, when it is turned inward, not because of rebellion but because of a lawful economic struggle between industry and labor, it should have no such indulgence. His command power is not such an absolute as might be implied from that office in a militaristic

[11] U.S. Const., Art. I, 8, cl. 15.

[12] 14 Stat. 29, 16 Stat. 143, 8 U.S.C. 55.

[13] 20 Stat. 152, 10 U.S.C. 15.

[14] In 1940, President Roosevelt proposed to transfer to Great Britain certain overage destroyers and small patrol boats then under construction. He did not presume to rely upon any claim of constitutional power as Commander in Chief. On the contrary, he was advised that such destroyers—if certified not to be essential to the defense of the United States—could be "transferred, exchanged, sold, or otherwise disposed of," because Congress had so authorized him. Accordingly, the destroyers were exchanged for air bases. In the same opinion, he was advised that Congress had prohibited the release or transfer of the so-called "mosquito boats" then under construction, so those boats were not transferred. Acquisition of Naval and Air Bases in Exchange for Over-age Destroyers, 39 Op. Atty. Gen. 484. See also Training of British Flying Students in the United States, 40 Op. Atty. Gen. 58.

system but is subject to limitations consistent with a constitutional Republic whose law and policy-making branch (646) is a representative Congress. The purpose of lodging dual titles in one man was to insure that the civilian would control the military, not to enable the military to subordinate the presidential office. No penance would ever expiate the sin against free government of holding that a President can escape control of executive powers by law through assuming his military role. What the power of command may include I do not try to envision, but I think it is not a military prerogative, without support of law, to seize persons or property because they are important or even essential for the military and naval establishment.

The third clause in which the Solicitor General finds seizure powers is that "he shall take Care that the Laws be faithfully executed ...."[15] That authority must be matched against words of the Fifth Amendment that "No person shall be ... deprived of life, liberty or property, without due process of law ...." One gives a governmental authority that reaches so far as there is law, the other gives a private right that authority shall go no farther. These signify about all there is of the principle that ours is a government of laws, not of men, and that we submit ourselves to rulers only if under rules.

The Solicitor General lastly grounds support of the seizure upon nebulous, inherent powers never expressly granted but said to have accrued to the office from the customs and claims of preceding administrations. The plea is for a resulting power to deal with a crisis or an emergency according to the necessities of the case, the unarticulated assumption being that necessity knows no law.

Loose and irresponsible use of adjectives colors all nonlegal and much legal discussion of presidential powers. (647) "Inherent" powers, "implied" powers, "incidental" powers, "plenary" powers, "war" powers and "emergency" powers are used, often interchangeably and without fixed or ascertainable meanings.

The vagueness and generality of the clauses that set forth presidential powers afford a plausible basis for pressures within and without an administration for presidential action beyond that supported by those whose responsibility it is to defend his actions in court. The claim of inherent and unrestricted presidential powers has long been a persuasive dialectical weapon in political controversy. While it is not surprising that counsel should grasp support from such unadjudicated claims of power, a

[15] U.S. Const., Art. II, 3.

judge cannot accept self-serving press statements of the attorney for one of the interested parties as authority in answering a constitutional question, even if the advocate was himself. But prudence has counseled that actual reliance on such nebulous claims stop short of provoking a judicial test.[16]

(648) The Solicitor General, acknowledging that Congress has never authorized the seizure here, says practice of prior Presidents has authorized it. He seeks color of legality from claimed executive precedents, chief of which is President Roosevelt's seizure on June 9, 1941, of the California plant of the North American Aviation Company. Its superficial similarities with the present case, upon analysis, yield to distinctions so decisive that it (649) cannot be regarded as even a precedent, much less an authority for the present seizure.[17]

[16] President Wilson, just before our entrance into World War I, went before the Congress and asked its approval of his decision to authorize merchant ships to carry defensive weapons. He said:

> "No doubt I already possess that authority without special warrant of law, by the plain implication of my constitutional duties and powers; but I prefer, in the present circumstances, not to act upon general implication. I wish to feel that the authority and the power of the Congress are behind me in whatever it may become necessary for me to do. We are jointly the servants of the people and must act together and in their spirit, so far as we can divine and interpret it." XVII Richardson, op. cit., 8211.

When our Government was itself in need of shipping whilst ships flying the flags of nations overrun by Hitler, as well as belligerent merchantmen, were immobilized in American harbors where they had taken refuge, President Roosevelt did not assume that it was in his power to seize such foreign vessels to make up our own deficit. He informed Congress: "I am satisfied, after consultation with the heads of the interested departments and agencies of the Government, that we should have statutory authority to take over any such vessels as our needs may require . . . ." 87 Cong. Rec. 3072 (77th Cong., 1st Sess.); The Public Papers and Addresses of Franklin D. Roosevelt, 1941 (Rosenman), 94. The necessary statutory authority was shortly forthcoming. 55 Stat. 242.

In his first inaugural address President Roosevelt pointed out two courses to obtain legislative remedies, one being to enact measures he was prepared to recommend, the other to enact measures "the Congress may build out of its experience and wisdom." He continued, "But in the event that the Congress shall fail to take one of these two courses, and in the event that the national emergency is still critical, I shall not evade the clear course of duty that will then confront me. I shall ask the Congress for the one remaining instrument to meet the crisis—broad Executive power to wage a war against the emergency, as great as the power that would be given to me if we were in fact invaded by a foreign foe." (Emphasis supplied.) The Public Papers and Addresses of Franklin D. Roosevelt, 1933 (Rosenman), 15.

On March 6, 1933, President Roosevelt proclaimed the Bank Holiday. The Proclamation did not invoke constitutional powers of the Executive but expressly and solely relied upon the Act of Congress of October 6, 1917, 40 Stat. 411, 5 (b), as amended. He relied steadily on legislation to empower him to deal with economic emergency. The Public Papers and Addresses of Franklin D. Roosevelt, 1933 (Rosenman), 24.

It is interesting to note Holdsworth's comment on the powers of legislation by proclamation when in the hands of the Tudors. "The extent to which they could be legally used was never finally settled in this century, because the Tudors made so tactful a use of their powers that no demand for the settlement of this question was raised." 4 Holdsworth, History of English Law, 104.

[17] The North American Aviation Company was under direct and binding contracts to supply defense items to the Government. No such contracts are claimed to exist here. Seizure of plants

The appeal, however, that we declare the existence of inherent powers ex necessitate to meet an emergency asks us to do what many think would be wise, although (650) it is something the forefathers omitted. They knew what emergencies were, knew the pressures they engender for authoritative action, knew, too, how they afford a ready pretext for usurpation. We may also suspect that they suspected that emergency powers would tend to kindle emergencies. Aside from suspension of the privilege of the writ of habeas corpus in time of rebellion or invasion, when the public safety may require it,[18] they made no express provision for exercise of extraordinary authority because of a crisis.[19] I do not think we rightfully may so amend their work, and, if we could, I am not convinced it would be wise to do so, although many modern nations have forthrightly recognized

which refused to comply with Government orders had been expressly authorized by Congress in 9 of the Selective Service Act of 1940, 54 Stat. 885, 892, so that the seizure of the North American plant was entirely consistent with congressional policy. The company might have objected on technical grounds to the seizure, but it was taken over with acquiescence, amounting to all but consent, of the owners who had admitted that the situation was beyond their control. The strike involved in the North American case was in violation of the union's collective agreement and the national labor leaders approved the seizure to end the strike. It was described as in the nature of an insurrection, a Communist-led political strike against the Government's lend-lease policy. Here we have only a loyal, lawful, but regrettable economic disagreement between management and labor. The North American plant contained government-owned machinery, material and goods in the process of production to which workmen were forcibly denied access by picketing strikers. Here no Government property is protected by the seizure. See New York Times of June 10, 1941, pp. 1, 14 and 16, for substantially accurate account of the proceedings and the conditions of violence at the North American plant.

The North American seizure was regarded as an execution of congressional policy. I do not regard it as a precedent for this, but, even if I did, I should not bind present judicial judgment by earlier partisan advocacy. Statements from a letter by the Attorney General to the Chairman of the Senate Committee on Labor and Public Welfare, dated February 2, 1949, with reference to pending labor legislation, while not cited by any of the parties here, are sometimes quoted as being in support of the "inherent" powers of the President. The proposed bill contained a mandatory provision that during certain investigations the disputants in a labor dispute should continue operations under the terms and conditions of employment existing prior to the beginning of the dispute. It made no provision as to how continuance should be enforced and specified no penalty for disobedience. The Attorney General advised that in appropriate circumstances the United States would have access to the courts to protect the national health, safety and welfare. This was the rule laid down by this Court in Texas & N. O. R. Co. v. Brotherhood of Railway Clerks, 281 U.S. 548. The Attorney General observed:

> "However, with regard to the question of the power of the Government under Title III, I might point out that the inherent power of the President to deal with emergencies that affect the health, safety and welfare of the entire Nation is exceedingly great. See Opinion of Attorney General Murphy of October 4, 1939 (39 Op. A. G. 344, 347); United States v. United Mine Workers of America, 330 U.S. 258 (1947)." See Hearings before the Senate Committee on Labor and Public Welfare on S. 249, 81st Cong., 1st Sess. 263.

Regardless of the general reference to "inherent powers," the citations were instances of congressional authorization. I do not suppose it is open to doubt that power to see that the laws are faithfully executed was ample basis for the specific advice given by the Attorney General in this letter.

[18] U.S. Const., Art. I, 9, cl. 2.

[19] I exclude, as in a very limited category by itself, the establishment of martial law. Cf. Ex parte Milligan, 4 Wall. 2; Duncan v. Kahanamoku, 327 U.S. 304.

that war and economic crises may upset the normal balance between liberty and authority. (651) Their experience with emergency powers may not be irrelevant to the argument here that we should say that the Executive, of his own volition, can invest himself with undefined emergency powers.

Germany, after the First World War, framed the Weimar Constitution, designed to secure her liberties in the Western tradition. However, the President of the Republic, without concurrence of the Reichstag, was empowered temporarily to suspend any or all individual rights if public safety and order were seriously disturbed or endangered. This proved a temptation to every government, whatever its shade of opinion, and in 13 years suspension of rights was invoked on more than 250 occasions. Finally, Hitler persuaded President Von Hindenberg to suspend all such rights, and they were never restored.[20]

The French Republic provided for a very different kind of emergency government known as the "state of siege." It differed from the German emergency dictatorship, particularly in that emergency powers could not be assumed at will by the Executive but could only be granted as a parliamentary measure. And it did not, as in Germany, result in a suspension or abrogation of law but was a legal institution governed by special legal rules and terminable by parliamentary authority.[21]

Great Britain also has fought both World Wars under a sort of temporary dictatorship created by legislation.[22] As Parliament is not bound by written constitutional limitations, it established a crisis government simply by (652) delegation to its Ministers of a larger measure than usual of its own unlimited power, which is exercised under its supervision by Ministers whom it may dismiss. This has been called the "high-water mark in the voluntary surrender of liberty," but, as Churchill put it, "Parliament stands custodian of these surrendered liberties, and its most sacred duty will be to restore them in their fullness when victory has crowned our exertions and our perseverance."[23] Thus, parliamentary control made emergency powers compatible with freedom. This contemporary foreign experience may be inconclusive as to the wisdom of lodging emergency powers somewhere in a modern

[20] 1 Nazi Conspiracy and Aggression 126–127; Rossiter, Constitutional Dictatorship, 33–61; Brecht, Prelude to Silence, 138.

[21] Rossiter, Constitutional Dictatorship, 117–129.

[22] Defence of the Realm Act, 1914, 4 & 5 Geo. V, c. 29, as amended, c. 63; Emergency Powers (Defence) Act, 1939, 2 & 3 Geo. VI, c. 62; Rossiter, Constitutional Dictatorship, 135–184.

[23] Churchill, The Unrelenting Struggle, 13. See also id., at 279–281.

government. But it suggests that emergency powers are consistent with free government only when their control is lodged elsewhere than in the Executive who exercises them. That is the safeguard that would be nullified by our adoption of the "inherent powers" formula. Nothing in my experience convinces me that such risks are warranted by any real necessity, although such powers would, of course, be an executive convenience. In the practical working of our Government we already have evolved a technique within the framework of the Constitution by which normal executive powers may be considerably expanded to meet an emergency. Congress may and has granted extraordinary authorities which lie dormant in normal times but may be called into play by the Executive in war or upon proclamation of a national emergency. In 1939, upon congressional request, the Attorney General listed ninety-nine such separate statutory grants by Congress of emergency or wartime executive powers.[24] They were invoked from time to time as need appeared. Under this procedure we retain Government (653) by law—special, temporary law, perhaps, but law nonetheless. The public may know the extent and limitations of the powers than can be asserted, and persons affected may be informed from the statute of their rights and duties.

In view of the ease, expedition and safety with which Congress can grant and has granted large emergency powers, certainly ample to embrace this crisis, I am quite unimpressed with the argument that we should affirm possession of them without statute. Such power either has no beginning or it has no end. If it exists, it need submit to no legal restraint. I am not alarmed that it would plunge us straightway into dictatorship, but it is at least a step in that wrong direction. As to whether there is imperative necessity for such powers, it is relevant to note the gap that exists between the President's paper powers and his real powers. The Constitution does not disclose the measure of the actual controls wielded by the modern presidential office. That instrument must be understood as an Eighteenth-Century sketch of a government hoped for, not as a blueprint of the Government that is. Vast accretions of federal power, eroded from that reserved by the States, have magnified the scope of presidential activity. Subtle shifts take place in the centers of real power that do not show on the face of the Constitution. Executive power has the advantage of concentration in a single head in whose choice the whole Nation has a part, making him the focus of public hopes and expectations.

[24] 39 Op. Atty. Gen. 348.

In drama, magnitude and finality his decisions so far overshadow any others that almost alone he fills the public eye and ear. No other personality in public life can begin to compete with him in access to the public mind through modern methods of communications. By his prestige as head of state and his influence upon public opinion he exerts a leverage upon those who are supposed (654) to check and balance his power which often cancels their effectiveness. Moreover, the rise of the party system has made a significant extraconstitutional supplement to real executive power. No appraisal of his necessities is realistic which overlooks that he heads a political system as well as a legal system. Party loyalties and interests, sometimes more binding than law, extend his effective control into branches of government other than his own and he often may win, as a political leader, what he cannot command under the Constitution. Indeed, Woodrow Wilson, commenting on the President as leader both of his party and of the Nation, observed, "If he rightly interpret the national thought and boldly insist upon it, he is irresistible .... His office is anything he has the sagacity and force to make it."[25] I cannot be brought to believe that this country will suffer if the Court refuses further to aggrandize the presidential office, already so potent and so relatively immune from judicial review,[26] at the expense of Congress.

But I have no illusion that any decision by this Court can keep power in the hands of Congress if it is not wise and timely in meeting its problems. A crisis that challenges the President equally, or perhaps primarily, challenges Congress. If not good law, there was worldly wisdom in the maxim attributed to Napoleon that "The tools belong to the man who can use them." We may say that power to legislate for emergencies belongs in the hands of Congress, but only Congress itself can prevent power from slipping through its fingers.

The essence of our free Government is "leave to live by no man's leave, underneath the law"—to be governed by those impersonal forces which we call law. Our Government (655) is fashioned to fulfill this concept so far as humanly possible. The Executive, except for recommendation and veto, has no legislative power. The executive action we have here originates in the individual will of the President and represents an exercise of authority without law. No one, perhaps not even the President, knows the limits of the power he may seek to exert in this instance and the parties affected cannot learn the limit of their rights. We do not know today what powers over labor

[25] Wilson, Constitutional Government in the United States, 68–69
[26] Rossiter, The Supreme Court and the Commander in Chief, 126–132.

or property would be claimed to flow from Government possession if we should legalize it, what rights to compensation would be claimed or recognized, or on what contingency it would end. With all its defects, delays and inconveniences, men have discovered no technique for long preserving free government except that the Executive be under the law, and that the law be made by parliamentary deliberations.

Such institutions may be destined to pass away. But it is the duty of the Court to be last, not first, to give them up.[27]

[27] We follow the judicial tradition instituted on a memorable Sunday in 1612, when King James took offense at the independence of his judges and, in rage, declared: "Then I am to be under the law—which it is treason to affirm." Chief Justice Coke replied to his King: "Thus wrote Bracton, 'The King ought not to be under any man, but he is under God and the Law.'" 12 Coke 65 (as to its verity, 18 Eng. Hist. Rev. 664–675); 1 Campbell, Lives of the Chief Justices (1849), 272.

4

Drafting Choices

Justice Jackson started writing his *Youngstown* opinion before the oral argument.[1] The expedited proceedings in the lower courts and the urgency of reaching a final decision gave the Supreme Court far less time than usual to issue its decision. Fortunately, since Jackson kept most of the drafts and notes for his concurrence, we can study how his thinking unfolded.[2] While he drew on his deep experience in the executive branch, he also relied on two written sources that were not given due credit in the opinion. A comparison of the opinion with Jackson's prior work also shows that he recycled some old material to save time. But he also cut some new material from the final version to use instead in a law review article on President Roosevelt's secret opinion about the legislative veto's constitutionality.

An Author at Work

The first draft of the concurrence is dated May 7. This was before the briefs were filed, which suggests that this draft was one of Jackson's "thinking to himself" memos, like his unpublished opinions in *Quirin* and *Hirabayashi*. He had probably read Judge Pine's District Court opinion and followed the press coverage. The May 7 draft contained a mix of typed and handwritten pages that addressed discrete issues; this draft shows that he was strongly inclined to conclude that the President acted unlawfully. Jackson's second draft, dated May 8, added details and this comment: "If the Government had chosen a course which could only be sustained by a virtual destruction of the Constitution as we have known it, it could not have done better."[3] At this point, though, Jackson did not know if he would be in the majority or in dissent because oral argument had not yet been held.

The Justice's third draft, dated May 22, was also rough but looked more like a complete opinion. This one was written with knowledge of the Court's likely decision. Justice Black had not circulated his draft majority opinion, but there was already an expectation among the Justices that several

The Actual Art of Governing. Gerard N. Magliocca, Oxford University Press. © Oxford University Press (2025).
DOI: 10.1093/9780197768563.003.0005

opinions would be filed.[4] Consequently, Jackson was now revising his work with an eye toward publication. By May 29, he had a fourth draft that included footnotes. It is unclear when Jackson first shared a draft with his law clerks, but the most likely answer is sometime between May 22 and 29. William H. Rehnquist recalled, "I am sure that this was the sort of opinion in which he felt no need for the help of clerks. We were shown the opinion in draft form, and as I recall, asked to find citations for some of the propositions it contained, but that was about the extent of our participation."[5] On June 2, the day that *Youngstown* came down, there is a final draft that is typeset in the official Court style and contains only small line edits and corrections.

Follow Gus

The most important judicial influence on the concurrence was an opinion by Judge Augustus N. Hand.[6] An undated handwritten note in Jackson's *Youngstown* file states: "The President has no power, in absence of legislative authority, to prohibit landing of a submarine cable. Opinion of A. N. Hand. United States v. Western Union Telegraph Co. 272 Fed 311."[7] The brief for the steel companies cited Judge Hand's 1921 opinion for the proposition that the President lacks "inherent or other power to legislate in the public interest."[8] *Western Union* also may have been in Jackson's mind independently. Just six months before *Youngstown*, he gave a speech in New York honoring Augustus Hand and his more famous cousin, Judge Learned Hand. In that address, Jackson said, "If I were to write a prescription for becoming the perfect district judge, it would be always to quote Learned and always to follow Gus."[9] He took his own advice in *Youngstown* and followed Gus by adopting a framework for presidential power that focused on whether Congress had authorized or rejected the executive action.

Western Union raised the question of whether the President could prevent a foreign underwater communication cable from being landed in the United States.[10] A telegraph company wanted to connect a cable from Barbados to Miami, but the President directed the Navy to block the landing,[11] and the United States then sued in federal court for an injunction. The case came before Judge Hand, who was then a federal district judge. There was no congressional authorization for the President to halt foreign cables, and thus Hand explained that an injunction was proper only if the President was given this power "expressly, or by implication, in the Constitution."[12]

"I cannot," Judge Hand wrote, "regard a failure by Congress to exercise its undoubted powers as proof that some other branch of the government has the right to do what Congress might readily have authorized." He then described some powers enumerated in Article II before rejecting the claim that the President's role as commander in chief covered Western Union's cable. Although "control of cables would be useful in time of war, it is nowhere suggested that there is any hostile purpose in the attempt to land the cables."[13] "The implications of the power contended for by the government," Hand observed, "are very great. If the President has the right, without any legislative sanction, to prevent the landing of cables, why has he not the right to prevent the importation of opium on the ground that it is a deleterious drug, or the importation of silk or steel because such importation may tend to reduce wages in this country and injure the national welfare?"[14] "In the same way," he said, "why does not the President, in the absence of any Act of Congress, have the right to refuse to admit foreigners to our shores, and to deport those aliens whose presence he regards as a public menace?"[15]

The United States also argued that the President's authority over cable landings could be sustained "because Congress has long acquiesced in executive regulation of such matters in cases where Congress has not acted."[16] (This anticipated Justice Frankfurter's argument in *Youngstown* that consistent executive action and congressional acquiescence could serve as a gloss on Article II.) Judge Hand discussed the main precedent, which was President Ulysses S. Grant's claim in 1875 that he could on his own authority deny the landing of a cable linked to a foreign firm with a monopoly.[17] "I have thought it most questionable," Hand said, "whether the power of the President to regulate cable connection is expressed or implied in the Constitution, but if Congress, which has control over foreign commerce, has chosen to allow the President to prevent physical connection between the shores of this country and of foreign nations by cables, telephones, radio devices, or pipe lines, the occasion and mode of such executive action would seem . . . to be a political question."[18] "I should doubt," Judge Hand went on, "whether the extent of the President's authority if based not upon an original prerogative but upon congressional acquiescence was a justiciable matter, and whether a court should interfere to define or support it; for the basis of the right would then depend on the interrelations and mutual accommodations of the Executive and Legislative Departments of the government, and not upon strict law."[19]

But Hand concluded that there was no congressional acquiescence. He reasoned that the Acts of Congress regulating international cables implied that the President was prohibited from acting on his own to block Western Union's cable. "[I]t seems unreasonable to hold," he wrote, "that Congress has not occupied the field and legislated so generally in regard to this defendant that it has withdrawn it from the exercise of executive power in respect to foreign cable connections."[20] Hand also concluded that the executive branch had not robustly asserted its authority in this area. He could find only two possible examples, and thus "the facts of the case do not appear to indicate a continuous current of legal opinion in the Departments of State and Justice which can be said to support the position now contended for by the government, and they certainly do not indicate any conscious acquiescence on the part of Congress."[21] As a result, "believing that the so-called executive power to restrict unauthorized foreign cable connections does not apply to this case, I deny the motion for a preliminary injunction."

Western Union contains the seeds of Jackson's famous three rough categories to assess presidential authority. First, Judge Hand read executive power in conjunction with Acts of Congress. Second, he said that an exercise of presidential authority could be valid even in the absence of Article II support or an Act of Congress if there was congressional silence. Third, he wrote that an implied exclusion of presidential action by Congress was possible and, indeed, had occurred with respect to foreign cable landings. Finally, Judge Hand made clear that the President's status as commander in chief did not justify any unilateral executive action that was plausibly about national security. But although Hand's logic permeates the *Youngstown* concurrence, Jackson did not acknowledge this fact in his opinion, citing *Western Union* only once in a footnote as one of many cases rejecting a claim of executive power without statutory authorization.[22]

The Bell Memo

A second unacknowledged influence on Jackson's concurrence was a Justice Department memo on "The President's Power in the Field of Foreign Relations," written in 1937 by Assistant Solicitor General Golden W. Bell.[23] While there is no direct evidence that Jackson used the Bell Memo, there is strong circumstantial evidence. First, we know that he was aware of the memo (even though it was not then publicly available), because a copy is

Figure 4.1 Judge Augustus N. Hand, the author of a District Court opinion that Justice Jackson used to construct his concurrence. Harvard Law Library.

in Jackson's personal papers.[24] Second, the memo used a distinctive turn of phrase that reappears in the *Youngstown* opinion. At one point, Bell wrote, "In the field of foreign relations, the Chief Executive moves in a zone of twilight where he may proceed with assurance of his powers under the

Constitution only when the people follow and approve."[25] Though Bell did not coin the phrase "zone of twilight," the odds that this image occurred to Jackson without seeing the memo are long. Third, the Bell Memo included some of the same themes, some of the same sources, some of the same quotations, and (most important of all) some of the same passages as the concurring opinion.[26] In short, Golden Bell is the unsung hero of the *Youngstown* concurrence.

Bell had been asked to consider the President's freedom to intervene in the Spanish Civil War and the Sino-Japanese War under the Neutrality Act of 1937. The Act imposed an arms embargo on belligerents and applied this limit to civil wars.[27] To assess the scope of the Act in relation to executive power, the Bell Memo started with the debate over President Washington's 1793 Neutrality Proclamation for the Anglo-French War.[28] Under the pen name "Pacificus," Alexander Hamilton wrote newspaper articles defending Washington's unilateral authority to issue the Proclamation.[29] James Madison, writing as "Helvedius," took the opposite view, arguing that only Congress could issue such a proclamation.[30] The Bell Memo then quoted President Jefferson's views about the war with the Barbary pirates and the Louisiana Purchase, which were inconsistent on the respective roles of the executive and Congress.[31] A few pages later, the memo discussed the dueling positions of Teddy Roosevelt and William Howard Taft regarding when a president could act without congressional authorization.[32] After that, Bell addressed the Court's decision in *United States v. Curtiss-Wright Export Corp.*, which describes the President's broad prerogative in foreign affairs in language that the memo dismissed as dicta.[33] Lastly, the memo quoted Woodrow Wilson's view on presidential power and on the link between that power and the President's role as a party leader.[34]

The Bell Memo's pragmatic assessment of presidential power also may have influenced Jackson.[35] The memo said that the scope of executive authority "is essentially practical and does not admit of a legalistic treatment that fails to take into account human nature in the individual and in the mass. . . . History corroborates the conclusion, while at the same time overturning any legal theory that does not accord with experience."[36] "In this sphere," the memo stated, "'the event is a great teacher.' The theory of Hamilton and the theory of Madison have been debated continuously—and the argument will persist. The two views have not been and cannot be reconciled in the realm of logic; in the practical world they converge." The memo summed up its analysis with the line about a "zone of twilight" where public

Figure 4.2 Golden W. Bell, the author of a Justice Department memo that footnotes in the *Youngstown* concurrence quoted without attribution. Library of Congress, Prints & Photographs Division, photograph by Harris & Ewing, [LC-DIG-hec-27111].

opinion was the crucial element of executive power. “If it be shocking,” the memo added, “to conclude that a President at one time under the Constitution has the power to do an act in respect of foreign relations, and that the same or another President under the same Constitution has not the power to do such an act at another time, the trouble is not with the conclusion but with the concept.” This theme resonates with Jackson’s hard-nosed assessment of presidential power in doubtful cases, although his experience had probably already taught him that lesson. The memo’s emphasis on public opinion also helps explain why Roosevelt—a popular president in 1941—was able to get away with the North American Aviation plant seizure while Truman—an unpopular president in 1952—was unable to make the steel seizure stick.

Jackson drew freely on the Bell Memo in his concurring opinion. To begin with, the Justice said in his concurrence that the historical sources “largely cancel each other." In a footnote, he described those conflicting sources as the Pacificus and Helvedius essays and the Taft and Theodore Roosevelt opinions on the presidency, just as the memo did.[37] Next, in two different notes Jackson used the same Jefferson quotations as the memo did, which helps explains the otherwise odd choice of these particular extracts.[38] Then in footnote 2 of the concurring opinion, Jackson used nearly the same language as the memo did to distinguish *Curtis-Wright*.[39] Furthermore, Jackson used two of the memo's Woodrow Wilson quotations, one in the opinion's text and one in a footnote.[40] Despite this ample sampling (maybe including the phrase "zone of twilight"), Jackson never gave Bell any credit.[41] The Justice could not have cited the memo because it was secret, but he could have recognized Bell's contribution in some other way.[42] As with Judge Hand's *Western Union* opinion, though, Jackson left the impression that he did all of the important work himself.

The Buffalo Law School Speech and FDR's Secret Memo

The final unacknowledged source for the concurrence was one of Justice Jackson's own articles. In May 1951, the Justice gave the inaugural Mitchell Lecture at Buffalo Law School, on "Wartime Security and Liberty Under Law."[43] This was a wide-ranging talk on the Bill of Rights, President Lincoln's suspension of the writ of habeas corpus during the Civil War, martial law, and *Korematsu*. In one section, Jackson discussed how some European nations responded to crises by providing for broad emergency powers, and then described how those constitutions operated in Weimar Germany, France, and Great Britain before and during World War II.[44] The sources for this information (according to the notes in the published version of the remarks) included Jackson's opening statement at the Nuremberg Trial and Clinton Rossiter's book on *Constitutional Dictatorship*, which was published in 1948.[45] The comparative emergency powers section of the Buffalo Law School address would be cut and pasted (with only light editing) directly into the Justice's *Youngstown* opinion.[46] In that opinion Jackson cited neither his Buffalo speech nor his Nuremberg address, though he did cite Rossiter's book.

Jackson also considered whether *Youngstown* was the appropriate occasion to disclose President Roosevelt's opinion attacking the constitutionality of the legislative veto. In a draft dated May 22, the Justice stated that he saw no reason why Congress could not terminate a grant of emergency power with a joint resolution. He then said, "In this respect, however, I must admit that I did not see eye to eye with the late President Roosevelt, and it is, perhaps, an appropriate time to fulfill his request that I should make known his personal view."[47] The Justice then described the Lend-Lease Act and FDR's contrary position before stating that "Since I felt unable to give him an opinion to that effect, he wrote one of his own, which he asked me to make known at some appropriate time. Since we are considering the powers of his office vis-à-vis the Congress this seems an appropriate time to take note of his view."[48] The May 29 draft moved the discussion of the secret opinion to a footnote.[49] And in the end, Jackson decided against revealing FDR's views in the *Youngstown* concurrence. Instead, he did so in a 1953 *Harvard Law Review* article.[50] Though the article offered a more detailed account of the Lend-Lease Act debate than the concurrence drafts had, Jackson may have taken some text that he left on the cutting-room floor in *Youngstown* for the Harvard article.[51]

Why did Jackson decide not to reveal the secret opinion in 1952? One possibility is that the constitutionality of a legislative veto was not at issue in *Youngstown*. A more thoughtful answer—given by Adam J. White in an article about the concurrence drafts—is that FDR's opinion belied Jackson's claim at oral argument and in his opinion that his statements and actions as attorney general should be discounted as precedents because he was acting as a partisan advocate for executive power.[52] In rejecting the President's request for an opinion declaring the legislative veto unconstitutional, Jackson took an independent position against executive power. Drawing attention to his independence as a presidential adviser would have undercut Jackson's claim that his support for the Northern American Aviation seizure did not bind him if that was a precedent for Truman's actions. But Jackson's extrajudicial thoughts on the relationship between the legislative veto and emergency power will be helpful for evaluating the proper scope of that power.

****

With this thorough grounding in the concurrence's text and context, let us now engage with the spirit and the ideas that make Justice Jackson's opinion so compelling.

PART 2
THEMES

5
Personal Reflections

Justice Jackson's concurrence begins by emphasizing his personal experience as a presidential adviser and closes by stating that the impersonal forces that we call law are the essence of free government. These two points reflect a deeper insight about how judges should decide cases.[1] The latter point represents blind justice, whereby judges set aside their personal thoughts and apply the law without fear or favor. The other represents wisdom, whereby judges draw on their own experience and reflect on the impact of any decision. Jackson's analysis in *Youngstown* is probably the most self-consciously wise opinion ever written by a Justice. Yet some of the concurrence's authority flows from the perception that its author was using—but at the same time rising above—his professional background to support the rule of law. Jackson's delicate balancing act may be impossible to replicate but contains instructive lessons on the art of judicial rhetoric.[2]

The Recusal Question

Before he started weaving his personal story into the concurrence, the Justice pondered whether his experience disqualified him from hearing *Youngstown* at all. His support for the North American Aviation property seizure as attorney general was discussed at oral argument. When Chief Justice Vinson delivered his dissent from the bench, he noted Jackson's prior view and then ad-libbed that changing one's mind was "evidence of strength" and that Jackson had stated his opinion in 1941 as strongly "as he ordinarily does now."[3] *The New York Times* reported that this last comment was followed by a burst of laughter in the courtroom that Jackson joined. But the Justice treated the issue seriously and did consider whether his involvement in the North American Aviation seizure meant that he should recuse himself from *Youngstown*.[4]

In his first draft, Jackson directly took on the recusal question with a nod to *Hamlet*: "To sit or not to sit."[5] "Candor requires me to state," he said, "that

The Actual Art of Governing. Gerard N. Magliocca, Oxford University Press. © Oxford University Press (2025).
DOI: 10.1093/9780197768563.003.0006

I have considered whether I should sit in this case, in view of having acted as an advisor to President Roosevelt in some Executive seizures prior to World War II and in the preparation for some others that were not consummated. No one, I suppose, would doubt that an ideal tribunal would be comprised of judges with no record to live up to and none to live down on the bench." But in practice the "custom of appointing Justices from the other branches of the Government frequently presents litigants with a bench whose judges have participated in legislative or Executive functions directly or indirectly involved. It is a question for each Justice to resolve, and I have concluded that my experience is too remote to carry any insurmountable predilections that warrant withdrawal and that practical experience with the problems of this case may contribute something to a debate as to the President's powers."[6] His next draft stated: "As Attorney General, it was my duty to advise President Roosevelt in urgent matters which raised sharp issues of presidential power that are cited as precedents here. Such a role might suggest withdrawal from this case. Having weighed all of those considerations, I have concluded instead that I may contribute some teachings of practical experience tempered by a decade of detached reflection to a theoretical debate that extends backward to the beginning and is likely to continue to the end of the Republic."[7]

In his final opinion, Jackson did not discuss recusal. That was the right decision. When a judge decides not to recuse, no reason for sitting is given in the opinion on the merits,[8] and to do so would be an irrelevant distraction. More important, Jackson made the right decision in not recusing. His executive experience was a source of valuable insights, and his active role in the North American Aviation seizure was not unfair to the parties in *Youngstown*, nor did it create any perception of unfairness. After all, Jackson's work was more than a decade old, involved another President, and had nothing to do with the steel industry. Moreover, a recusal could have led to a deadlocked Supreme Court in an important case, which is usually not a risk worth taking.[9]

Breaking the Fourth Wall

Jackson's concurrence is autobiographical in a way that no law clerk could have drafted, and some simple observations flow from that fact.[10] First, the intimate nature of the opinion explains why no other Justice joined. It is almost impossible to imagine another Justice signing an opinion with so many personal reflections by the author. By contrast, opinions that speak for the Court as opposed to an individual Justice must be impersonal because they require five votes and serve as institutional statements. Second, Jackson was forced to inject himself into the concurrence because his role in the North American Aviation seizure was raised by the briefs, in the oral argument, and in the Chief Justice's dissent. To ignore his own history in his opinion would have been unsatisfying. Professor Patricia Bellia makes the astute point that "Jackson's famous three-part framework initially developed not as an abstract tool for resolving presidential power disputes, but as a tool for contextualizing Justice Jackson's own advice to President Roosevelt and distinguishing it from the advice upon which President Truman acted."[11] Perhaps Jackson needed to convince himself before he could convince others. Though the prose in his opinions tended to be informal in a way that called attention to his individual perspective, none of his other opinions is as self-referential as this one.

Figure 5.1 Justice Robert H. Jackson. Library of Congress, Prints & Photographs Division, photograph by Harris & Ewing, [LC-DIG-hec-27903].

Judges tread on treacherous ground when they add personality to opinions.[12] Most of the time, such statements are unpersuasive because they are irrelevant. In other cases, they can come across as emotional outbursts rather than reasoned judgment.[13] One controversial example is the opening of Justice Frankfurter's dissent to Jackson's opinion in *Barnette* (the flag-salute case): "One who belongs to the most vilified and persecuted minority in history is not likely to be insensible to the freedoms guaranteed by our Constitution."[14] Frankfurter's statement (during the Second World War) that he was Jewish certainly grabs the reader's attention and sets up his argument that he was not deciding the case based on his personal views.[15] But Frankfurter's choice was sharply criticized—even by his own law clerk—as a distraction that undercut the rest of his analysis.[16]

A judge's personal reflection can also be gratuitous, because the reflection could just as easily have come from almost any person of a similar age.[17] Jackson provided an example in his unpublished draft in *Brown v. Board of Education*.[18] In that draft, he wrote: "One whose impressionable years were spent in public schools in a region where Negro pupils were very few and where economic, social and political motives united against segregating them is predisposed to the conclusion that segregation elsewhere has outlived whatever justification it may have had."[19] Later in the draft, he added: "My little experience in a nonsegregated school does not teach that to mingle closely with white pupils fully solves the Negro's psychological or educational problem."[20] The problem is that millions of Americans in 1954 could have said the same thing but reached a different conclusion. That suggests that Jackson's childhood experience offered no special insight into the constitutionality of racial segregation in schools.

A more basic challenge involved in including personal grace notes in a judicial opinion is that the United States is "a nation of laws and not of men."[21] Charisma or individuality is the antithesis of law, which is a collective enterprise.[22] Some Justices try to square that circle by stating that their legal view in a case is contrary to their personal view. The most notable examples are those in which a judge disagrees with a precedent but nonetheless affirms that precedent.[23] Then the message is that law requires a judge to set aside his or her personality, as symbolized by the tradition of judges wearing black robes in court and as practiced by judges refraining from partisan political statements.[24] To make an opinion more persuasive, a judge could also pretend that one's personal views are different from one's legal views, much as Mark Antony called Caesar's assassins "honorable men" in Shakespeare's version of the funeral oration.[25] To an underappreciated extent, Jackson's use of his past experience in *Youngstown* was more constructed than candid, though it will take a little time and patience to see why.[26]

Initially, Jackson offered an inside account of the North American Aviation seizure to explain why that action was not a precedent for Truman's steel-mill seizure. "If we simplify both occasions to the mere statement: 'The President seizes a manufacturing plant,'" he said in his first draft, "there is a similarity of subject, verb, and object. Hardly another qualification can be added that does not point to difference rather than likeness."[27] He then listed several factual differences, such as (1) the existence of federal contracts with the North American Aviation plant, (2) the presence of government property in the plant, (3) the strike's violation of the union's collective-bargaining agreement, and (4) the consent of the owners of that plant to the seizure. But it was the alleged communist involvement in the North American Aviation strike that was the decisive factor: "As the sole survivor of the group that was present when the seizure order was signed, I may say that it was this situation, communicated to the meeting in the President's office, that finally decided the seizure."[28] Here Jackson was acting as a fact witness who could not be cross-examined. Worse still, he was the only living witness, so his version of the facts could not be challenged. In his second draft, he retained the point with the first-person claim that Roosevelt's seizure, "at least as I knew it," did not support Truman's.[29] But later drafts eliminated the "I was there" references and cut back the entire discussion. Instead of spending pages on the issue as he had in early drafts, Jackson's final opinion used just two sentences and a note to say that North American Aviation "cannot be regarded as even a precedent, much less an authority for the present seizure."[30]

Jackson instead leaned on his personal experience to suggest that he would not have advised President Truman to seize and operate the steel mills unilaterally. "Whatever legal advice a President may get from those whose responsibility it is to defend his actions if they are attacked in court," he wrote in the May 22 draft, "there are seldom lacking irresponsible official and unofficial advisors who urge dramatic action, let the court decide what they may."[31] "[P]rudence," he went on, "counselled a moderation that would stop short of provoking a judicial test and a long line of court decisions and warned that a questioned seizure at least would need all the constitutional backing possible."[32] The Justice also wrote, in language that was largely retained in the final text, that advice to the President on his powers as commander in chief should pay attention to legislation that curbed executive authority. While Jackson deleted the "irresponsible" line in the next draft, he refined the prudence and statutory points and added citations.[33] For prudence, he quoted William Searle Holdsworth's classic history of English law, which said that the Tudor monarchs such as Queen Elizabeth I were so tactful in using their powers that no judicial or parliamentary definition of them was requested. The implication was twofold. First, Truman's act was not tactful because it provoked a judicial test. Second, Jackson's advice to Roosevelt on the North American Aviation seizure *was* tactful because no legal challenge was made. As for mindfulness of Congress, Jackson cited his own opinions as attorney general (without pointing out that they were his) on the destroyer deal and on another matter in which he advised FDR that his freedom of action was limited by an Act of Congress.[34]

The shift from personal narrator to personal sage was an improvement. But drawing on experience to say "I would not have advised this" is still problematic.[35] Reasonable officials often disagree about open-ended constitutional questions. And a government decision can be unwise and constitutional at the same time. Jackson's reputation and experience did give his constitutional opinion more credibility, but reputations are not impersonal. Consider for a moment how Jackson's opinion would be viewed if he had instead voted to uphold Truman's action. In that hypothetical, he could easily have used his privileged knowledge of the North American Aviation seizure as a justification. Such a ruling, though, might have looked more like the biased judgment of a former presidential adviser. Readers could well have thought that Jackson was simply interested in supporting President Truman, who had appointed him the Nuremberg prosecutor, or in justifying his prior work as attorney general.[36] One of the concurrence's secret weapons is that Jackson ruled against the President in a way that confounded expectations. But where did those expectations come from?

The Myth of Jackson's Turnabout

A common misunderstanding of the concurrence is that Jackson changed his position on the constitutionality of presidential property seizures because he was a judge. Chief Justice John Roberts made this claim at his confirmation hearing: "[O]ne reason people admire Justice Jackson so much is that although he had strong views as Attorney General, he recognized, when he became a member of the Supreme Court, that his job had changed, and he was not the President's lawyer, he was not the chief lawyer in the executive branch, he was a Justice sitting in review of some of the decisions of the Executive. And he took a different perspective."[37] Likewise, Professor Noah Feldman states that *Youngstown* "required Jackson to revisit and reverse the position on executive power that he had taken while working for Roosevelt."[38] They are incorrect. Jackson went out of his way to say that North American Aviation was not authority for the steel seizure and that he was not changing his view. Why, then, do some people think that he switched sides?

The answer is that Justice Jackson sprinkled his concurrence with lines implying that he might not have personally agreed with President Roosevelt's action in 1941. One was that "a judge cannot accept self-serving press statements of the attorney for one of the interested parties as authority for one of the interested parties, even if the advocate was himself." The press statement at issue was the one that Jackson issued in defense of the North American Aviation seizure.[39] His use of "self-serving" left the impression that the statement was a public-relations exercise on behalf of a client rather than sound analysis by an attorney. Jackson also stated in a footnote that he did not consider North American Aviation a precedent for Truman's seizure, and that "even if I did, I should not bind present judicial judgment by earlier partisan advocacy." The use of "partisan" suggested that Jackson had been representing his client rather than expressing his own position. Finally, there was a wink-and-a-nod reference in the concurrence's final footnote, where Jackson quoted Chief Justice Edward Coke's line to King James I that the "King ought not to be under any man, but he is under God and the Law."[40] Coke was Queen Elizabeth I's attorney general before he became a judge, and thus the reference implied that there was a parallel between Coke and Jackson. In one draft, Jackson made the comparison more explicit by prefacing Coke's quote with the line that he "had been a subservient, partisan Attorney General but . . . lives in history as an exemplary judge."[41] While the final opinion did not include this line, judges and professors who knew their English legal history would probably have understood the coded reference.

Justice Jackson was exercising poetic license in these passages. He was not a particularly partisan attorney general, and he did disagree with Roosevelt when he thought the law was against the President. Furthermore, Jackson did think that the North American Aviation seizure was lawful. But because his advice was confidential and could not be contradicted by any living witness,

Jackson was free to suggest that his private view on North American Aviation might have been different from his public claim. This may explain why he thought better of using his *Youngstown* opinion to reveal his disagreement with FDR on the constitutionality of legislative vetoes. A disclosure would have exposed their lawyer-client relationship and made plain that Jackson was not just the President's yes-man. With that background, Jackson's defense of the North American Aviation seizure in 1941 could not be dismissed as advocacy. Thus, the concurring opinion is an ambiguous text in which Justice Jackson embraces and distances himself from his personal experience at the same time. The most plausible reading is that the Justice complicated his personal role for persuasive effect.[42]

Nevertheless, the concurrence did capture a larger truth: Judges should be open to changing their minds. Justice Jackson cheerfully said as much in a solo opinion from 1950 that expressly disavowed another of his opinions as attorney general.[43] "I am entitled to say of that opinion," he wrote, "what any discriminating reader must think of it—that it was as foggy as the statute that the Attorney General was asked to interpret." After explaining why his prior view was incorrect, Jackson quoted some Justices and other famous people who recanted their previous views, including Baron Westbury's statement in the House of Lords that "I can only say that I am amazed that a man of my intelligence should have been guilty of giving such an opinion."[44] "If there are other ways of gracefully and good-naturedly surrendering former views to a better considered position," Jackson concluded, "I invoke them all." Two years later, in *Youngstown*, he said nothing like this about his press statement on the North American Aviation seizure. This again suggests that his comments in the concurrence about not being bound by prior advocacy were more rhetorical than real.

There was a Justice in the *Youngstown* majority who comes closer to the archetype that some have claimed Jackson represents: Tom Clark. Justice Clark was President Truman's attorney general before he joined the Court and in that role had expressed support for broad presidential power. In 1949, Clark told the Senate that "the inherent power of the President to deal with emergencies that affect the health, safety and welfare of the entire Nation is exceedingly great."[45] Justice Clark's service in the Truman Administration and this prior statement even led to calls for his recusal in *Youngstown*, which Jackson retained in his case file.[46] But Clark too voted against the steel seizure, noting with his own autobiographical twist that, in describing the President's authority to meet emergencies, "I care not whether one calls it 'residual,' 'inherent,' 'moral,' 'implied,' 'aggregate,' 'emergency,' or otherwise. I am of the conviction that those who have had the gratifying experience of being the President's lawyer have used one or more of these adjectives only with the utmost of sincerity and the highest of purpose."[47] Jackson defended Justice Clark in a footnote of the concurrence by quoting Clark's statement to the Senate and then saying that "[r]egardless of the general reference to 'inherent powers,' the citations were instances of congressional authorization."[48] Why Jackson defended Clark is unclear, though it was a way of underscoring his own argument that congressional authorization was critical in assessing executive power. Or maybe he was just doing Justice Clark a favor, given that they were voting the same way notwithstanding Clark's prior service for Truman.

In the end, Justice Jackson's reliance on experience reflected his broader attitude as a self-taught lawyer. What he had learned on the job was more trustworthy than what he called "the conventional materials of judicial decision, which seem unduly to accentuate doctrine and legal fiction."[49] But since these conventional materials are the building blocks of law, how did Jackson understand the proper method of constitutional interpretation in *Youngstown*?

6
Relativity

Justice Jackson's *Youngstown* concurrence is the only Supreme Court opinion that uses Einstein's term "relativity."[1] Jackson used that word to describe the relationship between Congress and the President, but the term also captures the spirit of his interpretive method.[2] He dismissed bright-line rules and orthodox legal authorities such as doctrine, history, and text in favor of a flexible structural analysis that took into account the presidency's informal institutional advantages over Congress.[3] Reading the Constitution in relative terms was an outgrowth of Jackson's faith in experience over theory, especially experience shaped by war.[4] One result was what he called "a somewhat over-simplified grouping of practical situations in which a President may doubt, or others may challenge, his powers"—a formulation that is today recited as a formal mantra in separation-of-powers cases. The transformation of Jackson's anti-doctrinal opinion into doctrine is an expression of the discomfort that many lawyers feel in openly interpreting the Constitution in a way that focuses on balance and heightens uncertainty.

Sidelining Standard Sources

The concurring opinion in *Youngstown* begins by stressing what it is not rather than what it is.[5] In his second sentence, Jackson downplays "conventional materials of judicial decision which seem unduly to accentuate doctrine and legal fiction." This is an unusual statement for a judge, since judges make doctrine by deciding cases.[6] Why did Jackson not want to accentuate the positive in his work? The answer is that he thought doctrine was often an unsound tool for creating constitutional law.[7] In *The Struggle for Judicial Supremacy*, a book he wrote before joining the Court, Jackson explained his skepticism of common-law reasoning in constitutional cases. First, he observed that lawyers did not possess "the rounded and comprehensive wisdom to govern all society."[8] Second, "doctrine has

The Actual Art of Governing. Gerard N. Magliocca, Oxford University Press. © Oxford University Press (2025).
DOI: 10.1093/9780197768563.003.0007

another characteristic which sets it quite apart from all science and from most philosophy. Legal learning is built around the principle known as *stare decisis*. It means that on the same point of law yesterday's decision shall govern today's decision. Like a coral reef, the common law thus becomes a structure of fossils."[9] While these "fossils" were a force for stability on private-law subjects such as contracts and property, "in constitutional law they are the most powerful influence in forming and supporting reactionary opinions. The judge who can take refuge in a precedent does not need to justify his decision. . . . He may 'reluctantly feel himself bound' by a doctrine, supported by a respected historical name, that he would not be able to justify to contemporary opinion or under modern conditions." Finally, Jackson argued that doctrine was too dependent on legal fictions, by which he meant false statements that are useful even though people know that they are false.[10] (One example is that, for certain purposes, a corporation may be treated a person.)[11] Fictions are a byproduct of doctrine because a judge must take precedents seriously even if they do not fit new circumstances well. Jackson said that courts often resolve that dilemma by "resorting to fiction to explain facts where modern learning would resort to facts to clarify fictions."[12] Indeed, one reason why Jackson's opinions are highly regarded is that he frequently punctured legal fictions in order to express a more candid view of what the Supreme Court was doing.[13]

Next, the concurrence downplayed the value of history in constitutional interpretation. Here is Jackson's famous line on that issue: "Just what our forefathers did envision, or would have envisioned had they foreseen modern conditions, must be divined from materials almost as enigmatic as the dreams Joseph was called upon to interpret for Pharaoh."[14] In the biblical story from Genesis, Pharaoh dreamed that he was standing by the Nile and saw seven fat cows emerge from the river.[15] He then saw seven scraggly cows emerge and eat the fat cows. In the next dream, Pharaoh saw seven healthy heads of grain growing on one stem. He then saw seven withered heads of grain swallow the healthy grain. Nobody at the royal court understood these dreams, but Joseph (who was then in prison) had been given the gift of divination by God. He told Pharaoh that there would be seven years of plenty followed by seven years of famine, and thus food should be stored during the fat years to stave off hunger in the lean years. The moral of this story, which would have been obvious to most Americans in 1952, is that only divine revelation could resolve what the Framers intended for the modern world.[16]

Jackson did not entirely reject history, just as he did not entirely reject doctrine. After all, later in the opinion he concluded that the forefathers probably did not create the presidency with George III in mind and that they were suspicious of emergency powers. Evidently some of what the forefathers envisioned could be ascertained. Jackson was also perfectly willing to rely on recent history in the form of legislative or executive practice. Nonetheless, the Justice was inclined to think that remote history was usually inconclusive.[17] Writing for the Court in *Cramer v. United States*, a landmark 1945 treason case, Jackson said that historical materials were "of little help; necessity as well as desire taught a concept that differed from all historical models in the drafting of our treason clause."[18] Twenty-first-century Supreme Court opinions, by contrast, rarely say that the drafting or ratification history of a constitutional provision is unhelpful. Indeed, originalist judges, given their assumption that a legal principle can almost always be derived from the original public meaning, sometimes struggle to explain the relevance of post-ratification practice.[19]

Jackson was equally skeptical of a literal reading of the text. He criticized "the rigidity dictated by doctrinaire textualism" because "[s]ome clauses could be made almost unworkable, as well as immutable, by refusal to indulge some latitude of interpretation for changing times." Moreover, the "actual art of governing under our Constitution does not and cannot conform to judicial definitions of the power of any of its branches based on isolated clauses or even single Articles torn from context." His jabs at textualism could be read as a criticism of Justice Black's opinion in *Youngstown*, but his life in the executive branch had also taught him that there was a big difference between the written and the actual Constitution,[20] particularly in times of crisis. Lawyers are understandably inclined toward functionalism when necessity is knocking loudly at the door, and Jackson's public service was dominated by dramatic events that were not amenable to textual solutions. As he said after the Court-packing fight, "Our forefathers never expected finally to solve the social and economic problems of their own day, much less those of all days to come, in the 4500 words of the original instrument. The chief purpose was to devise mechanics and to create a form of political organization, so that questions as they arise might always be answered by a peaceful method, and by a democratic process. The ultimate test of the Constitution is not doctrinal, but administrative."[21]

The Balanced Power Structure of the Republic

Consistent with this administrative premise, the *Youngstown* concurrence relies on a structural mode of interpretation.[22] Structural reasoning tends to be deductive and looks more like civil law than common law, which is in keeping with Jackson's skepticism of common-law thinking.[23] A structural opinion usually draws inferences from the text that give the government the best chance to function effectively.[24] In *M'Culloch v. Maryland*, Chief Justice John Marshall's opinion upheld the constitutionality of the National Bank by arguing that Congress must "be entrusted with ample means" for the execution of the powers granted by Article 1, Section 8, of the Constitution.[25] To conclude otherwise would leave federal authority crippled. The Chief Justice also said that the states lacked the power to single out federal institutions for taxation, because "the power to tax involves the power to destroy," and that states could not destroy or undermine constitutional federal entities.[26] A nonjudicial example of structural reasoning was President Lincoln's First Inaugural Address, in which he claimed that secession was unconstitutional in a democracy, in part because there was no logical limit to that idea.[27] If states can secede from the nation, then counties can secede from a state and towns can secede from a county. Lincoln also contended that secession was contrary to the spirit of democracy, which requires that losers concede defeat and remain as a loyal opposition rather than quitting.[28]

A recurring theme in Jackson's philosophy was that the Court's function was to keep the Constitution's structure balanced. For instance, his 1941 book stated that "[t]he Constitution, in making the balance between different parts of our government a legal rather than a political question, casts the Court as the most philosophical of our political departments. It keeps the most fundamental equilibriums of our society, such as that between centralization and localism."[29] Over a decade later, in his posthumously published Godkin Lectures, Jackson repeated this idea: "It is hard to conceive a task more fundamentally political than to maintain amidst changing conditions the balance between the executive and legislative branches of our federal system."[30] Not surprisingly, then, the first paragraph of the *Youngstown* opinion stresses that we must not "lose sight of enduring consequences upon the balanced power structure of our Republic." Later in the concurrence, the Justice referred to the "equilibrium established by our constitutional system." Our balanced power structure was assumed rather than proved.

Jackson then offered a second structural premise, which was that the Constitution "contemplates that practice will integrate the dispersed powers into a workable government. It enjoins upon its branches separateness but interdependence, autonomy but reciprocity." Justices quote this passage more than any other from the concurring opinion, usually in defending a functional reading of separation of powers against a more formal view.[31] From his structural observations, Jackson drew the inference that "[p]residential powers are not fixed but fluctuate, depending upon their disjunction or conjunction with those of Congress."[32] He then used "this factor of relativity" to distinguish roughly among situations when the President was acting with congressional authorization, without such authorization, or against congressional will.[33] The takeaway for now is that the rest of the concurrence proceeds on the assumption that executive power must be read with sensitivity to the essential counterbalance provided by Congress. For instance, Jackson said that the President cannot "escape control of executive powers by law" and that "emergency powers are consistent with free government only when their control is lodged elsewhere than in the Executive who exercises them." These are references to Congress, as the opinion's conclusion makes clear: "With all of its defects, delays and inconveniences, men have discovered no technique for long preserving free government except that the Executive be under the law, and that the law be made by parliamentary deliberations."

A third structural point in *Youngstown* is comparative.[34] Jackson copied a passage from one of his articles that surveyed the German, French, and British invocations of emergency powers before World War II. From those written and unwritten constitutions, he drew the conclusion that Weimar Germany took the wrong path by giving its president the right to declare an emergency on his own, as this had aided Hitler's rise to power.[35] France and Britain, by contrast, took the better path by requiring parliamentary approval for any emergency authority and by allowing their parliaments to withdraw that authority at any time. As a result, "parliamentary control made emergency powers compatible with freedom." Jackson also noted that Congress had already given the President many extraordinary powers in line with the French and British models, though none of them covered seizing steel factories. This sort of comparative structural logic, rare in American judicial opinions, was an outgrowth of Jackson's experience at Nuremberg.[36]

Fourth, Jackson made an informal structural argument based on the "gap that exists between the President's paper powers and his real powers."

For example, he pointed out—probably with Franklin D. Roosevelt's "Fireside Chats" in mind—that the President can seize the media spotlight in a way that Congress cannot.[37] He noted that our Constitution, unlike most democratic constitutions, makes the President head of state as well as head of government, which gives his actions an extra layer of legitimacy. And he wrote that the President leads his political party, which gives him powerful tools to persuade Congress when his party controls both chambers. I will say more about all three of these points later, but the conclusion that Jackson drew was that these were all reasons to read the President's formal powers more narrowly, since the executive's informal resources often allow him to "cancel the effectiveness" of the checks and balances available to Congress.

An inquiry into the actual art of governing (whether abroad or at home) complements a structural analysis.[38] Since a structural interpretation assumes that the Constitution contemplates a workable government, there is every reason to ask how governing works. Practice is different from judicial doctrine, consisting of what Judge Augustus N. Hand called the "interrelations and mutual accommodations of the Executive and Legislative Departments of the government."[39] Justice Jackson's interest in institutional custom was in keeping with his lifelong preference for learning by doing. But this method also flowed from Jackson's insight that the presidency was a "sketch," akin to an experiment. There were no national presidents anywhere in 1787; thus, any ideas about how that office would function could be only tentative. Put another way, a distinction can be drawn between constitutional principles that are ratified in view of well-worn structures or long-standing rights, where the original public meaning should receive deference, and others that are novel and so must be judged to a greater extent on their post-ratification evolution.

Part of the concurrence's power comes from its heavy reliance on structural reasoning.[40] A reader does not need to know anything about the Constitution's text, history, or doctrine to understand Jackson's opinion. His work reads like an essay more comparable to Chief Justice Marshall's most famous opinions, which cite no cases.[41] Structural opinions also look more like geometric proofs that begin with an axiom and then proceed step-by-step to a logical and inescapable conclusion—QED. But constitutional law is not geometry. No legal conclusion is incontrovertible, as each must be tested in an adversarial process. There is a rhetorical advantage, though, in presenting a legal conclusion as something like a geometric proof.[42] The resulting analysis usually flows directly from the text and sounds authoritative without being wooden. A structural opinion is also simply more convincing in a case about the Constitution's structure, as was true in *Youngstown*.[43] Finally, there is a practical bent to structural reasoning that is appealing and can bridge ideological divisions.[44]

What are the weak points in Jackson's interpretive method? One possibility is that, although the Constitution ought to be viewed through a structural lens, Jackson did so incorrectly.[45] A second thought is that a structural take was wrong in *Youngstown* because the case involved a constitutional right. Jackson did mention the Fifth Amendment's Due Process Clause and the Third Amendment in passing, but he said nothing about the Takings Clause or the fact that Truman seized the steel mills without any promise of compensation to their owners.[46] These two criticisms can be blended into a third, which is that Jackson's structural analysis was too simplistic.[47] The only factor of relativity that he identified was the relationship between Congress and the President. What about constitutional rights more generally? In one draft, Jackson nodded in this direction by saying that whether a presidential act should be upheld "may depend somewhat upon the nature of the action with a tendency to sustain it if it relates to some functioning of government other than one affecting the liberties of the people."[48] But the Justice did not follow up on this idea, nor did he consider the relevance of other structural pillars such as federalism and judicial independence.[49] Similarly, he ignored other potential threats to our balanced power structure, such as broad executive enforcement discretion or undue congressional generosity in granting the President power.[50] A single opinion cannot see around every corner.

The relativity of Jackson's concurrence can also be challenged on the ground that its search for balance leads only to confusion. Often it is unclear which of the concurrence's three rough categories applies to a given case. Within one of those categories, Jackson frankly stated that the legal dispute would fall within a "zone of twilight." And even when the proper category is clear and there is no zone of twilight, assessing the proper relationship between the President and Congress is fraught with difficulties. Professor Sanford Levinson once explained that "[t]o ask whether Congress has explicitly authorized, remained silent, or explicitly prohibited some presidential action is at best to begin analysis, certainly not to complete it."[51] Granted, Jackson offered structural insights beyond his three rough categories, but they do not advance the cause much further in most cases. One problem is that Jackson was inevitably creating doctrine to address a constitutional problem even though he thought that doctrine was not a good tool for resolving those problems. Another complication is that using his personal experience as the preface to his structural argument gives the opinion an "I know it when I see it" flavor in judging the appropriate relativity of presidential and congressional action. That might leave others who lack that experience less confident in their ability to match his judgment.[52]

On the other hand, Jackson's structural analysis can be misinterpreted as providing a false sense of security.[53] In my own experience teaching constitutional law, students gravitate to the three categories as a safe harbor in a world of contradictory authorities. They sound like rules, even though Jackson went out of his way to say that they were not. Courts and scholars also tend to recite the three categories as a formula before starting their analysis. The cardinal sin in any separation-of-powers dispute is not to quote Jackson's categories.[54] But this begs the question of whether Jackson's rough categories have become the very thing that he ridiculed—a legal fiction. To answer that question, we must examine each of the three categories in more detail.

7
Widest Latitude

Category One in Jackson's *Youngstown* concurrence states: "When the President acts pursuant to an express or implied authorization of Congress, his authority is at its maximum, for it includes all that he possesses in his own right plus all that Congress can delegate. In these circumstances, and in these only, may he be said (for what it may be worth) to personify the federal sovereignty. If his act is held unconstitutional under these circumstances, it usually means that the Federal Government as an undivided whole lacks power. A seizure executed by the President pursuant to an Act of Congress would be supported by the strongest of presumptions and the widest latitude of judicial interpretation, and the burden of persuasion would rest heavily upon any who might attack it."

Justice Jackson's first rough category appears simple. If Congress authorizes a presidential action, then the action is presumed constitutional. The action can still be unconstitutional, but only if Congress and the President lack the required authority. But this leaves some important questions unanswered.[1] First, how should statutes be read to determine whether Congress authorized a presidential action? Second, is there any internal limit on Congress's ability to delegate power to the President? Third, why don't Presidents always seek legislative authorization if that will increase their odds of prevailing in the courts? Lastly, why does Congress often shy away from giving the President an authorization?

On Reading Statutes

Statutory construction is the key that unlocks Jackson's three rough boxes. The relativity of executive and congressional action cannot be assessed without interpreting Acts of Congress. Legislative authorization creates a presumption of validity; legislative silence creates no such presumption; legislative prohibition creates a presumption against validity. Though statutory meaning matters a great deal for this constitutional analysis, the concurrence

The Actual Art of Governing. Gerard N. Magliocca, Oxford University Press. © Oxford University Press (2025).
DOI: 10.1093/9780197768563.003.0008

says almost nothing about how statutes should be interpreted.[2] Jackson also said that congressional authorization of a presidential action could be implied, thereby providing the widest latitude for courts to place an action into that category. Consequently, the concurring opinion's critics argue that judges can easily put the cart before the horse by first deciding that an executive action is lawful or unlawful and then reverse-engineering a statutory reading to support those conclusions.[3]

Jackson's rationales for the destroyers-for-bases agreement and the North American Aviation seizure exemplify this criticism. In defense of the former, Attorney General Jackson construed a law that barred the President from selling warships unless they were unfit for service as granting authority to trade battle-ready warships for leases on British bases. (Justice Jackson repeated this interpretation in footnote 14 of the concurrence.) This was not a close statutory question. Why, then, did Jackson reach such a conclusion? Maybe because he thought that Roosevelt really needed the power to exchange destroyers in order to save Britain from the Nazis. Similarly, in 1941 he claimed that the North American Aviation seizure was in part "an execution of congressional policy," but he did not say what laws stated that policy. In footnote 17 of the concurrence, he wrote that the Selective Service Act of 1940 authorized the President to seize plants that refused to fill military orders for equipment, and stated that there had been orders at North American Aviation that were not being filled.[4] But the owners of the North American Aviation factory were not refusing to fill the orders; rather, they could not fill the orders due to the strike.[5] Once again, Jackson's statutory interpretation (long after the fact) was strained. But as before, his view may have been shaped by his larger view that FDR had the constitutional authority to act.

Even if judges approach statutory issues unencumbered by a view of the constitutional merits, ascertaining whether Congress has authorized an executive action can be difficult. For example, at the start of Judge Samuel Alito's Supreme Court confirmation hearing in 2006, Senator Arlen Specter stated, "This hearing comes at a time of great national concern about the balance between civil rights and the President's national security authority. The President's constitutional powers as commander in chief to conduct electronic surveillance appear to conflict with what Congress has said in the Foreign Intelligence Surveillance Act. This conflict involves very major considerations raised by Justice Jackson's historic concurrence in the *Youngstown* steel seizure cases."[6] Senator Specter was referring to the Bush

Administration's electronic surveillance of suspected terrorists without a court warrant, contrary to the terms of FISA.[7] Specter's invocation of Jackson was ironic, since as attorney general Jackson had backed (albeit reluctantly) the surveillance of alleged foreign spies without statutory authorization. In any event, the Bush Administration countered that Congress had authorized the NSA program in its Authorization of Military Force resolution, passed after the terrorist attacks of September 11, 2001.[8] Both claims were plausible, and the answer determined whether the program was presumptively valid or invalid under Jackson's framework. The concurring opinion could not and did not seek to answer these sorts of charged statutory issues.

The Nondelegation Doctrine

Nevertheless, there are many cases in which congressional authorization of executive action is clear enough. At that point, the typical reading of the concurrence is that the President's act may be held unlawful only if some constitutional prohibition is violated (for example, the First Amendment). The Supreme Court later explained that invalidating a measure that falls into Jackson's first category "would mean that the federal government as a whole lacked the power exercised by the President."[9] Most scholars echo this view and argue that Jackson did not consider or credit the claim under the "nondelegation doctrine" that there is some internal limit on Congress's authority to delegate power to the President.[10] The nondelegation doctrine comes from two Supreme Court decisions of 1935 holding that Congress went too far in giving the President power to regulate the national economy.[11] Though the Court has not invoked the doctrine since then, scholars and judges freely speculate about whether or how nondelegation might return.[12] In *Youngstown*, the Court was not reviewing a delegation of legislative power to seize the steel mills. Understandably, then, Jackson did not spend much time addressing the scope of permissible delegation. But he did not ignore the nondelegation question entirely; in fact, he spoke directly to that point, though that discussion came in a footnote and thus is often overlooked.[13]

The text of the concurrence states that the President's power is at its peak when he can add "all that Congress can delegate" to his Article II authority. What does "all that Congress can delegate" mean? A clue comes one sentence later: "If his act is held unconstitutional under these circumstances [in other words, when Congress authorized executive action], it usually means that the Federal Government as an undivided whole lacks power."[14] Notice that Jackson qualified this comment with the word "usually."[15] This qualification implies that there is an internal limit on what Congress can delegate. Early drafts of the concurrence support this reading. There Jackson cited the nondelegation cases from 1935 for the point that executive action in Category One can be invalidated.[16] Footnote 2 in the final opinion, which came right after the phrase "all that Congress can delegate," confirms that reading. That note says that "[T]he strict limitation upon congressional delegations of power to the President over internal affairs does not apply with respect to delegations of power in external affairs."[17] So instead of rejecting or overlooking the nondelegation doctrine, Jackson instead wrote that the doctrine did exist for domestic affairs.

But what was the scope of that doctrine? The answer is unclear, but a brief written by Solicitor General Jackson sheds some light.[18] *Currin v. Wallace* was a 1938 Supreme Court case that upheld a federal statute regulating tobacco.[19] In *Currin*, the Court rejected the claim that the statute violated the nondelegation doctrine in granting expansive authority to the secretary of agriculture.[20] One of the solicitor general's arguments in his brief defending the law, which the Court did not address, was that the nondelegation doctrine should apply only if Congress gave power directly to the President.[21] Jackson's reasoning was that the Court's 1935 nondelegation precedents both involved direct grants of presidential authority.[22] He said that any expansion of those precedents to the rest of the executive branch or to independent agencies was unsupported by the Constitution's text, structure, and history.[23] Jackson also contended that delegations to the President raised separation-of-powers concerns that were absent when Congress gave power to a creature of Congress (for example, the Agriculture Department) that was under its scrutiny and control.[24] The solicitor general explained the Court's two nondelegation cases this way: "The executive was there endowed with nonexecutive functions. The legislative power was there delegated to the President, whose powers are in many respects independent of the Congress. It is generally held that the Judiciary will not assume nonjudicial functions, and that Congress cannot assume nonlegislative functions."[25] But the brief said little about how to assess whether delegations to the President involved nonexecutive functions.[26]

Traces of Jackson's *Currin* brief are visible in Category One of *Youngstown*. First, he refers to situations where only the President (not the executive branch generally) acts pursuant to an authorization by Congress.[27] Second, footnote 2 talks about the strict limitation upon congressional delegations of power to the President—again, not to the executive branch as a whole. Third, Category One—like the *Currin* brief—does not repudiate the Court's nondelegation decisions. Since the concurrence's framework for analyzing the relativity of congressional and executive action purports to be comprehensive, the nondelegation cases must go somewhere. And the only box they fit into is Category One.

Permission or Forgiveness?

Jackson revisited Category One later in the concurrence when he said that Presidents who doubted their authority to act asked Congress for legislation.[28] In footnote 16, he cited examples from Woodrow Wilson and Franklin D. Roosevelt that involved national-security matters.[29] Jackson also quoted from FDR's First Inaugural Address, which stated that if necessary he would ask Congress to give him "broad executive power to wage a war against the emergency, as great as the power that would be given to me if we were in fact invaded by a foreign foe."[30] The implication was that Roosevelt did not believe that he could exercise that kind of extraordinary power without an Act of Congress.

If Presidents are on stronger legal ground with congressional authorization, then why not always ask for new legislation? Perhaps Presidents simply want to act, daring someone to stop them. Perhaps they are confident that there is executive authority and see no need to consult Congress. The Office of Legal Counsel, the modern executive branch's source of constitutional guidance, explained in a 1986 opinion that presidential requests for statutory authority "may reflect a practical spirit of courtesy and compromise rather than any concession" that he cannot act without a statute.[31] A President may also believe there is no chance that Congress will say yes.[32] But there are deeper explanations. If Congress declines to act on a presidential request or rejects the request, that will present a political and legal problem for the President if he then acts on his own.[33] The political problem is that the President would suffer a high-profile defeat that would expose the lack of public support for his policy. The legal problem is that he would be hard-pressed in a court challenge to say that his action comes within Category One. New legislation would not be necessary if existing laws were sufficient. At least, that is what opponents of the President's decision would say. And courts could reason that because Congress affirmatively rejected the request, then the case falls into Category Three (implied prohibition) and makes the executive action presumptively unconstitutional.[34]

Presidents may not want to take these risks. There may be situations where the politics dictate that the prudent course involves a request to Congress.[35] But a president could conclude that he is better off leaving Congress's view unclear, or could claim that, under some creative interpretation, older statutes authorize his action.[36] Presidents also have the option of acting secretly without congressional approval, although that tactic can backfire if the secret spills out. Due to the Roosevelt Administration's clandestine wire-tapping program, Jackson knew all about this possibility. Indeed, he may have alluded to that program in the concurrence by warning that a President's conduct "of foreign affairs is so largely uncontrolled, and often even is unknown."

In the end, Presidents must make sound judgments after carefully considering the law, public opinion, and the consequences. It is not a coincidence that Jackson's footnote on presidential requests for congressional authorization ended with a reference to the tactful use of power by the Tudor monarchs. One of their Stuart successors—King Charles I—had acted without Parliament's approval one too many times and lost the Crown (and his head). The message was that Presidents should think carefully about whether to approach Congress before going it alone. And President Truman, in Jackson's view, made the wrong call in 1952.

The Napoleonic Coda

While the concurring opinion urged Presidents to ask Congress for authority when in doubt, Jackson worried that Congress would not respond. The last allusion to Category One came near the end of the opinion, when he wrote that the Court could not "keep power in the hands of Congress if it is not wise and timely in meeting its problems. A crisis that challenges the President equally, or perhaps primarily, challenges Congress." What followed was a line, attributed to Napoleon I, claiming that "[t]he tools belong to the man who can use them."[37] Napoleon is an unusual authority for an American judicial opinion, and (not surprisingly) the concurrence is the only Supreme Court opinion that purports to quote him.[38] But Lyndon B. Johnson expressed the same idea when he said, "Power is where power goes."[39] In other words, action can create power. In one draft, Jackson explained, "As crisis follows crisis, if Congress allows its attention to be diverted by trivia, its leadership of the Nation weakened by absorption in sectional tasks, its impact weakened by partisan division, the weight of public opinion will surely shift effective power to a centralized Executive in spite of all the essays this Court can promulgate."[40] The risk is that Congress will not occupy Category One often enough and will leave a vacuum for a President with a Napoleon complex to fill.[41] And some might argue that this is a fact, not just a hazard, in modern politics.[42]

Figure 7.1 Napoleon I crossing the Alps at St. Bernard. Painting by Jean-Louis David.

While Congress is sometimes just unable or unwilling to agree on a law authorizing presidential action, there may also be structural explanations for congressional inaction. First, the Senate filibuster, which was rare in Jackson's day, now commonly requires sixty votes to pass legislation. Second, Congress is not permitted to condition a grant of authority by saying that the authority may be withdrawn whenever Congress (and only Congress) wants.[43] The validity of the legislative veto was a bone of contention between Roosevelt and Jackson regarding the Lend-Lease Act. But the practice was constitutional when *Youngstown* was decided and made it easier for Congress to grant power by reassuring the skeptics that the power could be recalled without needing to override a presidential veto. Without that assurance, Congress may be more reluctant to grant authority, for fear that the grant can never be clawed back.[44] Last but not least, Jackson undercut Congress's role through his second rough category—the zone of twilight. Since the concurrence says that presidential authority can exist when Congress is silent, Congress does not always need to authorize executive action when his constitutional authority is doubtful or nonexistent. Cautious members might prefer to let the President proceed with their tacit approval, because tacit approval can easily turn into tacit disapproval if there is a public backlash.[45]

Throughout the concurrence, Jackson's executive experience tempered his view of the Constitution's structure. His strong preference was that law made by parliamentary deliberations should control the President. But he knew that this was not always possible or wise. Prepare to enter the twilight zone.[46]

8
Imponderables

Category Two of the Jackson concurrence states: "When the President acts in absence of either a congressional grant or denial of authority, he can only rely upon his own independent powers, but there is a zone of twilight in which he and Congress may have concurrent authority, or in which its distribution is uncertain. Therefore, congressional inertia, indifference or quiescence may sometimes, at least as a practical matter, enable, if not invite, measures on independent presidential responsibility. In this area, any actual test of power is likely to depend on the imperatives of events and contemporary imponderables rather than on abstract theories of law."

As much as lawyers love Justice Jackson's concurrence, they hate his second rough category.[1] Category Two may be canny political analysis, but as legal authority Jackson's language is, as Professor (and former Judge) Michael McConnell once said, "decidedly unhelpful. If these considerations are imponderable, how can the judge ponder them?"[2] Other scholars contend that Category Two is "useless," "confounds matters," and "provides precious little guidance."[3] Indeed, the leading study of Category Two cases shows that courts avoid putting cases in the zone of twilight if they can and are hopelessly divided about how to decide those cases when they must.[4]

There is a way out of this morass. The best reading of the *Youngstown* concurrence is that cases in the zone of twilight present non-justiciable political questions when no other constitutional claim is being made.[5] This conclusion flows from a careful reading of the concurrence, the evolution of Jackson's drafts, and Judge Augustus N. Hand's similar point in the *Western Union Telegraph* case that the Justice relied on.[6] Treating Category Two cases as non-justiciable also reflects the wisdom gleaned from decades of experience in the courts, which should resolve the concurrence's ambiguities in favor of non-justiciability.[7] Finally, relieving courts of the burden of settling disputes between Congress and the President when no statutes apply would

The Actual Art of Governing. Gerard N. Magliocca, Oxford University Press. © Oxford University Press (2025).
DOI: 10.1093/9780197768563.003.0009

allow those branches to work out informal norms capable of adapting to new or unexpected challenges.[8]

Wrestling with the Problem

For many lawyers, Category Two is a breath of fresh air. Judges rarely say that legal questions can be uncertain or can turn on the unexpected. In other words, few admit that there is a zone of twilight. A typical opinion confidently explains its reasoning and rejects contrary arguments as if there is no doubt about the correct result. But that is a legal fiction. Judges sometimes do think that a case is close, and sometimes change their mind during deliberations.[9] Why not then say so? The concern may be that expressions of doubt will make them look indecisive or undermine the authority of the decision.[10] Or their interpretive approach may not allow for the possibility of indeterminacy, and thus may require the pretense of certainty. Jackson's frankness was an outgrowth of his disdain for legal fictions and his belief in a pragmatic method that balanced competing interests. The scales of justice sometimes seesaw before they reach a final resting position.

But the language of Category Two never says anything about judicial review or courts. By contrast, in Category One Jackson talks about giving "the widest latitude of judicial interpretation" to presidential actions. And in Category Three he says that "[c]ourts can sustain exclusive Presidential control" only by denying Congress's power. Why did Category Two omit any references to judicial interpretation or courts? One hypothesis is that Jackson did not think that the courts should be involved at all, and believed instead that the "actual test of power" involved only public opinion and the competing interests of Congress and the President. To test that hypothesis and unravel the mystery of Category Two, we must first understand what he had in mind when he was considering that concept.[11]

An undated note in the Justice's Youngstown files provides the first sketch of Category Two, listing the main factors to consider where there was no statutory guidance:

Nature of exertion
Measure necessity
Meaning of silence and inaction
Gravitation—inertia
Airport.[12]

Look again at the final item in this list. "Airport" did not mean that Jackson had a flight to catch; it instead referred to Washington National Airport and his work on that project as solicitor general.[13] Congress did not authorize the construction of that airport, but President Roosevelt went ahead anyway on his own authority, and nobody could stop him in the courts because there was no justiciable question. While Jackson conceded in his reminiscences that FDR might have exceeded his constitutional power by building the airport, there were strong counterarguments. The need for a new national airport was great, no individual right was invaded, and Congress was not likely to act. Thus, the example that Jackson initially considered for Category Two was not justiciable. Moreover, no grand issues of national security were contemplated.[14]

Next, the opinion that inspired Jackson's three categories contemplated that some cases within Category Two would be non-justiciable. In *Western Union Telegraph*, Judge Augustus Hand considered the argument that congressional acquiescence in executive actions to prevent underwater communication cable landings could sustain that action if Congress had not legislated on the matter.[15] Hand said that in that instance the executive act would seem "to be a political question" and doubted whether this "was a justiciable matter and whether a court should interfere to define or support it, in which case the basis of right would then depend on the interrelations and mutual accommodations of the executive and legislative departments of the government and not upon strict law."[16] Like Jackson in *Youngstown*, Judge Hand concluded that the President did not have the relevant authority because Congress had by statute excluded him from acting, and thus the court should rule on the merits. In fairness, Hand did not say that all cases of executive action in the absence of congressional action would be non-justiciable. Again, though, Jackson was using a model for Category Two that discussed political questions and did not involve an armed conflict. I stress the latter point because so much of the literature on the *Youngstown* concurrence focuses on foreign affairs, overlooking the fact that most of the opinion was about domestic affairs.[17]

Jackson's drafts of *Youngstown* were ambivalent about judicial review in the twilight zone. The May 8 draft prefaced the three rough classifications by saying that "the Judiciary must make [sic] a different approach to these classes of questioned acts of the Executive."[18] And in Category Two, "[i]t is quite probable that the extent to which [presidential] action should be judicially sustained under such circumstances may depend somewhat upon the nature of the action with a tendency to sustain it if it relates to some functioning of government other than one affecting the liberties of the people." His May 22 draft, though, omitted both the reference to the judiciary from the prefatory language and the related comment on judicial review within Category Two itself.[19] In his May 29 draft he added a footnote, which became footnote 3 of the final version of the opinion, that cited some Supreme Court cases within Category Two.[20] Do these citations mean that Category Two situations should be subject to judicial review notwithstanding the omission of courts or the judiciary from the final text of the opinion?

A careful examination of the cases that Jackson cited in footnote 3 does not yield a clear answer. His main example was President Lincoln's suspension of the writ of habeas corpus in 1861.[21] Lincoln suspended the writ on his own authority while Congress was out of session, even though the Constitution probably permits only Congress to suspend the writ.[22] The suspension was challenged in *Ex Parte Merryman*,[23] a case decided by Chief Justice Roger B. Taney acting on his own, which held that the President lacked the authority to suspend the writ but did not free the prisoner who was detained without charge,[24] probably because the Chief Justice thought that military officials would not comply.[25] Two years later, Congress passed the Habeas Corpus Suspension Act, which straddled on the issue of whether Lincoln's initial suspension was lawful or whether Congress was retroactively authorizing the President's action.[26] Jackson cited *Merryman* to say that a court should *not* have intervened in what he saw as a Category Two case. In the final pages of *The Struggle for Judicial Supremacy*, he called Taney's opinion "one of the most admirable and pathetic documents in American judicial annals" and said that "[o]ne such precedent is enough!"[27] Consequently, *Merryman* (and the larger debate about habeas suspension during the Civil War) is more consistent with a non-justiciability reading of Category Two that allows the elected branches to work out their differences.

Jackson's other examples in footnote 3 are confusing or ambiguous. First, he included a compare citation to *Myers v. United States*[28] and *Humphrey's Executor v. United States*,[29] which expressed contrasting views on the President's authority to remove executive officials.[30] But Jackson also cited those cases as Category Three decisions in footnote 4 of the concurrence.[31]

The better view is that they do not fall within Category Two at all. Both *Myers* and *Humphrey's Executor* involved Acts of Congress that the President challenged as unconstitutional: they are not examples of congressional silence.[32] Next, Jackson referred to *Hirabayashi*, which upheld the curfew imposed on Japanese-Americans during World War II.[33] But that was also not a zone-of-twilight example; since Congress had authorized the curfew before the Court heard the case, it was instead a Category One decision.[34] Finally, Jackson cited two cases about the application of martial law during the Civil War.[35] In the first, the Supreme Court held that it lacked jurisdiction to review the military conviction of Representative Clement Vallandigham, a leading war critic.[36] This holding is consistent with the view that Category Two cases are non-justiciable. In the other, the Court reversed the military conviction of Lambdin Milligan for providing aid and comfort to the Confederacy on the ground that he could be convicted by only a civil court.[37] *Ex Parte Milligan* is thus the only example that Jackson offered of a Category Two case that a court was right to decide on the merits.[38] On the other hand, his experience with *Ex Parte Quirin*, in which he entertained the idea that the Court should not have reviewed the military trial of the Nazi saboteurs, renders the *Milligan* example complicated at best.[39] Footnote 29 of the concurring opinion also says that martial law should be treated as "a very limited category by itself," which further muddies the waters.

Accordingly, there are good reasons to think that Category Two cases should be treated as non-justiciable. The text, drafting background, and case law cited in *Youngstown* support this interpretation, while support for a contrary reading is weak. That said, the pragmatic spirit of the concurrence calls for an examination of how courts have read Category Two.

What Do Courts Do in Category Two?

In a 2021 article called "The Elusive Zone of Twilight," Professors Michael Coenen and Scott M. Sullivan conducted a comprehensive analysis of all Category Two cases.[40] One of their conclusions was that courts tend to read statutes as either authorizing or barring executive action.[41] This finding is not shocking, as Categories One and Three rest on a presumption of constitutionality or unconstitutionality that avoids the uncertainty of Category Two. Moreover, the lack of guidance in the concurrence about how statutes should be read gives courts ample discretion to keep cases away from Category Two. Another conclusion by Coenen and Sullivan was that courts sometimes say that Category Two cases are non-justiciable.[42] But when the courts cannot escape Category Two and gamely try to decide such cases, they flounder. Why? In part because judges are not suited to evaluate "the imperatives of events and contemporary imponderables." These are the domain of politicians and generals (such as Napoleon), who must often take critical decisions in fluid situations with incomplete information.[43] Jackson also said that "congressional inertia, indifference or quiescence may sometimes, at least as a practical matter, enable, if not invite, measures on independent presidential responsibility." But how are judges supposed to determine whether congressional inaction is inviting presidential action?[44]

Broadly speaking, courts have taken four approaches to answering that question:

- First, treat congressional silence as authorization for presidential authority.[45] The trouble is that this method conflates Category Two with Category One and expands executive power.
- Second, treat congressional acquiescence in related presidential acts as authorization.[46] This approach builds on Judge Hand's observation in *Western Union Telegraph*, although he thought that this situation was a political question rather than a reason to rule for the President on the merits. One problem here is that it is far from clear how much past practice is required to turn congressional acquiescence into authorization. The options range from Justice Frankfurter's high standard in his *Youngstown* concurrence ("a systemic, unbroken, executive practice, long pursued to the knowledge of Congress and never before questioned") to a single past example.[47]
- Third, use what Coenen and Sullivan call a "general tenor" analysis, in which courts attempt to read the legislative tea leaves to discern signs of approval or disapproval, without the actual, concrete approval or disapproval from Congress that would move the case into Category One or Category Three.[48]
- Fourth, focus on the signals sent by the executive branch or on more general concerns such as resolving "a major crisis."[49]

Even if some of these strategies are better than others, the inability of courts to converge on a single approach for resolving Category Two disputes counsels against interpreting that part of the concurrence as justiciable.

Trust the Elected Branches (but Verify)

Finally, there are practical reasons to think that Category Two cases should not be subject to judicial review.[50] First, asking courts to decide these cases when there are no statutes makes mistakes more likely. Jackson's executive experience may have given him confidence that judges could work out sensible constitutional solutions in the absence of positive law, but most judges (especially today) lack his professional background.[51] Second, fixing judicial errors in this area is not so easy. Congress can respond to a misguided Category Two decision by enacting legislation that permits or rejects executive power.[52] But when legislation seeks to curb executive authority, the President can wield his veto pen and usually freeze an opinion in his favor. Thus, there is a structural bias in favor of the White House when courts rule in Category Two cases. Most important, for most of our history courts did not get involved in disputes between Congress and the President, and that worked out just fine.[53] Unlike individuals, who need courts to protect them from abuses of power, the elected branches have powerful tools that they can deploy to protect their respective interests.[54] Eventually some political settlement will be reached, because these institutions cannot live without each other.[55] Unwritten precepts evolve from these clashes and form a flexible system that allows both sides to adapt to new challenges in a way that litigation cannot.[56] Lastly, the actual number of cases in which Congress has not acted, the President lacks clear Article II authority, and no other legal claim is being made is small.[57]

One objection to non-justiciability in Category Two could be that a President might be able to exceed his statutory and Article II powers because Congress is controlled in part by his party and will let him do what he wants. The *Youngstown* concurrence acknowledged this reality, but that risk does not by itself justify judicial review. Executive power is sometimes a function of public opinion "and does not admit of a legalistic treatment."[58] Public opinion is an effective (though finicky) check on executive overreach. Presidents who soar to new heights of unilateral authority often crash and burn a couple of years later.[59] But if the voters approve of a course of action by one or more Presidents, then that becomes a new baseline in the sense that Congress either will not legislate against the authority or might legislate in its favor, as occurred for Lincoln's suspension of habeas corpus. At a minimum, courts should stay their hand and let that process play out.[60] They would do better to keep out entirely.

In sum, a holistic reading of the concurrence supports the view that Category Two cases where the President lacks Article II authority should not be subject to judicial review. But what if the President has Article II authority and Congress attempts to restrict that power?

9
Lowest Ebb

Category Three of the Jackson concurrence states: "When the President takes measures incompatible with the expressed or implied will of Congress, his power is at its lowest ebb, for then he can rely only upon his own constitutional powers minus any constitutional powers of Congress over the matter. Courts can sustain exclusive presidential control in such a case only by disabling the Congress from acting upon the subject. Presidential claim to a power at once so conclusive and preclusive must be scrutinized with caution, for what is at stake is the equilibrium established by our constitutional system."

The third rough category of relativity is framed by the President's veto shield and Article II swords.[1] Congress can pass legislation limiting executive authority, and (according to Jackson) it did so in the context of President Truman's steel seizure. But this legislation must either be accepted by the President or enacted over his veto, which gives the executive branch a robust defense. In some instances, Congress may not regulate the executive at all because Article II gives a power to the President alone. Jackson stressed, though, that claims of exclusive presidential authority "must be scrutinized with caution" to keep the Constitution in balance. As a result, most of the concurring opinion focused on the proper reading of Article II.

Incompatibility

Jackson concluded that the steel seizure was incompatible with the will of Congress because the legislature "has not left seizure of private property an open field but has covered it by three statutory policies inconsistent with this seizure." He summarized the options that President Truman could have pursued (the Taft-Hartley Act, the Selective Service Act, and the Defense Production Act), and stated that the President's unilateral approach was therefore not "necessitated or invited by failure of Congress to legislate."[2]

The Actual Art of Governing. Gerard N. Magliocca, Oxford University Press. © Oxford University Press (2025).
DOI: 10.1093/9780197768563.003.0010

Consequently, "we can sustain the President only by holding that seizure of such strike-bound industries is within his domain and beyond control by Congress." Category Three gives Congress an incentive to legislate by augmenting the authority of that action in any subsequent judicial contest with the President.[3] If clear federal legislation is enacted, there is no zone of twilight.

The first point worth making about Jackson's application of the standard is that the phrase "implied will of Congress" was doing some work.[4] Congress never expressly prohibited the President from seizing private property under circumstances comparable to the steel strike, as Chief Justice Vinson noted in his dissent.[5] To be sure, Congress did reject giving the President that power in the Taft-Hartley Act debate, but that is not the same as enacting an express prohibition.[6] In one draft, Jackson contended that the "plain implications" of the Taft-Hartley Act "are that the President is not alone to determine for himself without evidence whether the strike creates a national emergency."[7] But the Chief Justice's dissent argued that the steel seizure was consistent with the broader Korean War policy laid down by Congress in other statutes and military appropriations.[8] Though Jackson's reading of the statutes was better, a judge who was inclined to uphold the seizure could have plausibly said that Congress had not spoken clearly (Category Two) or that there was implied authorization (Category One).[9]

The second point is that these statutes were either signed by Truman or enacted over his veto. One implication of that structural feature is that courts need not construe these restrictive statutes narrowly in order to protect executive authority because Presidents can defend their freedom of action well enough on their own. But should the courts take notice of presidential vetoes that are sustained by Congress? In a 2021 article, Professor Kristin E. Eichensehr argued that, when a bill is passed by Congress and vetoed, "the expressed congressional opposition to the president's view should be used to narrowly construe the underlying statutory or constitutional authority the President is claiming if that authority is ambiguous."[10] If that is correct, then the symmetrical claim can be made that restrictive statutes enacted over the president's veto should also be read narrowly, so as to acknowledge presidential opposition to Congress's view about the underlying authority. But Jackson did not make any such claim about the Taft-Hartley Act, which was enacted over Truman's veto criticizing the legislation's "ineffective and discriminatory emergency procedure for dealing with major strikes affecting the public health or safety."[11] Perhaps the two situations (a successful veto of a law restricting the President, and a veto override of a law that does the same) are dissimilar. Maybe courts should never interpret a law in the President's favor when Congress overrides a veto, because overrides are far rarer than vetoes. Or maybe courts should simply ignore most vetoes and overrides in construing statutes.[12]

As for constitutional analysis, Jackson offered few examples for Category Three. Footnote 4 did discuss the dispute over when Congress can limit the President's ability to remove executive officials, again citing *Humphrey's Executor* and *Myers*.[13] These decisions (broadly speaking) stand for the proposition that Congress can restrict the President's dismissal authority, but not when Article II gives exclusive authority to the executive.[14] In his drafts, Jackson also invoked the Tenure of Office Act, which restricted President Andrew Johnson's power to remove Cabinet members during Reconstruction and was vetoed by Johnson as unconstitutional.[15] The Justice's more intriguing example (in his first draft) was the Lend-Lease Act's legislative veto.[16] One way of viewing legislative vetoes is that they restrict the President's veto power. If so, then the legislative veto's constitutionality would turn on whether the executive veto is an exclusive presidential authority like the pardon power.[17]

What is clear is that Jackson viewed assertions of exclusive executive authority with great skepticism. In one draft, he stated that these claims "should be scrutinized with severity and required to meet the burden of justification."[18] In another draft, he said that the President carried "the burden of clear justification" in Category Three cases.[19] The Supreme Court would not quote Justice Jackson's language about Category Three until *Trump v. United States* in 2024.[20] And in that case, the Court omitted his warning about using "caution" before finding exclusive Article II power that barred some criminal liability for ex-Presidents.[21]

The Vesting Clause

Justice Byron White once told his law clerk, "You write very well. Justice Jackson had that problem too."[22] His point was that style is sometimes the enemy of substance. This problem shows up in Category Three and in Jackson's initial analysis of Article II. In Category Three, he wrote that the President's power "is at its lowest ebb." This is an evocative image, but it can be misleading. The President's exclusive Article II powers, such as the pardon power, do not fluctuate because of congressional action;[23] only the powers granted by Congress or those in the zone of twilight do.[24] If seizing the steel mills was within one of the President's fixed constitutional powers, then Truman's action was lawful no matter what Congress did. Jackson added that the executive's enumerated powers must receive "the scope and elasticity afforded by what seem to be reasonable practical implications instead of the rigidity dictated by a doctrinaire textualism."[25] But what are these enumerated powers, and how did they apply to the steel seizure?

The first textual clause that Jackson discussed was the first sentence of Article II: "The executive Power shall be vested in a President of the United States of America."[26] He then quoted the Government's brief, which said that the Vesting Clause "constitutes a grant of all the executive powers of which the Government is capable." Jackson's response was that this reading made the listing of specific executive powers in Article II superfluous.[27] Furthermore, "[t]he example of such unlimited executive power that must have most impressed the forefathers was the prerogative exercised by George III, and the description of its evils in the Declaration of Independence leads me to doubt that they were creating their new Executive in his image."[28] In one early draft, he wrote: "No government, except those of the Fascist and Communist dictators, is based on that doctrine, the teaching of which is as subversive of the principles of American Government as any doctrine for which the Communists are in jail."[29] In another draft, he wrote, "The argument that the President possesses all power that is not expressly taken from him by the Constitution is a complete legal and historical perversion which may have been entertained by some political figures but, so far as I know, has never had the endorsement of any responsible legal officer of the Government."[30] Thus, Jackson concluded that the Vesting Clause was nothing more than "an allocation to the presidential office of the generic powers thereafter stated."

This rather glib analysis is widely panned.[31] Taken literally, Jackson was saying that Article II gives the President only the powers listed in the text. But there are several problems with that reading.[32] First, Article I of the Constitution starts with "All legislative Powers herein granted shall be vested in a Congress of the United States."[33] The first line of Article II, though, omits the phrase "herein granted." From that omission, an inference can be drawn that the President is not limited to the powers enumerated in the text.[34] Second, presidents regularly exercise powers that are not in the text of the Constitution, are not powers of Congress, and are not controversial. For example, the President's only textual foreign-policy powers are to receive ambassadors, make treaties (if the Senate concurs with a two-thirds vote), and appoint ambassadors (if the Senate concurs by a majority vote).[35] "If these three things were all the President could do," Professor McConnell notes, "it would be impossible to conduct foreign policy."[36] Third, there is a distinguished line of argument, tracing back to Alexander Hamilton, that the Vesting Clause does confer substantive power on the President.[37] Finally, enumerating specific powers does not imply that the list is exclusive. A list can also clarify and limit authority. For example, the pardon power is limited to offenses against the United States and cannot be exercised in impeachment cases.[38]

Jackson's initial drafts took the view that the Vesting Clause did grant some power to the President. In one, he said that the "obvious meaning" of the provision was that "the Executive power appropriate to the form of Government created by the entire Constitution is what is vested in the President and that on any given issue a study of its interrelated powers and responsibilities must determine the question."[39] The idea that the Vesting Clause must be read together with the Constitution's "interrelated" structure was another expression of Jackson's relativity approach to executive authority. His statement also correctly rejected the claim that the Vesting Clause gives the President all potential executive power. As he wrote in a later draft, "It must be obvious that all 'Executive Power of which the Government is capable,' as claimed by the Government, either has no beginning or no end."[40]

But what power does the Vesting Clause grant that is less than everything but more than nothing? Scholars are divided on that question, although hardly anyone thinks that the Vesting Clause authorized President Truman's steel-company seizure.[41] One test comes from Justice Frankfurter's concurring opinion in *Youngstown*: "[A] systemic, unbroken, executive practice, long pursued to the knowledge of the Congress and never before questioned . . . may be treated as a gloss on 'executive Power' vested in the President by [Section] 1 of Art. II."[42] Another test flows from Justice Black's opinion and holds that the Vesting Clause does not give the President legislative powers such as the taking of property.[43] These are not the only two options. The point is that Jackson was on notice that there were plausible substantive readings of the Vesting Clause. He just did not work through that issue carefully.

Take Care

The concurrence briefly addressed the claim that the Take Care Clause of Article II—stating that the President "shall take Care that the Laws be faithfully executed"[44]—supported the seizure. Jackson replied that this "authority must be matched against words of the Fifth Amendment that 'No person shall be . . . deprived of life, liberty, or property, without due process of law.' One gives the government authority that reaches so far as there is law, the other gives a private right that authority shall go no farther." The upshot was that the take-care obligation applies only if there is law to execute.[45] Jackson was saying that in this case there was no law for Truman to execute.[46] This was a restatement of his view that Congress did not authorize (and thus implicitly barred) the seizure of private property for national security. But his quoting of the Due Process Clause strongly suggests that the Take Care Clause does not confer exclusive authority on the President. Only a law or a court judgment can activate the Take Care Clause and give the President law to execute, though the power, once activated, may well be exclusive.

Chief Justice Vinson's dissenting opinion argued that the Take Care Clause was "the central idea of the office" and justified President Truman's seizure.[47] "Faced with the duty of executing the defense programs which Congress had enacted and the disastrous effects that any stoppage in steel production would have on those programs," Vinson said, "the President acted to preserve those programs."[48] This was a restatement of the Chief Justice's view that Congress did not expressly prohibit (and impliedly approved of) the seizure of private property for the nation's security. He also endorsed Theodore Roosevelt's "stewardship" theory of the executive, which was that the President was a servant of the people and is "bound to serve the people affirmatively in cases where the Constitution does not explicitly forbid him to render the service."[49] While this may accurately describe the President's moral duty, neither Jackson nor the Court backed this expansive interpretation as a legal principle.

The Vesting and Take Care Clauses are not the only possible sources of exclusive presidential authority in Article II. Indeed, the concurrence's longest section focused on the strongest textual provision for President Truman's action—the Commander-in-Chief Clause. And in that passage, Jackson deepened his discussion of the relationship between Congress and the President by focusing on the ways in which Congress can limit the executive branch on the most consequential subject of all—war.

10
Commander in Chief

President Truman's executive order for the steel seizure invoked his authority as the "Commander in Chief of the armed forces of the United States."[1] The actual language in Article II is, "The President shall be Commander in Chief of the Army and Navy of the United States, and of the Militia of the several States, when called into the actual Service of the United States."[2] "These cryptic words," Justice Jackson wrote, "have given rise to some of the most persistent controversies in our constitutional history." He again alluded to his prior experience in saying that "what authority goes with the name has plagued Presidential advisers who would not waive or narrow it by nonassertion yet cannot say where it begins or ends." Jackson's answer to that question in *Youngstown* cannot be properly understood without reflecting on how the Manhattan Project and the Cold War transformed the commander in chief's role.[3] With that global context in mind, Jackson's concurrence gave the President broad latitude to use force overseas and rendered formal declarations of war obsolete. On the other hand, Jackson was sensitive to Congress's power of the purse and its domestic military authority to preserve the "balanced power structure of the Republic." The same goes for the Justice's attention to the Constitution's distinction between civil and military authority, especially in the immediate aftermath of Truman's removal of General Douglas MacArthur as the commander of the Korean War.

The Bomb and the National Security State

In 1952, the commander in chief could destroy much of the world on his own. This power was unimaginable to the Framers and unavailable to any of President Truman's predecessors. Garry Wills, in his perceptive book *Bomb Power*, explains that the development of nuclear weapons was a watershed for executive authority.[4] In part, that was because the Manhattan Project was viewed as a spectacular success that justified the use of secrecy and military control. The more important point, though, was that the use of nuclear

The Actual Art of Governing. Gerard N. Magliocca, Oxford University Press. © Oxford University Press (2025).
DOI: 10.1093/9780197768563.003.0011

weapons was understood—then and now—as a tactical decision that rested entirely in the President's discretion. "If the President has the sole authority to launch nation-destroying weapons," Wills wrote, then the President can claim "license to use every other power at his disposal that might safeguard that supreme necessity."[5] President Truman made this argument in his national address about the steel seizure by declaring that "if steel production stops, we will have to cut down and delay the atomic energy program."[6] The Government's brief in *Youngstown* also discussed the relationship between steel and atomic weapons and included a quotation on that issue from the chair of the Atomic Energy Commission.[7]

The idea that the greatest power includes all lesser powers is hard to resist. In an episode of the classic British comedy *Yes, Prime Minister*, the PM is frustrated to learn that the law bars him from hiring a cook for his official residence at 10 Downing Street and asks, "You mean I have the power to blow up the world but not to ask for scrambled eggs?"[8] On a more serious note, the Court sometimes invokes the power to impose a draft as support for other curbs on liberty or property.[9] For example, in an infamous 1927 opinion upholding a state law requiring the forced sterilization of women with intellectual disabilities, the Court said: "We have seen more than once that the public welfare may call upon the best citizens for their lives. It would be strange if it could not call upon those who already sap the strength of the State for these lesser sacrifices. . . ."[10] Likewise, the Chief Justice's dissent in *Youngstown* said that the steel seizure and the military draft were "[s]imilarly unpleasant" but lawful.[11] All constitutional limitations on the state's power over individuals would dissolve, though, if this conscription logic was routinely accepted.

Until 1945, presidential authority did not need to be evaluated against an existential backdrop. But the Bomb and the Cold War reinforced the trend toward executive power in the international realm. There would be no return to the isolationism that Attorney General Jackson confronted when he wrote the opinion supporting Roosevelt's destroyers-for-bases deal. America's new international responsibilities and military deployments dramatically expanded the President's jurisdiction. More covert operations would be launched under the President's exclusive control, including the wiretapping program that Jackson himself supervised. And once the Soviet Union developed its own atomic bomb in 1949, it was feared that any foreign incident could rapidly escalate into an emergency that would require a secret presidential response. The classic example is the Cuban Missile Crisis,

Figure 10.1 The mushroom cloud after the nuclear detonation at Nagasaki. Library of Congress. United States Army Air Forces. 1945. [LC-DIG-ds-05458]

during which President John F. Kennedy and his advisers made the pivotal decisions without input from Congress or the public.[12]

In response to these breathtaking changes, Congress reorganized the executive branch. First, the Atomic Energy Commission was created in 1946 to provide for civilian (rather than military) control over atomic bombs.[13] Second, in 1947 Congress passed the National Security Act, a landmark statute creating the National Security Council, the Joint Chiefs of Staff, the Central Intelligence Agency, and the Defense Department.[14] Congress emphasized the importance of civilian control over these new institutions by providing that the secretary of defense could not have been an active military officer for at least ten years and the CIA director would not be subject to or have authority over military officials.[15] *Youngstown* was the Supreme Court's most significant contribution to this high-level conversation about what most assumed was a permanent change to our tradition of neutrality with a small peacetime military.

The Undeclared War to End All Declared Wars

The Korean War was the first stress test of these new institutional arrangements and revealed some weaknesses. When President Truman committed troops to South Korea in 1950, he did not seek a war declaration from Congress.[16] Nevertheless, the solicitor general told the Supreme Court at oral argument that the steel seizure should be upheld because "this is wartime."[17] That comment drew sharp questions from the bench, with Jackson pointing out that there was no declaration of war against North Korea and that the President described the operation as a police action. None of the *Youngstown* opinions referred to the conflict as the Korean War;[18] Jackson instead referred to the "Korean enterprise" that was "perhaps a de facto war."

In early drafts of the concurrence, Jackson considered the idea that the absence of a declaration of war was relevant for interpreting the Commander-in-Chief Clause. At one point, he explained that "[a]ny action which the President may lawfully initiate on his own cannot be deemed in law to be a war or to be a foundation for a claim to war powers. . . . No doctrine that the Court could promulgate would seem to me more sinister and alarming than that a President can vastly enlarge his mastery over the internal affairs of the country by his own unauthorized commitment of the nation's armed forces to some foreign venture."[19] Here the Justice implied that the President's military authority should be read more narrowly because there was no war declaration. Jackson removed the language about "any action" but retained the word "unauthorized" to describe a president's commitment of troops overseas until the final draft of the opinion.[20] In that June 2nd draft, though, "unauthorized" was crossed out in ink. He then concluded that he did not "find it necessary or appropriate to consider the legal status of the Korean enterprise to discountenance argument based on it." In other words, Congress's failure to declare war was not dispositive.[21]

In this respect, the *Youngstown* concurrence helped legitimate de facto wars.[22] No President asked for a formal war declaration after 1952 and Congress never issued one, though there were congressional authorizations of force that could be viewed as functional war declarations.[23] There is no longer any need for a formal declaration. A war declaration would give the President more power and could have authorized Truman's seizure.[24] But the absence of such a declaration did nothing to stop him from conducting a muscular foreign policy. Jackson's edits to the opinion suggest that he wrestled with this problem before settling on the conclusion that the President needed flexibility to respond to crises abroad.

Rather than curtailing the President's authority to fight undeclared wars overseas, the concurrence instead focused on limiting their domestic fallout. "[T]he theme that appears most strongly in Justice Jackson's concurrence in *Youngstown*," the Office of Legal Counsel later explained, was "the fear of presidential bootstrapping."[25] Jackson rejected the idea that the Commander-in-Chief Clause gave "support for any Presidential action, internal or external, involving the use of force." He did not accept the claim "that the President having, on his own responsibility, sent American troops abroad derives from that act 'affirmative power' to seize the means of producing a supply of steel for them." He also emphasized that bootstrapping was especially problematic because the President's foreign-policy actions were often "unknown," which reflected Jackson's own experience as attorney general and the Cold War's emphasis on secret operations. Finally, Jackson wrote that the President was not "Commander-in-Chief of the country, its industries and its inhabitants. He has no monopoly of 'war powers,' whatever they are"; war powers were instead shared with Congress.

The Balance of War Powers

Jackson wrote in one draft that "no concrete content can be given to this [commander-in-chief] power without reference to the correlative powers of Congress."[26] This idea was consistent with the concurrence's broader approach—as expressed by the three rough categories—that executive authority must be read in relation to congressional authority. What are Congress's military powers? The Justice said that "[t]he Constitution expressly places in Congress power 'to raise and support Armies' and 'to provide and maintain a Navy.' This certainly lays upon Congress primary responsibility for supplying the armed forces."[27] That parliamentary tradition dated back to at least the English Bill of Rights.[28] Indeed, Presidents used to describe appropriations as "supply bills" in recognition of Congress's military-supply role.[29] "While Congress cannot deprive the President of the command of the army and navy," Jackson stated, "only Congress can provide him with an army or navy to command." He also noted that the Third Amendment says that—even in wartime—troops may not be quartered in private homes without the owner's consent unless Congress agrees.[30] Thus, the President cannot unilaterally "seize private housing to shelter his troops" even if he deems such seizure necessary for war. The implication was that the President also could not supply troops with private steel on his own or order workers to run the steel mills.[31]

Jackson then discussed Congress's authority to regulate the military. First, Congress "is empowered to make rules for the 'Government and Regulation of the land and naval forces,' by which it may to some unknown extent impinge upon even command functions."[32] Second, "[i]t was expressly left to Congress to 'provide for calling forth the Militia to execute the Laws of the Union, suppress Insurrections and repel invasions.'"[33] This mattered because "the militia rather than a standing army was contemplated as the military weapon of the Republic" and therefore "the Constitution's policy [was] that Congress, not the Executive, should control utilization of the war power as an instrument of domestic policy." The opinion then described statutes that direct when the commander in chief could use the military for domestic law enforcement. For example, during Reconstruction Congress provided that the President could use the armed forces to enforce civil rights in the South.[34] The political backlash to that action led to the enactment of the Posse Comitatus Act, also cited by Jackson, which largely prohibits the use of the army for domestic policing.[35] A draft of the concurrence said that the Act "has generally been thought adequate and constitutional to forbid the President to use the army for general strike-breaking purposes."[36] Since the steel seizure prevented a strike (albeit in favor of the workers), Jackson thought the Act did not permit a military justification for that action.

Although Jackson highlighted Congress's military powers, he went out of his way to buttress the President's unilateral authority to use force overseas. Executive-branch lawyers are fond of quoting this passage in the concurrence: "I should indulge the widest possible latitude of interpretation to sustain his exclusive function to command the instruments of national force, at least when turned against the outside world for the security of our society."[37] The seed of this idea was in an opinion issued by Attorney General Jackson in 1941, in which he said that "the President's authority has long been recognized as extending to the dispatch of armed forces outside of the United States, either on missions of good will or rescue, or for the purpose of protecting American lives or property or American interests."[38] Justice Jackson conceded that this was not always the constitutional understanding, as footnote 10 of his opinion quoted Jefferson's far more limited view of executive power in the fight against the Barbary pirates.

One challenge for the *Youngstown* framework is when the President strongly believes that national security demands military or economic aid to a foreign nation or group but Congress objects. This was the dilemma that preoccupied Attorney General Jackson when the President wanted to give vital assistance to Britain after the fall of France in 1940. Congress had enacted broad neutrality legislation in the 1930s to prevent Roosevelt from providing material support to any nation that might drag America into another European war. Jackson was able to find clever workarounds to this neutrality legislation, like trading destroyers for bases, though only through strained interpretations of older laws. While the President can circumvent congressional opposition to foreign aid by sending troops into these conflicts, that may impose a much higher political cost.

Likewise, Congress has often been frustrated by the concurrence's indulgence of unilateral executive military action abroad. The War Powers Act of 1973 was an attempt to restore the authority of Congress's power to declare war by creating a standing legislative framework for the use of troops overseas.[39] But the Act proved ineffective and is now seen as a failure. Though Congress can end a foreign adventure by cutting off money to the forces in the field, that action carries the risk of a backlash when soldiers are fighting and dying. As a result, Congress often issues sharp criticisms of the commander in chief's actions while doing nothing to stop them once they are underway. Only public opinion or enemy forces effectively restrain the President's adventures overseas.

Civil-Military Relations

Another powerful idea in the *Youngstown* opinion was that the steel seizure violated the unwritten constitutional principle that civil and military authority must be kept separate. "That military powers of the

Commander-in-Chief were not to supersede representative government of internal affairs seems obvious from the Constitution and from elementary American history," the Justice wrote. "His command is not such an absolute," Jackson added, "as might be implied from that office in a militaristic system but is subject to limitations consistent with a constitutional Republic whose law and policy-making branch is a representative Congress. The purpose of lodging dual titles in one man was to insure that the civilian would control the military, not to enable the military to subordinate the presidential office. No penance would ever expiate the sin against free government of holding that a President can escape control of executive powers by law through assuming his military role."[40]

The distinction between military and civil power is foundational to our constitutional order. In the Declaration of Independence, Congress said that King George III "has affected to render the Military independent of and superior to the Civil power."[41] The 1780 Massachusetts Constitution stated: "[T]he military power shall always be held in an exact subordination to the civil authority and be governed by it."[42] Martial law is thus highly disfavored. The Supreme Court declared in 1866 that such a doctrine "destroys every guarantee of the Constitution, and effectually renders the 'military independent of and superior to the civil power.' . . . Civil liberty and this kind of martial law cannot endure together; the antagonism is irreconcilable, and, in the conflict, one or the other must perish."[43] Concerns about the undue fusion of military and civil power were also behind Congress's decision to remove the atomic bomb from Army control and to prevent active or recently retired officers from serving as secretary of defense.

Just one year before *Youngstown*, the American people received a high-profile lesson about the superiority of civil over military authority. President Truman and his commander in Korea, Douglas MacArthur, clashed sharply over the appropriate response to China's decision to intervene in the war.[44] The final break came in March 1951 when General MacArthur sabotaged the White House's effort to arrange a ceasefire by issuing a provocative public statement to his Chinese counterpart.[45] Truman wrote in his memoir that the General's statement "was in open defiance of my orders as President and as Commander in Chief. This was a challenge to the President under the Constitution."[46] In announcing MacArthur's firing, Truman told the nation, "Full and vigorous debate on matters of national policy is a vital element in the constitutional system of our free democracy. It is fundamental, however, that military commanders must be governed by the policies and directives issued to them in the manner provided by our laws and Constitution."[47]

Figure 10.2 General Douglas MacArthur, whose removal by President Truman in 1951 set a powerful precedent for civilian control of the military. Library of Congress. U.S. Army. 1945. [LC-USZ62-21027]

While General MacArthur's removal led to calls for Truman's impeachment, many praised his decisive action to protect civilian supremacy.[48] Even a popular war hero was obliged to obey an unpopular President.[49]

Jackson's discussion in *Youngstown* upheld the principle behind MacArthur's dismissal by rejecting Truman's steel-seizure decision.

Military authority could not be permitted to subvert civil authority, and that was true whether the two realms were represented by different people or by the same person—the President. Driving this lesson home was especially important in 1952. Dwight D. Eisenhower was widely expected to run for President, and he won the Republican primary in New Hampshire shortly before Truman ordered the steel seizure.[50] His election in November as the first ex-general to serve as President since Ulysses S. Grant blurred the boundary between civil and military power. Fortunately, President Eisenhower turned out to be a good steward of this aspect of the Constitution, and before leaving office he made his most important rhetorical contribution by denouncing the merger of those two entities into the "military/industrial complex."[51]

Thus, the MacArthur firing and *Youngstown* set vital precedents for the Commander-in-Chief Clause at the start of the Cold War. But the concurrence did not stop with the possible textual sources for executive authority. There were also unenumerated and unspoken powers, especially in moments of crisis or panic.

11
Emergency!

Thomas Jefferson wrote in 1810 that "strict observance of the written law is doubtless *one* of the high duties of a good citizen, but it is not the *highest*. The laws of necessity, of self-preservation, of saving our country when in danger, are of higher obligation."[1] To fulfill what the Truman Administration saw as its highest duty in *Youngstown*, the solicitor general argued for what Justice Jackson described as the "power to deal with a crisis or an emergency according to the necessities of the case, the unarticulated assumption being that necessity knows no law."[2] In rejecting this request, Jackson relied on long-standing legislative practice and on an unarticulated premise that the Korean War was not a national emergency grave enough to justify unilateral executive action.[3] The concurrence's warnings about unchecked emergency power have gone largely unheeded by the Supreme Court and by Congress, perhaps because of crucial edits that Jackson made in the drafting process. But during the recent COVID-19 pandemic, state courts proved more sensitive to the opinion's deep logic.[4]

Separating the Lock from the Key

The linchpin of the concurrence's analysis on emergency powers was that the President could not define his own. No emergency powers are given to the President by the Constitution, even though the Framers "knew what emergencies were, knew the pressures they engender for authoritative action, knew, too, how they afford a ready pretext for usurpation."[5] "I do not think we rightfully may amend their work," Jackson explained, "and, if we could, I am not convinced it would be wise to do so, although many modern nations have forthrightly recognized that war and economic crisis may upset the normal balance between liberty and authority." He surveyed the European experience with emergency powers in a passage drawn from a book by Clinton Rossiter and from his own 1951 speech on "Wartime Security and

The Actual Art of Governing. Gerard N. Magliocca, Oxford University Press. © Oxford University Press (2025).
DOI: 10.1093/9780197768563.003.0012

Liberty." The lesson from Europe was that "emergency powers are consistent with free government only when their control is lodged elsewhere than in the Executive who exercises them." This was the case in France and Britain but not in Germany, where "Hitler persuaded President von Hindenburg to suspend all such rights, and they were never restored."[6]

The Justice then turned inward and observed that Congress could and often did give the President emergency powers when necessary. He cited a document provided to Congress by Attorney General Frank Murphy in 1939 listing ninety-nine statutes that provided such authority in specific circumstances.[7] "Under this procedure," Jackson wrote, "we retain Government by law—special, temporary law, perhaps, but law nonetheless." "In view of the ease, expedition, and safety with which Congress can grant and has granted large emergency powers . . . I am quite unimpressed with the argument that we should affirm possession of them without statute. Such power either has no beginning or it has no end." Here again the concurrence was emphasizing Congress's role in the constitutional structure and connecting that insight to parliamentary traditions elsewhere. This was another example in which Jackson was content to rely more on recent practice rather than on other tools of constitutional interpretation to extract the relevant legal principle; most of the statutes listed by the attorney general dated from World War I or later.[8]

Nevertheless, Jackson did not rule out the possibility that the President could exercise emergency power without statute. The zone of twilight left the door open when Congress was silent. In one draft, Jackson went further and declared: "I am not ready to say that no occasion can arise grave enough to warrant departures in particular instances from . . . the limitations of the Constitution. There may be occasions when preservation of our society will be more important than strict adherence to the Constitution. *Korematsu v. United States* 323 U.S. 214. But nothing here justifies such extreme and dangerous experimentation."[9] The draft citation to *Korematsu* might seem unexpected given that Jackson dissented in that case. He may have meant that the Court felt that the risk of Japanese sabotage within the United States was so great that the Bill of Rights could not be treated as what he would later describe as a "suicide pact."[10] What is clear, though, is that Jackson did not think the Korean War posed anything like that sort of danger.[11]

One of Jackson's drafts also made the point that Congress was free to condition grants of emergency power so that they could be withdrawn at any time. For example, the Lend-Lease Act gave the President broad discretion to provide military assistance to foreign nations but subjected that authority to a legislative veto.[12] President Roosevelt rejected the constitutionality of the legislative veto, and Jackson thought about revealing his disagreement with FDR in his *Youngstown* opinion. While thinking through that issue, he wrote that "I have never been able to see any reason why Congress may not keep effective control of any legislative policy by making the grant terminate at any time or upon any contingency, even its own joint resolution," by which he meant a majority vote of one or both houses of Congress that could not be vetoed by the President.[13] "[I]f emergency powers are ever to be conceded to the Executive department," the Justice mused, "he should not be allowed indefinitely to enhance his own power by his own act, but the invocation, extent, and termination of such powers shall all be defined by the legislative branch."[14] "[T]he ease, expedition, and safety with which Congress can grant and recall large emergency powers," he concluded, undermined the argument that the Constitution confers unilateral executive authority. But Jackson deleted the words "and recall" from the final version of the concurrence. This was an editorial decision that would have unfortunate consequences.[15]

The National Emergencies Act (Dubitante)

When Congress reformed emergency-power law in the 1970s, legislators looked to the *Youngstown* concurrence for guidance. Senator Frank Church, the architect of the National Emergencies Act of 1976, invoked "Justice Jackson's widely quoted and praised concurring opinion" and explained that "[the Senate] Special Committee on National Emergencies and Delegated Emergency Powers accepted Justice Jackson's outline as a basic guide in drafting legislation to curb the abusive use of emergency powers."[16] Instead of the piecemeal approach summarized by Attorney General Murphy in 1939, Congress created a uniform procedure for the President to declare a national emergency and access every grant of emergency power provided by another statute.[17] One significant implication of the National Emergencies Act was that there was no zone of twilight on that issue because Congress had enacted a comprehensive law. All executive emergency actions consistent with the Act fall into Category One and all inconsistent actions fall into Category Three. The Act's other crucial limit was that Congress could rescind the President's declaration of a national emergency through a legislative veto passed by both houses.[18] In Senator Church's words, "the legislative branch will be in a position to assert its ultimate authority."[19]

Seven years later, the Supreme Court in *INS v. Chadha* held federal legislative vetoes unconstitutional.[20] *Chadha* largely endorsed President Roosevelt's formal reasoning about that process, while noting Attorney General Jackson's contrary view.[21] What the Court lacked, though, was the discussion in his *Youngstown* draft about the importance of the legislative veto for the special case of emergency-powers statutes. Writing in dissent, Justice Byron White did observe that the decision would upend many federal laws, including the National Emergencies Act.[22] "Without the legislative veto," he wrote, "Congress is faced with a Hobson's choice: either to refrain from delegating the necessary authority, . . . or in the alternative, to abdicate its law-making function to the executive branch and independent agencies."[23] Justice White also quoted Jackson's *Youngstown* concurrence for the idea that separation of powers should be construed functionally.[24]

Congress responded to *Chadha* by removing the legislative veto from the National Emergencies Act.[25] This was a mistake. Congress should have reconsidered the entire statute. As the Act now stands, the President's invocation of emergency power does not end unless he agrees or two thirds of each House of Congress can enact a joint resolution over his veto.[26] No such override has ever happened, even though presidents have declared approximately forty emergencies that remain in effect today.[27] While the powers being exercised under these emergencies are modest, executive restraint may not endure. The most thorough analysis of the Act points out that the President could, among other things, test biological and chemical weapons on people without their consent, shut down the Internet, or suspend individual bank accounts without notice.[28]

Let us pause and reflect on the mismatch between Jackson's analysis and the current National Emergencies Act. First, the concurrence stressed that emergency powers are consistent with free government only when they are controlled by the legislature. Shorn of its legislative veto, though, the Act deprives Congress of effective control over the powers previously given. Second, the concurrence emphasized that emergency authority is "special, temporary law." But today emergencies are more likely to go on indefinitely because Congress cannot, in practice, end them. Third, Jackson expressed concern—both as solicitor general and in *Youngstown*—about the constitutionality of delegations made directly to the President on domestic affairs. The Act often does just that. Finally, Jackson's analysis of the nondelegation doctrine as solicitor general centered on laws giving the President legislative power.[29] The concurrence elaborated on that point by explaining that emergency authority is quintessentially legislative, which should mean that delegations of that authority directly to the President require extra scrutiny. Granted, the inconsistency between the Act and the concurrence would be clearer if Jackson had retained his draft language about the vital role of the legislative veto in checking emergency law. Nevertheless, the Act sits on unstable constitutional ground so long as the concurrence stands, especially since the Act has never been reviewed by the Supreme Court.

Consider a related example discussed in a law review article by then-Professor Amy Coney Barrett.[30] Professor Barrett asked whether Congress could delegate to the President the power to suspend habeas corpus whenever he thought the necessary constitutional conditions were present. Her answer was no. She contended that Congress must determine whether, as the Suspension Clause requires, a "Rebellion or Invasion" currently exists.[31] Suspension authority is also inherently legislative, which is why Lincoln's unilateral suspension at the start of the Civil War when Congress was out of session was (and remains) controversial.[32] This judgment cannot just be handed to the White House under a legislative delegation, because habeas corpus is meant to prevent arbitrary executive detention.[33] The writ's purpose would be subverted if the President could decide for himself when judicial limits on his detention power could be set aside. Furthermore, requiring a legislative decision close in time to a crisis that may require suspension promotes what Professor Barrett called "transparent, vigorous, and representative debate" that confers legitimacy on any subsequent action.[34] She concluded that the Suspension Clause "stands as an exception to the nondelegation doctrine, which emphasizes the extremely broad leeway that Congress enjoys in assigning responsibilities to the Executive Branch."[35]

Similar reasoning applies to the National Emergencies Act and calls into question its constitutionality under Category One of *Youngstown*. The suspension of habeas corpus, as the concurrence notes, is a legislative delegation of "extraordinary authority because of a crisis." Jackson also argued that legislative control of such emergency authority is essential for preserving liberty. While some delegation is permissible, the standing grants of exceptional authority pursuant to the National Emergencies Act mean that no "transparent, vigorous, and representative debate" occurs before the President declares an emergency. This is dangerous, because curbs on freedom and the circumvention of constitutional tradition should occur only when a current majority deems them necessary after robust discussion. This reasoning does not mean that all applications of the Act are unconstitutional. Some emergency powers are narrow and might be well-suited to the conditions facing the country when they are invoked. Others involve foreign affairs and are therefore not subject to a nondelegation doctrine challenge. Nevertheless, faithfulness to the *Youngstown* concurrence demands that courts read the Act narrowly and carefully consider specific nondelegation claims.[36]

The Concurrence During the Pandemic

One way of making the concurrence's discussion of emergency powers come alive is by seeing how its logic was applied to events that might be described as "almost too recent to be called history, but which are familiar to us all."[37] During the COVID-19 pandemic, state and local governments invoked emergency public-health laws to impose severe restrictions on daily life.[38] These new rules were greeted with sharp protests. In part, that was because these health laws were often enacted long before the pandemic and were largely unknown to the public. Moreover, they delegated broad powers to executive officials that could not always easily be recalled. Thus, in most state legislatures, no "transparent, vigorous, and representative debate" occurred about what should be done and what exceptions should be made. When challenges to these policies were mounted, state courts turned to *Youngstown* for guidance and did not reflexively uphold the emergency delegations.

In some states, the concurrence was used to invalidate legislative or executive action. For example, the Michigan Supreme Court cited Jackson's opinion in holding that, under the state constitution, the governor could not implement certain pandemic measures by executive order.[39] The court said that the emergency statute relied on by the governor (enacted in 1945) "authorizes indefinite exercise of emergency powers for perhaps months—or even years."[40] Quoting the concurrence for the proposition that emergency laws are "best characterized as 'temporary,'" the court held that the indefiniteness of the delegation, along with its "expansiveness" and "inadequate standards," meant that the law was unconstitutional under a nondelegation analysis.[41] Likewise, the Kentucky Supreme Court quoted Jackson's opinion at length in rejecting the claim of unilateral power by that state's governor to respond to COVID-19.[42] The Kentucky court's judgment was buttressed by the fact that the legislature enacted a fresh statute in 2021 (over an executive veto) to restrict the Governor's extraordinary authority.[43]

By contrast, the Massachusetts Supreme Judicial Court, citing Category One of *Youngstown*, upheld the state governor's exercise of delegated emergency power during the pandemic.[44] Citing the *Youngstown* upheld concurrence, the court stated: "Because the Governor was acting under an express authorization of the Legislature . . . his authority was, therefore, at its maximum." The court also observed, though, that the state statute permitted the legislature to make any part of the emergency inoperative through a legislative veto.[45] Thus, "not only have the [Governor's] emergency orders not precluded the legislative from exercising its full authority to pass laws, but the Legislature also has at its disposal a way to curb the Governor's powers . . . should it desire to do so, and it has not done so."[46] This was a supple reading that correctly intuited that the availability of a legislative veto makes broad delegations of emergency authority sustainable.[47]

Another thoughtful take on *Youngstown* and COVID-19 was offered by a justice of New Mexico's Supreme Court who concurred in that governor's exercise of emergency power.[48] The court upheld the governor's actions and quoted Jackson's canonical statement about the need for a "workable government."[49] Justice David K. Thomson concurred but expressed his concern about "the broad and vague statutes that grant emergency powers to the Governor."[50] In his words, "When a crisis first erupts, the question of whether the executive branch has exercised its police or emergency power within the structures of the Constitution can be indeterminate and at times vague. This is understandable because the need to immediately address a life-threatening situation does not necessarily allow for a full, open debate concerning all of the possibilities to arrive at a *best* and clearly constitutional response."[51] He then invoked, with a twist, the zone-of-twilight metaphor: "Extending Justice Jackson's analysis concerning the semi-permeable boundary between the proper exercise of federal executive and legislative power, the exercise of state executive power during a crisis or emergency may likewise fall within a zone of twilight, where the power to act is not the sole province of one branch of government." The upshot of his reasoning was that, as time passes, an emergency delegation should be read more restrictively.

Overall, the state courts that pondered the concurrence understood that Jackson did not say that every legislative delegation of emergency power is constitutional. It may be hoped that this lesson will percolate up and lead Congress to reform the National Emergencies Act or educate the US Supreme Court whenever a legal challenge to the Act is brought there during the next emergency.

12
The Modern Presidency

As the concurrence reached its conclusion, Justice Jackson returned to his theme that, from the perspective of a former presidential adviser, separation of powers should be understood in practical terms. He wrote that the gap "between the President's paper powers and his real powers" counseled against giving the White House the benefit of the constitutional doubt in a dispute with Congress.[1] Years of seeing Franklin D. Roosevelt in action told Jackson that modern presidents have substantial soft power due to their celebrity, singular role as head of state, and position as party leader. As a result, they can often persuade Congress to give them what they want. But persuade they must. To relieve them of that duty would throw away the hard-won limits on executive authority established since Magna Carta, which Jackson illustrated with a final dash of poetry by Kipling about England's long struggle to bring the Crown under the law.[2] The Supreme Court, though, has never cited or accepted the *Youngstown* concurrence's central lesson.

Outward Sameness, but Inner Change

Jackson's concurring opinion is part of a proud intellectual tradition that examines how constitutional practice compares to constitutional forms. Walter Bagehot pioneered this approach for the uncodified British Constitution, stating that "an observer who looks at the living reality will wonder at the contrast to the paper description. He will see in the life much which is not in the books; and he will not find in the rough practice many refinements of the literary theory."[3] Jackson read Bagehot and drew on one of his books for a 1949 dissent.[4] But Bagehot's greatest American disciple was Woodrow Wilson, who was a political scientist before entering politics.[5] In his groundbreaking book *Congressional Government*, Professor Wilson argued that the Constitution's formal structure belied the reality that power after the Civil War rested with congressional committee chairs who were not mentioned

The Actual Art of Governing. Gerard N. Magliocca, Oxford University Press. © Oxford University Press (2025).
DOI: 10.1093/9780197768563.003.0013

in the constitutional text.[6] Jackson's concurrence followed in that spirit in stating that "[s]ubtle shifts take place in the centers of real power that do not show on the face of the Constitution" and by quoting another book by Wilson about the executive's informal authority. Putting his ideas into practice, President Wilson exemplified Jackson's belief that the text "does not disclose the measure of the actual controls wielded by the modern presidential office." For example, Wilson broke with tradition by holding regular press conferences and by delivering speeches to a joint session of Congress outlining his legislative agenda and asking for support.[7] The *Youngstown* concurrence is still the most serious judicial effort to integrate our customary or political constitution with the written one.

Jackson's first political-science observation was that the federal government was far stronger and more concentrated than in George Washington's day. This was the result of changes in American society, constitutional amendments, and a New Deal revolution (in which Jackson played a major role) that read the powers of Congress more broadly.[8] The New Deal also ushered in a powerful administrative state, which increased the President's reach by providing personnel and expertise to carry out executive initiatives. While Congress does exercise oversight over agency work, the policy details are typically sorted out in practice by presidential appointees. These trends have continued unabated since 1952 and have strengthened the President's position relative to Congress and the courts, especially after the demise of the legislative veto.

The Justice's next functional point was that a modern President's ability to focus media attention gives the White House a large advantage over Congress and the courts. Until the twentieth century, Presidents generally refrained from personal campaigning and cultivated a reserved public image as the "Chief Magistrate." While Wilson's changes were innovative, FDR's use of the radio in his "Fireside Chats" was transformative. Jackson reflected that "[t]he radio listener liked the way Roosevelt just conversed by microphone. While others might orate, Roosevelt would simply talk as if to a neighbor; the country sat at its receiving sets, and each felt that he was being talked with."[9] Based on these strengths, he speculated that Roosevelt "probably would have been as great or greater a master of the newly devised television. That opens to his successors even larger possibilities for the communication of personality, sincerity, and thought."[10] Social-media outlets, of course, amplified this tendency in the twenty-first century by giving Presidents a powerful tool to bypass Congress and the press and appeal directly to voters.

Figure 12.1 Woodrow Wilson, whom Justice Jackson cited for his scholarship on the presidency. Library of Congress. Pach Brothers. 1912. [LC-USZ62-132907]

The unitary structure of the presidency enhances this media edge. Jackson was not the first person to emphasize that we have only one President: Alexander Hamilton discussed this in *The Federalist* #70.[11] But this fact takes on greater importance in a political environment in which media and celebrity count for more. Nine Justices or hundreds of members of Congress cannot match the President as "the focus of public hopes and expectations. In drama, magnitude, and finality his decisions so far overshadow any others that almost alone he fills the public eye and ear."[12] Jackson wrote after *Youngstown* that "a White House tenant who is a skillful manipulator of his extralegal influences may force an unwelcome program through Congress."[13] Put another way, the President is the only official with what Teddy Roosevelt called the "bully pulpit."[14]

Jackson's next savvy insight was that the President's prestige as head of state gives him "leverage upon those who are supposed to check and balance his power which often cancels their effectiveness." The United States is unusual in making its head of state and head of government the same person. In most democracies, those roles are divided in order to weaken the executive. As Winston Churchill once stated, "It is wise in human affairs, and in the government of men, to separate pomp from power."[15] There are many constitutional monarchies, but the British Crown and prime minister represent the most famous example of executive bicameralism. A different form involves a ceremonial president who is either elected or appointed and is distinct from the prime minister.[16] These institutions provide a unifying leader who stands above party politics, while denying the prime minister the trappings of the head of state. Another advantage of dividing the executive branch internally is that ceremonial heads of state are often designated as the commander in chief of the armed forces.[17] While this title does not come with command authority (except perhaps in dire emergencies), prime ministers are denied the rhetorical benefit of referring to themselves by that title when trying to convince the nation to go to war or to adopt controversial military decisions.

The *Youngstown* concurrence is the only judicial opinion that recognizes the President's status as our head of state and its relevance for constitutional analysis, although Jackson did not develop the point. Simply put, Presidents can use their symbolic role to persuade Congress and the American people to follow their lead. In the age of mass media, opportunities abound for a President to use events where he appears as head of state to make an appeal for his partisan agenda.[18] This sort of appeal became even more persuasive after World War II, when the President started being described as "the leader of the free world."[19] Presidents receive a political boost by meeting with apolitical heads of state or by representing the nation abroad. Foreign-policy and national-security issues lend themselves to presidential persuasion using the argument that certain measures are necessary to maintain our international reputation.

Jackson's final dose of reality was that the President is a party leader who twists arms in Congress. Political parties did not exist in 1787 when the Constitution was written. "The rise of the party system," he explained, "has made a significant extraconstitutional supplement to real executive power. No appraisal of his necessities is realistic which overlooks that he heads a political system as well as a legal system. Party loyalties and interests, sometimes more binding than law, extend his effective control into branches of government other than his own and he often may win, as a political leader, what he cannot command under the Constitution." The claim that party loyalties are sometimes more binding than law was an unusual admission in a judicial opinion, but again Jackson drew on his time with Roosevelt.[20] In his unfinished FDR memoir, the Justice stated that "[t]he Chief Magistrate does not succeed merely by being magisterial. He will fail as President if he fails as politician."[21] "Toward Congress," he said, "the President's attitude was somewhat mercurial. Congress itself is mercurial."[22] Roosevelt expected to make proposals and then have his legislative program "made effective through representatives of his party." One reason why Jackson may have been unimpressed by President Truman's claim of unilateral executive authority is because Truman made no real effort to convince his party's representatives to give him authority to seize the steel mills, even though Democrats controlled Congress.

Today Presidents exert even more influence over their party than Truman could. Robert Jackson lived in a world where party bosses were powerful and presidential candidates were not chosen by primaries. "How much those [party] organizations influenced their congressmen or senators, I would, of course, be unable to say," Jackson once recalled, "but probably considerably if they wanted to remain in office."[23] A Democratic President's reach within his party was also curtailed in the South by Jim Crow and the fierce local loyalties inspired by white supremacy.[24] Political reforms and cultural changes in the 1960s and 1970s weakened these fiefdoms and strengthened the President. In more recent times, party polarization unlike anything Jackson experienced makes presidential appeals to party identity more difficult for members of Congress to resist. Finally, the President's greater overall power today provides additional bargaining chips and leverage to whip the party into line.

Though the concurrence expressly says that there is a relationship between separation of powers and political parties, a leading scholarly article notes that "after decades of dissecting Justice Jackson's *Youngstown* opinion, neither the Supreme Court nor any other federal court has ever quoted this critical insight."[25] While courts are understandably reluctant to discuss political partisanship, Jackson's wisdom on this point is more relevant than ever. The fact is that Congress and the President check each other much more often when they are controlled by different parties.[26] Legislative scrutiny is more vigorous, impeachment investigations are more likely, and Congress is far less willing to give the executive broad authority or fund its requests. Jackson later explained that the concurrence was meant "to point out the inadequacies of judicial power to appraise or control the realistic balance of power between Congress and the President."[27]

After examining the President's "real powers," the concurrence concluded that courts should not give the executive the benefit of the doubt in a dispute with Congress. "I cannot be brought to believe," Jackson wrote," that this country will suffer if the Court refuses further to aggrandize the presidential office, already so potent and so relatively immune from judicial review, at the expense of Congress."[28] For this claim he cited another book by Clinton Rossiter.[29] Jackson may have used the book because Rossiter had showered praise on the Justice's opinions, especially his "clear, cold words" in *Korematsu*.[30] But Rossiter also observed that "it is extremely difficult for injured persons to obtain definitive judicial scrutiny" of presidential actions when they raise "a question so politically explosive that the very notion of 'government by lawsuit' becomes unthinkable."[31] He also shrewdly pointed out that attorneys needed to consider "the implications of this study for constitutional law in the atomic age."[32]

The Supreme Court has never accepted Jackson's admonition that Congress should prevail in close or doubtful separation-of-powers cases. As this point is the climax of the Justice's analysis on executive power, the Court's refusal to cite that part of the concurrence requires some explanation. One part of the answer may be the predominance of textual or formalist interpretive methods that are more focused on the Constitution's paper powers at the expense of its real powers.[33] Congress also asserted its authority more aggressively during and after Watergate, which may have led the Court to conclude that the informal advantages of the presidency were no longer so strong and that judicial action was therefore required.[34] A third possibility is that Jackson was exceptional among former executive-branch lawyers in thinking that the presidency should be judged skeptically. Many modern Justices serve in the executive branch before reaching the bench and may instead take the view that the President should be freed from the shackles imposed by Congress and the courts.[35]

The Old Issue

"Leave to live by no man's leave, underneath the law" is the poetic opening to the concurring opinion's closing. Jackson put this quotation in a draft that he decided not to publish in the final Japanese-American incarceration case—*Ex Parte Endo*.[36] Less than a year later, he would use the line to end his opening address to the Nuremberg tribunal.[37] It comes from "The Old Issue," a Rudyard Kipling poem published in 1899.[38] Jackson prized Kipling's verse. In a radio address in 1941, he closed with a Kipling quatrain from "For All We Have and Are."[39] He kept a line from the poet framed on his mantelpiece: "He travels fastest who travels alone."[40] And he had used Kipling in an opinion that he wrote for the Court in 1948.[41]

There is a double meaning to the use of "The Old Issue" in *Youngstown*, as the poem is an extended meditation on the legal struggle against arbitrary royal power. Kipling begins with a reference to "the King we schooled . . . in the eyot at Runnymede!" This refers to Magna Carta, a written concession from King John to the barons that was negotiated in 1215 on an isle (or eyot) in the Thames at Runnymede.[42] The next stanza invokes the execution of King Charles I in 1649 "round the scaffold . . . by Whitehall."[43] These landmark events were instrumental in establishing constitutional limits on the Crown, and they prompted the stanzas of celebration and caution that opened this book:

> All we have of freedom, all we use or know—
> This our fathers bought for us long and long ago.
> Ancient Right unnoticed as the breath we draw—
> Leave to live by no man's leave, underneath the Law.
> Lance and torch and tumult, steel and grey-goose wing
> Wrenched it, inch and ell and all, slowly from the King.[44]
> Till our fathers 'stablished, after bloody years,
> How our King is one with us, first among his peers.
> So they bought us freedom—not at little cost—
> Wherefore must we watch the King, lest our gain be lost.[45]

Kipling's point was that centuries of painful effort were required to create a constitutional monarchy. There was always a risk that tyranny could return.

The next section of "The Old Issue" described "what shall fall [i.e., befall] if the King return" and touched on many fundamental points in Anglo-American law. After stating that the King "shall mark our goings, question whence we came," it goes on to envision that the Crown would also "take a tribute, toll of all our ware; / He shall change our gold for arms—arms we may not bear."[46] The first line of the couplet is an allusion to the royal collecting of taxes or seizing of property to support war without consent of Parliament, which would find a modern parallel in President Truman's steel seizure without congressional authorization.[47] The second line is a reference to the right to bear arms in the English Bill of Rights, a right that was later incorporated into the Second Amendment.[48] The English Bill of Rights was enacted in response to another dangerous King—James II—who was forced to abdicate the throne by the Glorious Revolution of 1688.[49] The next stanza says that the King "shall break his Judges if they cross his word / He shall rule above the Law calling on the Lord."[50] The King's minions "shall deal our Justice: sell—deny—delay," a repudiation of Magna Carta's declaration that "To no-one will we sell or deny or delay right or justice."[51] In other dire warnings, he imagines that the land will be filled with "hosts of hurrying spies" and censorship will be imposed "lest we mock the King."[52] In the end: "Long-forgotten bondage, dwarfing heart and brain— / All our Fathers died to loose he shall bind again."

Jackson knew the deeper meaning of "[l]eave to live by no man's leave, underneath the Law" when he quoted the line at Nuremberg and in *Youngstown*. In both cases, he was speaking against arbitrary executive power and on behalf of "those impersonal forces which we call law." "The executive action we have here," he said, "originates in the individual will of the President and represents an exercise of authority without law. . . . With all its defects, delays and inconveniences, men have discovered no technique for long preserving free government except that the Executive be under the law, and that the law be made by parliamentary deliberations." In his final couplet, the Justice wrote that "[s]uch institutions may be destined to pass away." In a draft, he added, "Sometimes I fear it."[53] But "it is the duty of the Court to be last," he said, "not first, to give them up."

When President Nixon subverted the Constitution in the 1970s, the Court was asked to curb abuses of the executive's "real powers." Justice Jackson's concurrence met that moment.

PART 3

RESULTS

13
The Scandal

The concurring opinion in Youngstown was not an instant classic. A year after the case was decided, Professor Edward C. Corwin wrote about it in the *Columbia Law Review* and said that "Justice Jackson's rather desultory opinion contains little that is of direct pertinence to the constitutional issue."[1] After Jackson's death in 1954, though, Professor Louis Jaffe penned a tribute to the Justice in the *Harvard Law Review* and stated that the "concurrence is in my opinion a most brilliant exposition of 'undefined presidential powers' and their relation to legislation."[2] This sort of academic back-and-forth is par for the course for Supreme Court cases and rarely leads to a consensus that an opinion is exceptional. How, then, did Jackson's concurrence rise to such heights? The answer is that President Richard M. Nixon's abuses of power led lawyers and scholars to reconsider executive authority and search for a persuasive source that rejected what Arthur M. Schlesinger, Jr., called the "Imperial Presidency."[3] Their expedition discovered the concurring opinion. In *United States v. Nixon* and transformative federal legislation enacted after Watergate, Justice Jackson's wisdom started to become law.

The Wilderness Years

Prior to Richard Nixon's election in 1968, references to the *Youngstown* concurrence were few and far between.[4] The only notable quotation came in 1962 when Chief Justice Earl Warren used Jackson's passage about Pharaoh's dreams in a lecture at NYU.[5] But the ingredients for the opinion's expansion were at hand. America's growing involvement in Vietnam carried echoes of the Korean War. The Great Society would expand executive power through the creation of many new federal programs and agencies. President Nixon faced a Congress controlled by large Democratic majorities, which gave him an incentive to take unilateral steps and test the boundaries of his authority.[6] He did just that by bombing Cambodia without specific authorization from Congress, attempting to prevent publication of the Pentagon Papers

The Actual Art of Governing. Gerard N. Magliocca, Oxford University Press. © Oxford University Press (2025).
DOI: 10.1093/9780197768563.003.0014

on his own in the name of national security, and aggressively impounding appropriations (refusing to spend money authorized by Congress).[7]

Famous judicial opinions are not intrinsically great. A ruling typically receives special recognition because of factors that go beyond what the decision says.[8] In order to shine, an opinion must be useful for future lawyers and judges.[9] But whether a decision speaks to important questions that arise in later years is often a matter of chance.[10] The reputation of the opinion's author also matters.[11] Great opinions are not written by obscure judges;[12] it was Jackson's independent status as a superb jurist that gave the *Youngstown* concurrence an opportunity to enter the constitutional canon. Finally, for a separate opinion to achieve renown there must be a flaw in the Court's opinion. Though virtually everyone today thinks that *Youngstown* was correctly decided, Justice Black's decision was spare, because the case was heard on a rapid timetable and no opinion could mass the Court behind a single rationale. This left the door open for one of the concurrences to become the leading voice.

An opinion by a single Justice rarely becomes authoritative, but some dissents have achieved that status. A basic constraint on a solo opinion's potential is that a compelling analysis normally induces at least one other Justice to join. To write separately without colleagues typically means that the Justice is either significantly out of step with the prevailing mood or somewhat quirky and unwilling to make the changes necessary to attract more votes.[13] The most canonical lone opinion in the Court's history is Justice John Marshall Harlan's dissent in *Plessy v. Ferguson*, with its admonition that "our Constitution is color blind."[14] The dissent of Justice Oliver Wendell Holmes, Jr., in *Lochner v. New York* is also widely cited in challenges to unwritten constitutional rights.[15] Jackson himself contributed an example in *Korematsu*, with its arresting metaphor of a "loaded weapon."[16] But his opinion in *Youngstown* remains the only lone concurrence that reached the judicial summit and has stayed there.

The first indication that the concurrence might become essential reading came in 1971 when a federal circuit court was asked to evaluate the legality of affirmative action. *Contractors Association of Eastern Pennsylvania v. Secretary of Labor* involved President Nixon's executive order implementing the "Philadelphia Plan," which required bidders for federal construction contracts to hire a certain percentage of minority employees.[17] The Third Circuit's opinion began its analysis by stating that "[t]he limitations of Executive power have rarely been considered by the courts" but that *Youngstown* was one of those cases.[18] "From the six concurring

Figure 13.1 Richard Nixon. Library of Congress. Official White House Photograph. 1969–1974.

opinions and one dissenting opinion in that case," the Court stated, "the most significant guidance for present purposes may be found in that of Justice Jackson."[19] The Court quoted Jackson's three rough categories in full, which marks the first time that any court had done so. After canvassing executive practice on federal contracting going back to World War II, the

Court said that there was enough to support the Philadelphia Plan in the zone of twilight given Congress's acquiescence in those set-aside programs.[20] The Court then concluded that no Act of Congress barred the President from imposing affirmative action on federal contracts.[21]

That same year, a different federal circuit court turned to the concurrence in rejecting a constitutional challenge to the Vietnam War. *Massachusetts v. Laird* was triggered by a state law prohibiting military service by state inhabitants in an undeclared foreign war.[22] The First Circuit concluded that the power "to conduct undeclared hostilities" was shared by Congress and the President, which built on Jackson's view that a formal war declaration was unnecessary to support measures up to and including conscription.[23] The Court quoted Category Two of the concurring opinion as the legal standard "in the circumstance where powers are interrelated."[24] Within the zone of twilight, the Court stated that funding for the Vietnam War "reveals a prolonged period of Congressional support of executive activities," though that may not be an "express or implied ratification" of presidential conduct. "All we hold here," the Court concluded, "is that in a situation of prolonged but undeclared hostilities, where the executive continues to act not only in the absence of any conflicting Congressional claim of authority but with steady Congressional support, the Constitution has not been breached."[25]

These circuit rulings represented a step forward for Jackson's concurring opinion, but there was still no common understanding that his analysis deserved extraordinary respect. Circuit cases are not Supreme Court cases. And when William H. Rehnquist, who had served as Justice Jackson's law clerk during *Youngstown*, was nominated to the Supreme Court in 1971, he was asked no questions about the case during his Senate confirmation hearings. There was also no significant uptick in scholarly references to the concurrence.[26] But things would look very different a few years later after a "third-rate burglary" at Democratic National Headquarters and the subsequent cover-up.[27]

The Watergate Tapes Case

Watergate was an apt illustration of the modern presidential pathologies that informed Jackson's opinion.[28] First, the Nixon Administration's crimes and abuses of public trust were conducted secretly, often under the guise of national security. The concurrence expressed concern that much of what the President does is "largely uncontrolled" and "unknown" so long as national security is invoked. Second, these illegal or unconstitutional acts were undertaken in the President's capacity as a party leader to further his reelection in 1972, which dovetails with Jackson's discussion of the informal influence of partisanship on the presidency. Third, one of the three impeachment articles approved by the House Judiciary Committee charged Nixon with using the bully pulpit "for the purpose of deceiving the people of the United States," which connects to the importance that the concurrence attached to the President's public megaphone.[29] Fourth, Watergate reflected the President's "real power" in that many of the wrongs were conducted by staff members rather than officials subject to Senate confirmation, and funded by campaign contributions rather than by congressional appropriations.[30] The President's "paper powers" in the Constitution say nothing about any of that. Finally, President Nixon was accused of engaging in unlawful electronic surveillance—an issue Jackson knew well when he wrote his opinion—and was undone by his own surveillance of the Oval Office.

The sharpest dispute during Watergate was whether a special prosecutor could obtain President Nixon's White House tapes as part of the criminal investigation.[31] In the District Court, the President argued that executive privilege was an absolute shield against discovery and that to hold otherwise "would effectively destroy the status of the Executive Branch as an equal and coordinate element of government."[32] Special Prosecutor Archibald Cox's brief replied, "We enjoy a constitutional government of laws and not of men because each branch has acknowledged its duties under the functioning of the others."[33] The brief then quoted Jackson's "workable government" passage in defense of a relative view of separation of powers where the President's need for confidentiality must be weighed against the demands of criminal justice.[34] A page later, the brief discussed *Youngstown* in a footnote and stated that "Justice Jackson expressed the fundamental principle underlying the Court's decision" when he declared, 'With all its defects, delays and inconveniences, men have discovered no technique for long preserving free government except that the Executive be under the law.'"[35] Judge John J. Sirica's opinion rejecting the President's view repeated the "workable government" passage to support the point that "the Framers' intention to lodge the powers of government in separate bodies also included a plan for interaction between departments."[36] The D.C. Circuit, sitting *en banc*, affirmed Judge Sirica's decision and quoted the "defects, delays, and inconveniences" language of the concurrence in a footnote.[37] A week later, President Nixon fired Cox in the notorious "Saturday Night Massacre."[38] But the ensuing outcry forced Nixon to appoint another special prosecutor, Leon Jaworski, and a new tapes case arrived at the Supreme Court in July 1974.[39]

United States v. Nixon is one of the most consequential cases in American history and was the first to quote from Jackson's concurring opinion.[40] The Court's unanimous decision, written by Chief Justice Warren Burger, ordered Nixon to turn over the tapes and thereby hastened his resignation.[41] *Nixon* was the first opinion to hold that the President can claim "executive privilege."[42] In the process, the decision also turned Chief Justice Marshall's rulings in Aaron Burr's treason trial into a touchstone for constitutional reasoning.[43] *Nixon*'s less heralded jurisprudential innovation was its blessing of the *Youngstown* concurrence. The Court repeated Jackson's "workable government" passage to support the point that "the separate powers were not intended to operate with absolute independence."[44] "To read the Art[icle] II powers of the President as providing an absolute privilege as against a subpoena essential to enforcement of criminal statutes on no more than a generalized claim of the public interest in confidentiality of nonmilitary and nondiplomatic discussions," the Court continued, "would upset the constitutional balance of 'a workable government.'"[45] Three years later, the Court stated that *Nixon* "rejected the argument that the Constitution contemplates a complete division of authority between the three branches. Rather, the unanimous Court essentially embraced Mr. Justice Jackson's view, expressed in his concurrence in *Youngstown*."[46]

One lesson from this history is that the concurrence was in the right place at the right time during Watergate. A high-profile dispute about presidential power consumed the nation's life for two years before being ultimately tested in court. President Nixon's argument against giving up the most important evidence was that separation of powers should be understood in absolute terms that precluded a judicial order directing the President to turn over the tapes. Jackson's functional approach met the moment by offering a justification for balancing executive privilege against other constitutional interests, a balancing exercise that Nixon was bound to lose. The surprise here is that the Court's first citation of the concurrence did not involve the three rough categories for congressional-executive action and did not come in a case that

Figure 13.2 "Above Any Office." Herb Block, *Washington Post*, August 31, 1973. A 1949 Herblock Cartoon, © The Herb Block Foundation.

involved a dispute between Congress and the President. Instead, the opinion's contribution turned out to be its memorable expression of pragmatism and flexibility.

Scholarly and Congressional Embrace

Watergate was also a watershed for academic thinking about the concurrence. The most widely read account was Professor Schlesinger's 1973 book on *The Imperial Presidency*. This penetrating critique of executive power said that the opinion "set forth an analysis, brilliant then and classic now, of the American separation of powers."[47] Prominent law professors started jumping on the bandwagon even before *Nixon* was decided.[48] For example, the former dean of the Yale Law School, Eugene Rostow, wrote an article in 1972 declaring that Jackson's concurrence was "probably his finest opinion" and quoted the memes about Pharaoh's dream and workable government along with the three rough categories.[49] After *Nixon*, Professor Gerald Gunther revised his influential constitutional-law casebook to emphasize Jackson's discussion in *Youngstown*.[50] And Philip Kurland, a pillar of the University of Chicago Law School, called the concurrence the "[m]ost important opinion [Jackson] ever composed."[51] To be sure, acclaim for Jackson's opinion was not universal,[52] but the trend was unmistakable.

The same trend played out in Congress. Watergate and its aftermath marked the last period in which Congress was the most powerful branch of government. Sweeping laws enacted in the 1970s, sometimes over presidential vetoes, took power away from the executive.[53] Many of these statutes were grounded in Jackson's opinion. The National Emergencies Act was an example;[54] another was the Foreign Intelligence Surveillance Act.[55] Both statutes relied not on Jackson's functional constitutional approach, as *Nixon* did, but on the concurrence's view that comprehensive federal legislation on a topic where Congress and the President shared power barred unilateral executive action.

The *Youngstown* concurrence's three rough categories would not be cited by the Supreme Court until 1981, when Justice Jackson's law clerk from 1952 would write the majority opinion in *Dames & Moore v. Regan*.[56]

14
The Law Clerks

William H. Rehnquist walked into the Supreme Court for the first time less than four months before the oral argument in *Youngstown*.[1] Fresh out of Stanford Law School, he had been chosen to serve as one of Justice Jackson's two law clerks.[2] He followed the initial *Youngstown* proceedings with keen interest and attended the argument in the D.C. Circuit on the Government's stay motion.[3] Decades later, Chief Justice Rehnquist would reflect often on his initiation to high-stakes litigation.[4] Though he played no role in drafting the concurrence, the opinion would shape his thinking in significant constitutional cases such as *Dames & Moore* and *Morrison v. Olson*.[5] Rehnquist's most famous law clerk, John Roberts, would also pay homage to Justice Jackson's work. The *Youngstown* concurrence exerted a powerful influence on Chief Justice Roberts's 2024 opinion for the Court in *Trump v. United States*, though more in form than in function.[6]

Past as Prologue

In 1969, Rehnquist returned to Washington from private practice to serve in the Office of Legal Counsel, and he soon found himself relying on the concurrence. One of the many difficult issues that landed on his desk involved President Nixon's authority to bomb Cambodia, which was neutral in the Vietnam War but was being used by North Vietnam as a supply route to South Vietnam.[7] Rehnquist wrote a memo concluding that the President had the authority to act, in part based on his role as commander in chief.[8] To support that claim, he quoted Jackson's declaration in *Youngstown*: "We should not use this occasion to circumscribe, much less to contract, the lawful role of the President as Commander in Chief. I should indulge the widest latitude of interpretation to sustain his exclusive function to command the instruments of national force, at least when turned against the outside world for the security of our society."

The Actual Art of Governing. Gerard N. Magliocca, Oxford University Press. © Oxford University Press (2025).
DOI: 10.1093/9780197768563.003.0015

This first significant use of the concurrence drew criticism from anti-war lawyers. In a letter to the editor in the *New York Times*, they wrote: "It is ironic that Mr. Rehnquist, who served as a law clerk to Supreme Court Justice Robert Jackson, distorted Justice Jackson's classic opinion, in the steel seizure case."[9] They went on: "Justice Jackson demolished the Government's contention that the President under the commander-in-chief clause had the power to do 'anything, anywhere, that can be done with an army or navy.' Yet Mr. Rehnquist has in effect advanced that notion in his statements."

Following Rehnquist's confirmation to the Court in 1971, he continued to heap praise on the concurrence.[10] In a talk at Albany Law School, he observed that Justice Jackson's description of the three rough categories is "yet to be surpassed in its statesmanlike and lawyerlike analysis of the executive branch of the federal government."[11] Justice Rehnquist added, "I do not believe he would have written his concurring opinion in the *Steel Seizure Cases* had he not been exposed in the eleven years between 1941 and 1952 to this country's participation in a World War, to the experiences which he underwent as the prosecutor for the United States at the Nuremberg trials, to the beginnings of the 'Cold War' in the late forties and the early fifties of this century." It is also fair to say that Rehnquist would not have written his opinion for the Court in *Dames & Moore* in the way that he did but for his exposure to the concurrence's birth.[12]

Dames & Moore v. Regan

An international crisis gave Justice Rehnquist the opportunity to turn the concurring opinion into law. In December 1979, the American Embassy staff in Tehran was taken hostage after the overthrow of the Iranian Shah, who had been backed by the United States.[13] President Jimmy Carter responded by declaring a national emergency and freezing Iranian assets.[14] The hostages were released in 1981 under a bilateral agreement that terminated all outstanding court judgments against Iran and stipulated that any disputes would be submitted to arbitration.[15] President Carter and President Ronald Reagan issued executive orders to enforce this agreement.[16] Companies with judgments for damages against Iran (including the nationalization of their assets there) challenged presidential authority to set their attachments aside and extinguish their court cases.[17]

Figure 14.1 Justice William H. Rehnquist, who clerked for Justice Jackson during *Youngstown* and helped turn the concurrence into law in *Dames & Moore v. Regan*. Library of Congress. United States Supreme Court. 1972.

Two circuit courts that initially addressed these claims both quoted from the *Youngstown* concurrence.[18] The D.C. Circuit upheld the executive orders by using Justice Jackson's three rough categories.[19] The Court reasoned that a federal law authorized the President to nullify court attachments against Iran.[20] The First Circuit did the same.[21] As for extinguishing the court cases, the D.C. Circuit held that, although this fell into Category Two, the executive orders should be sustained because of congressional acquiescence to similar executive practice in the past.[22] The First Circuit went further and said that this case "well illustrates the imperative need to preserve a presidential flexibility sufficient to defuse an international crisis, in order to prevent the crisis from escalating or even leading to war," in a nod to the zone of twilight's emphasis on the imperatives of events and contemporary imponderables.[23] Indeed, the Court characterized the Iran hostage crisis as "a major crisis in foreign relations of this country."[24] Then-Judge Stephen Breyer concurred, but on the narrower ground that the Act of Congress authorizing the nullification of attachments also authorized wiping out the court cases at issue.[25]

The Supreme Court affirmed in a unanimous opinion by Rehnquist that cited Justice Jackson's handiwork early and often. *Dames & Moore* opened by saying "it is doubtless both futile and perhaps dangerous to find any epigrammatical explanation of how this country has been governed" and cited "the poverty of really useful and unambiguous authority applicable to concrete problems of executive power."[26] One page later, Rehnquist wrote that both parties agreed that the *Youngstown* concurrence "brings together as much combination of analysis and common sense as there is in this area."[27] He added that Jackson's opinion rejected a claim of "plenary and exclusive power of the President" and quoted the concurrence's passage about the forefathers not wanting to emulate George III.[28]

After stating the facts, Justice Rehnquist returned to his talisman and offered a refined assessment of Jackson's work. He wrote that the concurrence "elaborated in a general way the consequences of different types of interaction between the two democratic branches in assessing Presidential authority to act in any given case."[29] "Although we have in the past found and do today find Justice Jackson's classification of executive actions into three general categories useful," he continued, "Justice Jackson himself recognized that his three categories represented 'a somewhat over-simplified grouping.'"[30] Rehnquist then explained that "it is doubtless the case that executive action in any particular instance falls, not neatly in one of three pigeonholes, but rather at some point along a spectrum running from explicit congressional authorization to explicit congressional prohibition." "This is particularly true," he concluded, "as respects cases such as the one before us, involving responses to international crises the nature of which Congress can hardly have expected to anticipate in any detail." This marks the point where the concurrence's tripartite scheme became standard fare for courts, lawyers, scholars, and law students.

In applying the *Youngstown* concurrence to the executive orders implementing the Iran settlement, Justice Rehnquist spent most of his time on the President's authority to suspend court cases. The Court easily concluded, as did the circuit courts, that an Act of Congress authorized the President to nullify judicial attachments and freeze assets involving a foreign power.[31] After quoting Category One, the Court held that "we cannot say that petitioner has sustained that heavy burden" to overcome the strong presumption of constitutionality when the President acts with the support of a statute.[32] With respect to the suspension of the underlying claims, though, the Court offered a more complicated analysis. While no law authorized presidential action, some statutes were "highly relevant in the looser sense of indicating congressional acceptance of a broad scope for executive action in circumstances such as those presented in this case."[33] Rehnquist said that "the enactment of legislation closely related to the question of the President's authority in a particular case which evinces legislative intent to accord the President broad discretion may be considered to 'invite . . . measures on independent presidential responsibility.'"[34] Thus, *Dames & Moore* should probably be viewed as a Category Two decision on this point.[35]

Rehnquist's opinion in *Dames & Moore* is not as admired as its source material. One common criticism is that the Court's description of the three rough categories as falling along a spectrum made them more malleable and less useful.[36] A second problem is that *Dames & Moore* concluded that the relevant statutes did not authorize but tacitly invited executive action (Category Two), while in *Youngstown* Jackson said that the relevant statutes did not authorize but implicitly prohibited executive action (Category Three).[37] The difference between these two conclusions may be only in the eye of the beholder. A final concern is that Justice Rehnquist said nothing about the importance of resolving the Iran hostage crisis as the First Circuit had. Given that *Dames & Moore* was probably a zone-of-twilight case, some discussion of the policy implications was essential once the decision was made to reach the merits and rule for the President.[38]

Morrison v. Olson

After Rehnquist became the Chief Justice of the United States in 1986, he leaned on the concurrence in another high-profile case. In *Morrison v. Olson*, the Court upheld the validity of the portions of the Ethics in Government Act that established an independent counsel.[39] This post-Watergate reform permitted the appointment of a special federal prosecutor whom the President could fire only for cause.[40] Writing the *Morrison* decision, Rehnquist relied on Jackson's opinion to advance a flexible reading of separation of powers that permitted Congress to strip some prosecutorial discretion from the executive. "[W]e have never held," the Court said, "that the Constitution requires that the three branches of Government "operate with absolute independence." In the often-quoted words of Justice Jackson, "While the Constitution diffuses power the better to secure liberty, it also contemplates that practice will integrate the dispersed powers into a workable government. It enjoins upon its branches separateness but interdependence, autonomy but reciprocity."[41] This quotation was the same one that the Court had relied upon in *Nixon* to order the President to turn over his tapes to a different kind of special prosecutor.[42]

While *Morrison*'s holding remains intact, the opinion's functional reasoning no longer commands a Court majority.[43] Justice Antonin Scalia's lone dissent in *Morrison* said, "It is not for us to determine, and we have never presumed to determine, how much of the purely executive powers of government must be within the full control of the President. The Constitution prescribes that they *all* are."[44] "The Court," he continued, "has, nonetheless, replaced the clear constitutional prescription that the executive power belongs to the President with a 'balancing test.' What are the standards to determine how the balance is to be struck, that is, how much removal of presidential power is too much?"[45] Subsequent official removal cases have sided with the President and have not embraced Jackson's concurrence.[46] This trend in the cases can be described as the triumph of a more formal reading of separation of powers.

Ironically, though, Justice Scalia's dissent also made a powerful functional argument against upholding the independent-counsel provisions by quoting . . . Robert Jackson. Scalia ended his opinion by "considering the effect of the Act upon the fairness of the process."[47] To drive home the "vast power and immense discretion placed in the hands of a prosecutor," he quoted at length from Attorney General Jackson's speech on "The Federal Prosecutor" that was delivered to US Attorneys in 1940.[48] In this speech, which is today a staple in criminal-law classes, Jackson declared, "If the prosecutor is obliged to choose his case, it follows that he can choose his defendants. Therein is the most dangerous power of the prosecutor: that he will pick people that he thinks he should get, rather than cases that need to be prosecuted. . . . It is here that law enforcement becomes personal, and the real crime becomes that of being unpopular with the predominant or governing group, being attached to the wrong political views, or being personally obnoxious to or in the way of the prosecutor himself."[49] Scalia argued that presidential accountability was an important safeguard against the risk of prosecutorial abuse and that the independent-counsel provisions were dangerous because they removed that protection.[50] As a result, an argument can be made that the *Morrison* dissent and the Court's subsequent removal cases actually just reached a different functional judgment against robust congressional limits on the President's removal power.

The ambivalence (or incoherence) of the Court's executive removal jurisprudence can be traced back to the *Youngstown* concurrence itself. Recall that Jackson juxtaposed the Court's principal removal cases—*Myers v. United States* and *Humphrey's Executor v. United States*—in footnotes for Category Two and Category Three.[51] In other words, Jackson was unsure how to describe the constitutional boundary between Congress and the President on this point.[52] The Justice did say in his oral history that there was "a substantial difference in the nature of the offices" in the cases, and that "most lawyers would agree that the two cases were not parallel and the decisions not inconsistent."[53] But he did not offer a convincing explanation.

The Clerk's Clerk and *Trump v. United States*

John Roberts was one of Justice Rehnquist's law clerks in 1981 when the *Dames & Moore* decision came down. It is unclear if he worked on the case, but the *Youngstown* concurrence clearly made an impression.[54] Roberts would be the first Supreme Court nominee to discuss Jackson's concurring opinion in a Senate confirmation hearing.[55] After being confirmed as Rehnquist's successor in 2005, Chief Justice Roberts soon found himself calling on the concurrence in his own opinions. For example, in *Medellin v. Texas* the Chief Justice wrote for the Court holding that the President lacked the power to enforce decisions by the International Court of Justice without an enabling act from Congress.[56] The Chief Justice explained that "Justice Jackson's familiar tripartite scheme provides the accepted framework for evaluating executive action in this area."[57] He went on to say that a treaty is not legislation that can authorize executive action under Category One unless the treaty is clearly self-executing.[58] He also reasoned that there was no practice of or congressional acquiescence in presidential implementation of treaties without statutory authority that might sustain a Category Two claim.[59] In 2020, Chief Justice Roberts returned to Jackson's opinion to explain when President Trump was required to comply with a congressional subpoena. His opinion in *Trump v. Mazars USA* declared—citing the concurrence—that Congress and the President "have an ongoing relationship that the Framers intended to feature both rivalry and reciprocity."[60]

The Chief Justice's opinion in *Trump v. United States* was his most extended meditation on Justice Jackson's framework. *Trump* presented the question of whether an ex-President could claim immunity from criminal prosecution for official acts. Roberts opened and closed his analysis with Jackson's line about the need to evaluate separation of powers in connection with the "enduring consequences upon the balanced power structure of our Republic" rather than by focusing on "transient results" such as Trump's alleged misconduct.[61] He also noted that there were few precedents to guide the Court, citing Jackson's passage about "the poverty of really useful and unambiguous authority" on executive power.[62] But he then channeled the concurrence to conclude that presidential actions falling within an exclusive Article II power (Category Three) could not be the subject of federal criminal liability.[63] For all other official acts, the Chief Justice reasoned that the President was entitled to at least presumptive immunity.[64]

In other respects, the Chief Justice looked away from the concurrence.[65] First, he did not note or follow Jackson's advice that the President should not receive the benefit of the doubt in a constitutional contest with Acts of Congress, though in fairness no other Supreme Court case does either. Second, Roberts did not mention Jackson's warning that Category Three claims should be treated with caution. This omission is notable because the Chief Justice had invoked that analysis in a 2015 dissent.[66] Third, he used a legal fiction to disregard experience, rather than avoiding legal fiction to embrace experience. Roberts observed that no ex-President had ever faced criminal charges before Donald Trump and thus "[a]ll that our Nation's practice establishes on the subject is silence."[67] This statement is false. The nation's practice immediately after Watergate was *not* silent on the question of whether Richard Nixon could be criminally charged for his crimes. Executive practice, in the form of President Gerald Ford's pardon of Nixon, spoke loudly. President Ford's pardon stated: "As a result of certain acts or omissions occurring before his resignation from the Office of President, Richard Nixon has become liable to possible indictment and trial for offenses against the United States. Whether or not he shall be so prosecuted depends on findings of the appropriate grand jury and on the discretion of the authorized prosecutor."[68] The Chief Justice's conclusion that there was nothing but silence on that issue makes sense only by indulging the fiction that judicial doctrine is essential for relevant constitutional practice, which Jackson also cautioned against in *Youngstown*.

One conflict between the Chief Justice's opinion for the Court and the opinion by the D.C. Circuit that was vacated and remanded involved the relevance of Category Three. The D.C. Circuit read Jackson's concurrence to mean that an ex-President did not have any immunity for criminal acts: "The Indictment charges that former President Trump violated criminal laws of general applicability. Acting against laws enacted by the Congress, he exercised power that was at its 'lowest ebb.' Former President Trump lacked any lawful discretionary authority to defy federal criminal law and he is answerable in court for his conduct."[69] The Chief Justice instead read Category Three to mean that an ex-President could not be prosecuted for exercising his exclusive Article II authority while in office: "Congress cannot act on, and the courts cannot examine, the President's actions on subjects within his 'conclusive and preclusive' authority. It follows that an Act of Congress—either a specific one targeted at the President or a generally applicable one—may not criminalize the President's actions within his exclusive constitutional power."[70]

The criminal-immunity issue helps explain why Jackson described his three categories as rough and oversimplified. For instance, the Constitution contemplates that a President who is impeached and removed for treason or bribery can then be criminally prosecuted under a pertinent federal statute.[71] There is no exception for bribes taken to exercise an exclusive presidential power; thus the Supreme Court's statement that no criminal prosecution may be brought within the ambit of Category Three is erroneous dicta.[72] That said, the D.C. Circuit's equally broad claim that the President lacks any lawful discretionary authority to defy federal criminal law seems to rest on an unstated assumption that the Take Care Clause qualifies the President's exclusive Article II powers with a rule that he may not commit crimes as defined by Congress. But that argument proves too much, for Congress cannot regulate an exclusive Article II power by simply classifying the conduct as a crime.[73] Of course, nobody in 1952 thought that President Truman's seizure of the steel mills was a criminal robbery; thus, the issue of a post-presidential prosecution never arose after *Youngstown*. President Trump's alleged wrongdoing in connection with the January 6, 2021, insurrection at the Capitol presented a much harder case. But perhaps the failed Trump prosecution simply demonstrates the sagacity of Jackson's observation that sometimes it is best not to "provoke a judicial test" of uncertain government powers.

******

Opinions cannot become great without followers. William Rehnquist was the concurring opinion's most important champion. Chief Justice Roberts is carrying on that tradition. But the ongoing judicial conversation about the *Youngstown* concurrence calls to mind Judge Learned Hand's comment that some lessons are "never learned but never quite forgotten."[74]

Epilogue

A Lonely Landmark

In his 1941 book *The Struggle for Judicial Supremacy*, Robert Jackson wrote, "No doubt another day will find one of its tasks to be correction of mistakes that time will reveal in this structure in which we now take pride. . . . I bespeak the right of the future to undo our work when it no longer serves acceptably. The precedents of this period should receive only the respect due to the deeds of men who with earnest heart and troubled mind have sought gropingly but honestly for what was best for their day."[1] In that spirit, I end with some concluding thoughts and questions on how the *Youngstown* concurrence should inform the actual art of governing today.

Justice Jackson's concurring opinion was extraordinary. Its rhetoric disrupted judicial norms by discussing how his own experience in the executive branch shaped his thinking about executive power. Its interpretive method discarded traditional tools of text, history, and judicial doctrine in favor of structural and pragmatic considerations. Its vivid "zone of twilight" metaphor admitted that some constitutional questions are uncertain and cannot be resolved by legal tests. Its discussion of war and emergency powers for the new atomic age was deep and perceptive. And its frank assessment of the President's informal power as a party leader stands in sharp contrast to the Supreme Court's typical focus on the office's paper powers, drafted and ratified at a time when political parties were unknown. From start to finish, the *Youngstown* concurrence stands out.

In law, though, originality is not typically a virtue. Another way of describing an original idea is unprecedented. And opinions that are unprecedented and out of sync with prevailing norms are often treated as nails that must be hammered down. How did Jackson's concurrence avoid this fate? One answer is that Watergate and its immediate aftermath gave the opinion a purpose and turned the concurrence into a sort of constitutional shorthand for limiting executive power. Another is Jackson's sterling reputation, earned long before 1952. That reputation remains impeccable: he is one of the few deceased Justices who is regularly quoted by name in Supreme Court

The Actual Art of Governing. Gerard N. Magliocca, Oxford University Press. © Oxford University Press (2025).
DOI: 10.1093/9780197768563.003.0016

opinions.[2] Finally, there are the lucky accidents that Chief Justice Rehnquist was Jackson's law clerk during *Youngstown* and that one of Rehnquist's own law clerks had a close encounter with the concurrence before becoming the next Chief Justice.[3] Both treated Jackson as a model judge. As a result, there will probably have to be a change in the broader legal zeitgeist for the concurrence to lose its luster.

The greatest intellectual challenge to Jackson's opinion is the rise of originalism in constitutional discourse. Jackson brusquely dismissed that theory as akin to divining Pharaoh's dreams. To state the obvious, the *Youngstown* concurrence is in tension with the Supreme Court's current interpretive philosophy. While there is academic commentary pointing out this discrepancy, even the Court's most committed originalist—Justice Clarence Thomas—considers the *Youngstown* concurrence canonical.[4] And in 2024 the Court used Justice Jackson's opinion to construct *Trump v. United States*, with no Justice expressing any criticism of Jackson's reasoning.

The current dominance of originalism, though, suggests that the *Youngstown* concurrence will never become a jurisprudential model. Jackson broke the norms of judicial writing in his opinion, but the norms remained intact. Perhaps an opinion that is so personal cannot be replicated by others unless the stars perfectly align.[5] Perhaps the poetry of Jackson's prose was necessary for the concurrence's authority. If so, few Justices can be expected to reach those heights. Perhaps an analysis that rests on a practical foundation cannot be persuasive unless the author possesses considerable real-world experience on the subject. But few Justices can make that claim on any topic in the way that Jackson could for executive power. Finally, an effective structural opinion requires some consensus on the desired ends. *Youngstown* was decided by nine Justices appointed by Democratic presidents. While they disagreed about the legality of the steel seizure, they were singing from a common hymnbook. The same cannot be said about the average Supreme Court.

Nevertheless, a close reading of the concurring opinion in the light of our experience since 1952 suggests three areas for legislative and judicial reform. First, the National Emergencies Act is inconsistent with the deep logic of the concurrence on nondelegation and the proper scope of emergency powers. Congress should take notice and reform the Act. If not, courts should pay careful attention to applications of the Act to ensure that they remain within constitutional bounds. Second, courts should get out of the business of adjudicating Category Two cases that present no other legal claim and hold that they present nonjusticiable political questions. Jackson did not say that courts should reach the merits in these zone-of-twilight cases, and subsequent attempts to do so have proved unworkable in the absence of applicable statutory or constitutional law. Finally, the President should not receive the benefit of the doubt in constitutional contests with Congress. Though Jackson wrote this because of the dramatic expansion of informal executive influence, the Supreme Court ignored that part of his opinion even as that informal influence continued to swell. One explanation for that blind spot is that the Justices are no longer drawn from Congress as they were in Jackson's time, and they now experience Congress mainly through the unpleasant spectacle of a Senate confirmation hearing, something Jackson did not have to endure. Whatever the explanation, taking the *Youngstown* concurrence seriously means giving the separation-of-powers presumption to Congress when that institution speaks through statutes.

In the end, the *Youngstown* concurrence epitomizes Robert Jackson's belief that (as expressed by Kipling) "[h]e who travels fastest travels alone."[6] One man produced the best opinion ever written against one-man rule. Jackson wrote by himself, for himself, and about himself. He did not acknowledge the influence of Augustus N. Hand and Golden W. Bell on his reasoning. He rejected, as the only living witness, the Truman Administration's reliance on his support for the North American Aviation seizure. He discussed the issues in a unique style. Yet this singular opinion is now the quintessential statement of "those impersonal forces which we call law."

Notes

Introduction

1. Robert H. Jackson, "Founders Day Address" (Oct. 12, 1937), at 11, which is available online as part of the Robert H. Jackson Center Archive at: https://www.roberthjackson.org/wp-content/uploads/2015/01/Founders_Day_address_at_University_of_North_Carolina.pdf.
2. 343 U.S. 579, 634–655 (1952) (Jackson, J., concurring). This book omits page citations to Justice Jackson's concurrence since his opinion is reprinted in chapter 3, which the reader can simply consult to find the relevant quote or reference. There was once a practice of giving high-profile Supreme Court cases a nickname (e.g., the *Slaughterhouse Cases* or the *Civil Rights Cases*), but the practice is no longer followed. Most of the book thus refers to the *Steel Seizure Case* by its formal name—*Youngstown.*
3. See, e.g., Maeva Marcus, *Truman and the Steel Seizure Case*: *The Limits of Presidential Power* (Durham, NC: Duke University Press, 1994).
4. William H. Rehnquist, "Robert H. Jackson: A Perspective Twenty-Five Years Later," *Albany Law Review* 44 (1980), 539.
5. Sanford Levinson, "Speaking in the Name of the Law: Some Reflections on Professional Responsibility and Judicial Accountability," *University of St. Thomas Law Journal* 1, no. 1 (2003), 462; see Akhil Reed Amar, *The Law of the Land*: *A Grand Tour of Our Constitutional Republic* (New York: Basic Books, 2015), 72 ("It is Jackson's concurring opinion, and not Black's faux majority opinion, that has come to be viewed over time as canonical in the field of separation of powers"); Laurence H. Tribe, "Transcending the *Youngstown* Triptych: A Multidimensional Reappraisal of Separation of Powers Doctrine," *Yale Law Journal Forum* 126 (2016), 91 (calling the Youngstown concurrence "the very lodestar of the Court's separation-of-powers jurisprudence").
6. See 418 U.S. 683 (1974); 603 U.S. 593 (2024).
7. See Neal Katyal, "*Hamdan v. Rumsfeld*: The Legal Academy Goes to Practice," *Harvard Law Review* 120 (2006), 99; Stephen P. Vladeck, "Foreign Affairs Originalism in *Youngstown*'s Shadow," *Saint Louis University Law Journal* 53, no. 1 (2008), 34.
8. Michael McConnell, *The President Who Would Not Be King: Executive Power Under the Constitution* (Princeton, NJ: Princeton University Press, 2020), 278.
9. See Stephen Skowronek, *The Politics Presidents Make: Leadership from John Adams to Bill Clinton* (Cambridge, MA: Harvard University Press, 1997), 20 ("[T]he presidency is a governing institution inherently hostile to inherited governing arrangements" [italics omitted]).
10. For an example of Justice Jackson's elaboration of New Deal constitutionalism, see Wickard v. Filburn, 317 U.S. 111 (1942) (setting forth a broad reading of the Commerce Clause). On the larger constitutional dimensions of the New Deal, see Bruce Ackerman, *We the People*, vol. 2: *Transformations* (Cambridge, MA: Harvard University Press, 1998), 279–282.

Chapter 1

1. The basic facts of Jackson's biography are drawn from Jackson, *That Man: An Insider's Portrait of Franklin D. Roosevelt*, edited by John Q. Barrett (New York: Oxford University Press, 2003); Eugene Gerhart, *America's Advocate: Robert H. Jackson* (Indianapolis: Bobbs-Merrill, 1958); and the unpublished manuscript "Reminiscences of Robert H. Jackson" (edited by Harlan B. Phillips, 1955), available at Columbia University. Jamestown is now the home of the Robert H. Jackson Center, which is a significant source of research support.
2. See, e.g., Gerard N. Magliocca, *Washington's Heir: The Life of Justice Bushrod Washington* (New York: Oxford University Press, 2022), 12–13 (describing Washington's legal apprenticeship with James Wilson).

3. See David Cannadine, *Mellon: An American Life* (New York: Knopf, 2006), 525–534; ibid. at 534 (stating that Jackson described Mellon as "the most difficult man that I ever cross-examined").
4. Laura Kalman, *FDR's Gambit: The Court Packing Fight and the Rise of Legal Liberalism* (New York: Oxford University Press, 2022), 151 (quoting Joseph Alsop on the testimony); see Robert H. Jackson, "Testimony Before the Senate Judiciary Committee on the Reorganization of the Judiciary," Mar. 11, 1937, at https://www.roberthjackson.org/wp-content/uploads/2015/01/Reorganization_of_Federal_Judiciary.pdf.
5. See Noah Feldman, *Scorpions: The Battles and Triumphs of FDR's Great Supreme Court Justices* (New York: Twelve, 2010), 129 ("Jackson was an amazingly successful solicitor general, by far the greatest on record. He won thirty-eight of his forty-four cases, a record unlikely ever to be surpassed").
6. See, e.g., Melvin I. Urofsky, *Louis D. Brandeis: A Life* (New York: Pantheon, 2009), 749. I say "allegedly" because there is no direct source for this statement, but in his oral history Jackson said that Brandeis made the comment to Felix Frankfurter and Thomas Corcoran. Frankfurter later repeated Brandeis's statement to Jackson's biographer, Eugene C. Gerhart.
7. See, e.g., "Nomination of John G. Roberts, Jr. to be Chief Justice of the United States: Hearing Before the S. Judiciary Comm.," 109th Cong. 385 (2005) (calling Justice Jackson one of the best writers to serve on the Court); Akhil Reed Amar, *The Law of the Land: A Grand Tour of Our Constitutional Republic* (New York: Basic, 2015), 56 (stating that Jackson "wrote with style and flair—better than any of his peers or precursors, with the possible exception of John Marshall—and in this respect he set a high bar for all that followed"); Ray v. Blair, 343 U.S. 214, 232 (1952) (Jackson, J., dissenting) (paraphrasing a line from Gilbert and Sullivan's *H.M.S. Pinafore* to describe presidential electors); Craig v. Harney, 331 U.S. 367, 396 (1947) (Jackson, J., dissenting) (quoting Milton's "Lycidas"); Everson v. Board of Ed. of Ewing Tp., 330 U.S. 1, 19 (1947) (Jackson, J., dissenting) (quoting Byron's "Don Juan"); David M. O'Brian, *Justice Robert H. Jackson's Unpublished Opinion in* Brown v. Board (Lawrence: University Press of Kansas, 2017), 25 (observing that Jackson referred to Matthew Arnold's "Stanzas from the Grand Chartreuse" in his book on *The Struggle for Judicial Supremacy* and in his unpublished draft opinion in *Brown*).
8. 319 U.S. 624 (1943); see Charles Alan Wright, "My Favorite Opinion—The Second Flag-Salute Case," *Texas Law Review* 74 (1996), 1299 (discussing *Barnette* and then stating: "Robert Jackson was, to my taste, the best writer to ever sit on the Court").
9. *Barnette*, 319 U.S. at 639.
10. Ibid. at 642.
11. Ibid. at 641.
12. *That Man*, 47. *That Man* was a book about Franklin D. Roosevelt that Jackson began in 1952 but never completed.
13. See ibid. at 47–48; see also William R. Casto, *Advising the President: Attorney General Robert H. Jackson and Franklin D. Roosevelt* (Lawrence: University Press of Kansas, 2018), 22–25 (describing the discussion in detail). The solicitor general does not ordinarily get involved in policy issues, which indicates that Jackson was continuing to serve FDR as a troubleshooter.
14. *That Man*, 48. The next two quotations in the text come from this same page.
15. 308 U.S. 338 (1939).
16. *That Man*, 68. The best account of the wiretapping issue is Neal Katyal and Richard Caplan, "The Surprisingly Stronger Case for the Legality of the NSA Surveillance Program: The FDR Precedent," *Stanford Law Review* 60 (2008), 1024–1076.
17. *That Man*, 68 (quoting "FDR Confidential Memorandum for the Attorney General," in Robert H. Jackson papers, Library of Congress, Manuscript Division, Box 94).
18. *That Man*, 69. In his oral history, Jackson said that he kept close tabs on Hoover but that "[t]here might have been some circumstances under which I wasn't available and he didn't [seek authorization for a wiretap]." See "Reminiscences of Robert H. Jackson," 972. There are reasons to doubt that Jackson closely supervised all the wiretaps. See Casto, *Advising the President*, 38.
19. See Katyal and Caplan, "Surprisingly Stronger Case," 1052–1060. For a fine biography of Hoover that delves into his work with Jackson and with Roosevelt, see Beverly Gage, *G-Man: J. Edgar Hoover and the Making of the American Century* (New York: Viking, 2022).

20. *That Man*, 68. In another case where Jackson was involved as an adviser, FDR was prepared to defy a Supreme Court decision if it came out the wrong way until such time as Congress provided a statutory remedy. For the full story, see Gerard N. Magliocca, "The Gold Clause Cases and Constitutional Necessity," *Florida Law Review* 64 (2012), 1243–78.
21. "Reminiscences of Robert H. Jackson," 984.
22. In 1952, Jackson wrote an account of the destroyer deal, which was edited after his death by his son and by E. Barrett Prettyman, Jr., Jackson's final clerk. See *That Man*, 81–82. The text relies on that account for the facts and background of the deal. See ibid. at 82–103.
23. See, e.g., Roy Jenkins, *Churchill: A Biography* (New York: Plume, 2002), 627.
24. See In the Matter of Acquisition of Naval and Air Bases in Exchange for Overage Destroyers, 39 Op. A.G. 484–496 (1940). The first part of the opinion explained why the deal could be undertaken as an executive agreement rather than as a treaty or a binding obligation that required an Act of Congress. See ibid. at 485–488.
25. See ibid. at 492. Jackson concluded that the President lacked statutory authority to send Britain ships that were under construction. See ibid. at 494–496. Not long before the deal was announced, Congress passed a statutory amendment stating that naval material could not be sold or transferred unless the Chief of Naval Operations certified that the material was not essential to national defense. See ibid. at 490 (quoting § 14(a) of the Act of June 28, 1940, ch. 440, 54 Stat. 681). Jackson noted that a constitutional question existed insofar as this amendment was read to strip authority from the President, but he concluded that this issue need not be resolved in order for the destroyer deal to proceed. See ibid.
26. See ibid. at 489 (referring to the Act of March 3, 1883, § 5, ch. 141, 22 Stat. 582, 599–600). The quotation from the statute in the text comes from the same page.
27. Professor Casto describes Jackson's analysis as "frivolous," Casto, *Advising the President*, 72, but I need not go that far in order to make my point. It is worth noting that the title of this statutory section was "Appraisal and sale of vessels stricken from Navy Register as unfit for service."
28. The facts of the seizure are drawn from President Roosevelt's Exec. Order No. 8773 (6 Fed. Reg. 2777, 1941), Jackson's *Youngstown* concurrence, and Casto, *Advising the President*, 90–92.
29. See 89 Cong. Rec. 3992 (1943) (reprinting in full the attorney general's statement of June 10, 1941). It is unclear why this text was not issued as a formal opinion.
30. See, e.g., Maeva Marcus, *Truman and the Steel Seizure Case: The Limits of Presidential Power* (Durham, NC: Duke University Press, 1994), 155–156, 161–162, 171–172.
31. The principal source for this story is Robert H. Jackson, "A Presidential Legal Opinion," *Harvard Law Review* 66 (1953), 1353–1361.
32. See Lend-Lease Act, Pub. L. 77–11, 55 Stat. 32 (1941).
33. See ibid. at § 5(c): "After June 30, 1943, or after the passage of a concurrent resolution of the two Houses before June 30, 1943, which declares that the powers conferred by or pursuant to subsection (a) are no longer necessary to promote the defense of the United States, neither the President nor the head of any department or agency shall exercise any of the powers conferred by or pursuant to subsection (a)."
34. Jackson, "Presidential Legal Opinion," 1354.
35. See ibid. (quoting FDR's memo to Jackson stating that "the emergency was so great that I signed the bill in spite of a clearly unconstitutional provision contained in it"); ibid. at 1356–1357 (describing the political situation in Congress).
36. Ibid. at 1355. Jackson recalled that he "regarded the question as interesting but rather academic," which was true for the Lend-Lease Act, but not more generally.
37. Ibid. at 1353.
38. Ibid. at 1358. In 1983, the Supreme Court endorsed FDR's view and held that the legislative veto was unconstitutional. See INS v. Chadha, 462 U.S. 919 (1983).
39. Jackson, "Presidential Legal Opinion," 1359 (quoting a note from FDR to Jackson dated April 7, 1941). The President's legal opinion is in Box 57 of the Jackson Papers.
40. See ibid. at 1360 (discussing Jackson's uncertainty about how to handle FDR's request).
41. See *Ex Parte* Endo, 323 U.S. 283 (1944); Korematsu v. United States 323 U.S. 214 (1944); Hirabayashi v. United States, 320 U.S. 81 (1943).
42. See Korematsu, 323 U.S. at 242–248 (Jackson, J., dissenting).
43. 317 U.S. 1 (1942). The account of Quirin in the text comes from the Court's opinion, Justice Jackson's unpublished opinion in the case (see Jackson Papers, "Memorandum: Ex Parte

Quirin," Box 124), and Amanda L. Tyler, *Habeas Corpus in Wartime: From the Tower of London to Guantanamo Bay*. (New York: Oxford University Press, 2017), 253–260. The quotations in the text are from Jackson's unpublished opinion. Jackson's draft in Quirin was probably the source for his description of the Bill of Rights in Barnette. Compare Barnette, 319 U.S. at 639 (referring to "the majestic generalities of the Bill of Rights"), with Jackson Papers, *supra* (referring to "the majestic generalities of the Bill of Rights").

44. See, e.g., Brad Snyder, *Democratic Justice: Felix Frankfurter, the Supreme Court, and the Making of the Liberal Establishment* (New York: Norton, 2022), 398.
45. Chapter 8 explains that Jackson referred in *Youngstown* to Civil War cases about military commissions, though he did not cite *Quirin*.
46. The text draws from the Court's opinion in Hirabayashi, 320 U.S. 81 (1943). For Jackson's draft, see Jackson Papers, "Undated Draft: Hirabayashi v. United States, Box 128, and Tyler, *Habeas Corpus in Wartime*, 231–33; see also Dennis J. Hutchinson, "'The Achilles Heel' of the Constitution: Justice Jackson and the Japanese Exclusion Cases," *Supreme Court Review*, 2002, 459–476. The quotations in the text come from Jackson's Hirabayashi draft. The Hirabayashi draft was probably the source for Jackson's line that the Court should not "convert the constitutional Bill of Rights into a suicide pact." Terminiello v. City of Chicago, 337 U.S. 1, 37 (1949) (Jackson, J., dissenting); see Jackson Papers, *supra* ("We must not hedge the war power with restrictions which will make the Constitution a suicide pact").
47. There were concurring opinions by Justice Douglas, Justice Murphy, and Justice Rutledge. See Hirabayashi, 320 U.S. at 106–109 (Douglas, J., concurring); ibid. at 109–14 (Murphy, J., concurring); ibid. at 114 (Rutledge, J., concurring).
48. See Korematsu v. United States 323 U.S. 214 (1944); see also Trump v. Hawaii, 585 U.S. 667, 710 (2018), quoting Justice Jackson's dissent ("*Korematsu* was gravely wrong the day it was decided, has been overruled in the court of history, and—to be clear—'has no place in law under the Constitution'").
49. See *Korematsu*, 323 U.S. at 242–248 (Jackson, J., dissenting).
50. Ibid. at 246 (Jackson, J., dissenting). The next quotation in the text comes from the same page.
51. Ibid. at 247 (Jackson, J., dissenting).
52. Ibid. at 248 (Jackson, J., dissenting). There was similar language in his *Hirabayashi* draft.
53. For some background on Jackson's work in Germany, see Bernard D. Meltzer, "Robert H. Jackson: Nuremberg's Architect and Advocate," *Albany Law Review* 55 (2004), 55–65; Robert H. Jackson, "Nuremberg in Retrospect: Legal Answer to International Lawlessness," at https://www.roberthjackson.org/speech-and-writing/nuremberg-in-retrospect-legal-answer-to-international-lawlessness/.
54. "Report to the President from Justice Robert H. Jackson, Chief of Counsel for the United States in the Prosecution of Axis War Criminals," *American Journal of International Law* 39 (1945), 187 (stating that the report was given in June 1945).
55. Feldman, *Scorpions*, 281; see Roger K. Newman, *Hugo Black: A Biography* (New York: Pantheon, 1994), 340 (stating Justice Black's view that the war-crimes trials were unlawful and a mistake); see also William Safire, ed., *Lend Me Your Ears: Great Speeches in History* (New York: Norton, 2004), 714–718 (reproducing an edited version of Senator Robert Taft's argument against the legality of the war-crimes trials).
56. See R. T. Jones, ed., *The Collected Poems of Rudyard Kipling* (Ware, UK: Wordsworth, 1994), 307. Portions of Jackson's opening address at Nuremberg can be viewed at https://www.youtube.com/watch?v=EJj6NcWHkDE.
57. Robert H. Jackson, "Justice Jackson Weighs Nuremberg's Lessons," *The New York Times*, June 16, 1946, at 60.
58. See "Reminiscences of Robert H. Jackson," 1220–1221; cf. Telford Taylor, *The Anatomy of the Nuremberg Trials* (New York: Knopf, 1992), 316–317 (noting that Winston Churchill's "Iron Curtain" speech was delivered while the proceedings were underway).
59. Robert H. Jackson, "Wartime Security and Liberty Under Law," *Buffalo Law Review* 1 (1951), 104.
60. See Casto, *Advising the President*, 98; see also Snyder, *Democratic Justice*, 601 (quoting Justice Felix Frankfurter's view that Nuremberg "had a profound influence on [Jackson's] endeavor to understand the human situation").
61. Robert H. Jackson, "Nuremberg Trial of the Major Nazi Leaders," Jan. 24, 1947, at https://www.roberthjackson.org/speech-and-writing/nuremberg-trial-of-the-major-nazi-leaders/.

62. See, e.g., Shaughnessy v. United States *ex rel.* Mezei, 345 U.S. 206, 225–226 (1953) (Jackson, J., dissenting) (invoking the Nazi practice of "protective custody" to denounce the equivalent treatment of an alien); Dennis v. United States, 341 U.S. 494, 577 (1950) (Jackson, J., concurring); see also ibid. at 578, n.16 (pointing out the ineffectiveness of Weimar Germany's efforts to criminalize the Nazi Party).
63. See Terminiello, 337 U.S. at 23–24 (Jackson, J., dissenting); see also Patrick Schmidt, "'The Dilemma to a Free People': Justice Robert Jackson, Walter Bagehot, and the Creation of a Conservative Jurisprudence," *Law and History Review* 20 (2002), 517–539 (providing a nuanced analysis of Jackson's Terminiello dissent).
64. Dennis, 341 U.S. at 577.

Chapter 2

1. The best account of the facts in Youngstown is Maeva Marcus, *Truman and the Steel Seizure Case: The Limits of Presidential Power* (1977; reprint, Durham, NC: Duke University Press, 1994). Other sources include the opinions in Youngstown Sheet & Steel Tube Co. v. Sawyer, 343 U.S. 579 (1952) and William H. Rehnquist, "Constitutional Law and Public Opinion," *Suffolk U. L. Review* 20 (1986), 751–769.
2. See Youngstown, 343 U.S. at 868–869 (reproducing the entire text of Executive Order No. 10, 340). Before the seizure, the President referred the dispute to the Wage Stabilization Board; the Board proposed a settlement that was not accepted by April. See ibid. at 582–583.
3. See David McCullough, *Truman* (New York: Simon & Schuster, 1992), 892–893. Truman was eligible to run for another term because the recently ratified Twenty-Second Amendment did not apply to him. See U.S. Const. amend. XXII, § 1 ("[T]his Article shall not apply to any person holding the office of President when this Article was proposed by the Congress. . . .").
4. See McCullough, *Truman*, 891–892. Truman's approval rating in the Gallup Poll was 22 percent in February and 28 percent in April. See https://www.presidency.ucsb.edu/statistics/data/harry-s-truman-public-approval.
5. See Rehnquist, "Public Opinion," 766–767.
6. Republicans held the White House for twenty-four consecutive years from 1861 (Abraham Lincoln) to 1885 (Chester A. Arthur).
7. See United States v. Nixon, 418 U.S. 683 (1974).
8. Pub. L. 80–101, 61 Stat. 136, 155–156 (1947).
9. See McCullough, *Truman*, 565–66, 898; Patricia L. Bellia, "The Story of the Steel Seizure Case," in *Presidential Power Stories*, ed. Christopher H. Schroeder and Curtis A. Bradley, 233–285 (New York: Foundation Press, 2008), 256. The President's official explanation for not using Taft-Hartley was that the Act "did not fit the needs of the present situation." Harry S. Truman, "Radio and Television Address to the American People on the Need for Government Operation of the Steel Mills" (April 8, 1952), in 1952–53 Harry S. Truman, Containing the Public Messages, Speeches, and Statements of the President (Washington, DC: Government Printing Office, 1961–1966), 246–250 [hereinafter "Truman Address"]. For instance, Truman said that he could not impose a cooling-off period until after a board of inquiry issued a report, which meant that steel production would be suspended for a week or two. See ibid. at 251. He also pointed out that the union had been working without a collective bargaining agreement since January and that another delay would not solve the problem. See ibid.
10. Pub. L. 80–759, 62 Stat. 625.
11. See Marcus, *Steel Seizure*, 76–77.
12. See Patricia Bellia, "Executive Power in Youngstown's Shadow," *Constitutional Commentary* 19 (2002), 101–02.
13. Defense Production Act of 1950, Pub. L. 81-774, 64 Stat. 799; see Matthew Steilen, "Life and Afterlife in the *Steel Seizure Case*," *Buffalo Law Review* 70 (2022), 883.
14. See Marcus, *Steel Seizure*, 75; Oral Argument Transcript in Youngstown at 17 [hereinafter Oral Argument Transcript], 9–13. The transcript is not paginated; I have supplied page numbers by simply counting them.
15. Legend says that Chief Justice Vinson, who was appointed by Truman and was a close friend, advised the President that the seizure was constitutional. See Noah Feldman, *Scorpions: The Battles and Triumphs of FDR's Great Supreme Court Justices* (New York: Twelve, 2010), 358. The President's attorney general, James McGrath, resigned a day before the executive order was issued because of an unrelated corruption investigation. See Marcus, *Steel Seizure*,

35. Thus, while Youngstown was litigated, the Justice Department was under the interim leadership of Solicitor General Perlman.

16. "Truman Address," 246. The next three quotations come from the same page of the speech.
17. Youngstown, 343 U.S. at 868.
18. See Truman Papers, "Special Message to the Congress Reporting on the Situation in the Steel Industry," April 9, 1952, at 251.
19. See Truman Papers, "The President's News Conference," April 17, 1952, at 272. See also Neal Devins and Louis Fisher, "The Steel Seizure Case: One of a Kind?" *Constitutional Commentary* 19 (2002), 67 (putting this statement into some context).
20. Truman Papers, "The President's News Conference," April 17, 1952, at 272–273.
21. See Marcus, *Steel Seizure*, 102; Rehnquist, "Public Opinion," 755.
22. See Marcus, *Steel Seizure*, 111; Bellia, "Story of the Steel Seizure Case," 245. Judge Pine could have avoided the constitutional issue by holding that the steel companies were not entitled to an injunction, even if the seizure was unlawful. Perhaps the only available remedy was damages. But Judge Pine and the Supreme Court showed little interest in this argument.
23. The transcript of the hearing that is quoted in the text is reproduced in Bellia, "Story of the Steel Seizure Case," 249–250.
24. See Joseph Paull, "U.S. Argues President Is Above Courts," *Washington Post*, April 25, 1952, at 1.
25. See Joseph Loftus, "President's Power Is Not Restricted, Says U. S. Lawyer," *New York Times*, April 26, 1952, at 1.
26. Marcus, *Steel Seizure*, 125–26; see Rehnquist, "Public Opinion," 765 (stating that the Government's position "shocked almost every observer of the Washington scene").
27. See Youngstown Steel & Tube Co. v. Sawyer, 103 F. Supp. 569 (D.D.C. 1952), affirmed by 343 U.S. 579.
28. See ibid. at 573–575; ibid. at 575 ("[I]t is difficult to follow [the] argument that several prior acts apparently unauthorized by law, but never questioned in the courts, by repetition clothe a later unauthorized act with the cloak of legality").
29. Ibid. at 577.
30. See Memorandum from CGN, "Presidential Seizure Power," May 8, 1952, in Jackson Papers, Box 176, at 1.
31. See Youngstown, 343 U.S. at 584. The Court's decision to grant review without letting the circuit court weigh in was unusual but not unprecedented.
32. Brad Snyder, *Democratic Justice: Felix Frankfurter, the Supreme Court, and the Making of the Liberal Establishment* (New York: Norton, 2022), 551 (quoting a letter from Justice Frankfurter to C. C. Burlingham).
33. See McCullough, *Truman*, 900; see also George Martin, *CCB: The Life and Century of Charles C. Burlingham, New York's First Citizen* (New York: Hill and Wang, 2005), 249–253 (providing some background on Davis and on his unsuccessful run for the Presidency in 1924).
34. Oral Argument Transcript at 17.
35. See Marcus, *Steel Seizure*, 169; Snyder, *Democratic Justice*, 551–552.
36. William H. Rehnquist, *The Supreme Court*, rev. ed. (New York: Vintage, 2002), 185. The oral argument confirms the intensity of the questioning and the friction between the SG and the Court. At one point, Justice Frankfurter commented, "Doctor Johnson, said, you know, you can give a person knowledge, but not understanding." Perlman replied, "If that is meant for me, it is a dirty dig." Oral argument transcript at 38.
37. Robert H. Jackson, *That Man: An Insider's Portrait of Franklin D. Roosevelt*, ed. John Q. Barrett (New York: Oxford University Press, 2003), 1. Jackson said that he began writing his FDR book because of Youngstown. See ibid.
38. Oral Argument Transcript at 41.
39. Ibid. at 42. The next two quotations in the text come from the same page of the transcript.
40. Chief Justice Rehnquist recalled that "I virtually glowed with satisfaction at Jackson's comment." Rehnquist, *Supreme Court*, 186.
41. See *That Man*, 216 n.28 (quoting a letter dated May 13, 1952).
42. Oral Argument Transcript at 78. The transcript contains an error on this page that makes the solicitor general's comment look like a question from Justice Frankfurter, but the context and scholarly analysis make clear that Perlman made the comment. See Marcus, *Steel Seizure*, 173; Snyder, *Democratic Justice*, 553.

43. See William R. Casto, *Advising the President: Attorney General Robert H. Jackson and Franklin D. Roosevelt* (Lawrence: University Press of Kansas, 2018), 93. The Chief Justice cited this example in his dissent. See Youngstown, 343 U.S. at 695 (Vinson, C.J., dissenting).
44. Snyder, *Democratic Justice*, 554.
45. Rehnquist, *Supreme Court*, 186.
46. See Robert H. Jackson Papers, Library of Congress, Manuscript Division, Box 176 (containing Justice Jackson's tally sheet for Youngstown). The quotation in the text comes from Justice Jackson's tally sheet.
47. Justice Black wrote the Court's opinion because he was the most senior Justice in the majority and assigned the case to himself. Chief Justice Vinson, the Court's most senior member, was in dissent.
48. Youngstown, 343 U.S. at 589 (statement of Frankfurter, J.). Justice Frankfurter's unusual statement is not part of his concurrence.
49. Ibid. at 582. The Constitution describes this role as "Commander in Chief of the Army and Navy of the United States." See U.S. Const., art. II, § 2, cl. 1.
50. Youngstown, 343 U.S. at 585.
51. Ibid. at 586. Justice Black was quoting the Government's brief, though without a specific citation. The next quotation in the text comes from the same page of the opinion.
52. Ibid. at 587.
53. Ibid. at 588.
54. See Roger K. Newman, *Hugo Black: A Biography* (New York: Pantheon, 1994), 125–230 (describing Black's Senate career). Black did offer a partial explanation: "The preamble of the order, like that of many statutes, sets out reasons why the President believes certain policies should be adopted, proclaims those policies as rules of conduct to be followed, and again, like a statute, authorizes a government official to promulgate additional rules and regulations consistent with the policy proclaimed and needed to carry that policy into execution." Youngstown, 343 U.S. at 588. The fact that Truman's executive order looked like a statute is unhelpful, as that would mean that the form of a document determines the constitutional answer. But the idea that "rules of conduct to be followed" could be understood as lawmaking if they are significant rules of conduct, like government seizure and operation of the steel industry, does make some sense.
55. Youngstown, 343 U.S. at 588.
56. Ibid. at 589. The next quotation in the text also comes from this page.
57. See ibid. at 593–97 (Frankfurter, J., concurring).
58. Ibid. at 598 (Frankfurter, J., concurring).
59. See ibid. at 598–602 (Frankfurter, J., concurring).
60. See ibid. at 602 (Frankfurter, J., concurring) ("It cannot be contended that the President would have had power to issue this order had Congress explicitly negated such authority in formal legislation. Congress has expressed its will to withhold this power from the President as though it had said so in so many words").
61. Ibid. at 603–4 (Frankfurter, J., concurring).
62. Ibid. at 610 (Frankfurter, J., concurring).
63. Ibid. at 610–11 (Frankfurter, J., concurring).
64. Ibid. at 613 (Frankfurter, J., concurring).
65. See ibid. at 629–32 (Douglas, J., concurring); U.S. Const., amend. V ("[N]or shall private property be taken for public use, without just compensation").
66. Youngstown, 343 U.S. at 630–31 (Douglas, J., concurring).
67. Ibid. at 631 (Douglas, J., concurring).
68. Ibid. at 631–32 (Douglas, J., concurring).
69. Ibid. at 633 (Douglas, J., concurring).
70. See ibid. at 655–60 (Burton, J., concurring); Jim Newton, *Justice for All: Earl Warren and the Nation He Made* (New York: Riverhead, 2006), 263–264 (providing background on Justice Burton). Justice Burton was the only member of the majority besides Jackson who stated that he concurred in the Court's opinion and its judgment. See Youngstown, 343 U.S. at 655 (Burton, J., concurring).
71. Youngstown, 343 U.S. at 658–659 (Burton, J., concurring).
72. Ibid. at 659 (Burton, J., concurring). The next quotation in the text comes from the same page.
73. Ibid. at 659 (Burton, J., concurring).

74. Ibid. at 660 (Burton, J., concurring).
75. See ibid. at 660–667 (Clark, J., concurring in the judgment); see also Marcus, *Steel Seizure*, 190 (giving some background on Justice Clark).
76. Ibid. at 662 (Clark, J., concurring in the judgment). The next quotation in the text comes from the same page.
77. Ibid. at 662–666 (Clark, J., concurring in the judgment).
78. See ibid. at 667–710 (Vinson, C.J., dissenting). A draft of Vinson's dissent is among Jackson's Youngstown papers with critical notes in the margin, such as "No" and "meaning what?"
79. Ibid. at 668 (Vinson, J., dissenting). The next quotation in the text comes from the same page.
80. Ibid. at 668 (Vinson, C.J., dissenting).
81. See ibid. at 670–672 (Vinson, C.J., dissenting).
82. Ibid. at 683 (Vinson, C.J., dissenting).
83. Ibid. at 700 (Vinson, C.J., dissenting).
84. See ibid. at 701–03 (Vinson, C.J., dissenting).
85. Ibid. at 704 (Vinson, C.J., dissenting).
86. Ibid. at 708–709 (Vinson, C.J., dissenting).
87. One oft-quoted story about Truman's attitude was his comment at a barbeque that Justice Black held for the President and the other Justices not long after the decision: "Hugo, I don't much care for your law, but, by golly, this bourbon is good." McCullough, *Truman*, 901.
88. "Text of Truman Address to Congress Asking Steel Seizure Power," *New York Times*, June 11, 1952, at 25.
89. See Marcus, *Steel Seizure*, 251–53; McCullough, *Truman*, 901–903.
90. See Marcus, *Steel Seizure*, 212–14; Devins and Fisher, "One of a Kind," 70–71.
91. Marcus, *Steel Seizure*, 213 (quoting the *Los Angeles Times* of June 3, 1952).
92. According to the press reports and William Rehnquist's account, Justice Jackson did not deliver a summary of his opinion from the bench. See Rehnquist, *Supreme Court*, 188.

Chapter 4

1. My principal secondary source on the drafting of the concurrence is Adam J. White, "Justice Jackson's Draft Opinions in the Steel Seizure Cases," *Albany Law Review* 69 (2006), 1107–1133; see ibid. at 1109 (noting that the first drafts were dated May 7th and 8th, a few days before oral argument). White lays out the chronology of the drafting (see ibid. at 1109–1110), though some uncertainties exist about specific pages or edits.
2. Robert H. Jackson papers, Library of Congress, Manuscript Division, Box 176. The drafts are not always clearly paginated and sometimes consist of loose sheets inserted into a prior typescript. Thus, I sometimes refer to the drafts only by date (if the date is known).
3. Jackson Papers, Box 176, May 8 Draft at 4.
4. See Brad Snyder, *Democratic Justice: Felix Frankfurter, the Supreme Court, and the Making of the Liberal Establishment* (New York: Norton, 2022), 554 (describing Justice Frankfurter's suggestion at conference that all the justices write opinions).
5. William H. Rehnquist, *The Supreme Court* (New York: Vintage, 2002), 188. Rehnquist and his senior co-clerk George Niebank asked the Justice if he wanted a memo on some procedural and remedial issues relevant to the certiorari petition. See "Memorandum of CGN and WHR to RHJ" (undated), in Jackson Papers, Box 176. Jackson apparently declined.
6. There is no biography of Augustus N. Hand, but the preeminent biography of Learned Hand describes his cousin. See Gerald Gunther, *Learned Hand: The Man and the Judge*, 2nd ed. (New York: Oxford University Press, 2011), 557–558.
7. Jackson Papers, Undated Handwritten Note, Box 176; see United States v. Western Union Telegraph Co., 272 F. 311 (S.D.N.Y 1921). The Western Union case was affirmed on appeal, 272 F. 893 (2d Cir. 1921) (per curiam), but the parties reached a settlement before Supreme Court review and the final appeal was dismissed. See 260 U.S. 754 (1922).
8. Brief of Petitioner at 41, Youngstown Sheet & Tube Co. v. Sawyer, 343 U.S. 579 (May 10, 1952).
9. Robert H. Jackson, "Why Learned and Augustus Hand Became Great" (Dec. 13, 1951), at https://www.roberthjackson.org/wp-content/uploads/2020/06/why-learned-and-augustus-hand-became-great.pdf, at 43.
10. See Western Union, 272 U.S. at 311–312 (stating the facts).

11. The President objected that the cable was connected to Brazil through a British firm with a monopoly from the Brazilian government. See ibid. at 312. He was willing to grant a permit if the cable was not connected "with a line enjoying an exclusive foreign monopoly." Ibid.
12. Ibid. at 313. The next quotation in the text comes from the same page.
13. Ibid. at 314–315.
14. Ibid. at 315.
15. Ibid. Judge Hand explained that the British Crown lacked the prerogative power to exclude aliens, which cut against the argument that the President possessed that power. See ibid. at 315–316. He also quoted A. V. Dicey, the esteemed British constitutional scholar, for the idea that "there are times of tumult or invasion when for the sake of legality itself the rules of law must be broken. The course which the government must then take is clear. The ministry must break the law and trust for protection to an act of indemnity. A statute of this kind is (as already pointed out) the last and supreme exercise of parliamentary sovereignty. It legalizes illegality." Ibid. at 315.
16. Ibid. at 316.
17. See ibid. at 316–317 (citing President Grant's Message to Congress in December 1875). Hand explained that subsequent officials "have done little more than follow a precedent set by President Grant under circumstances differing from the present. It is very easy for any official to follow a general departmental custom when his department has once taken the position and the assertion of the position must be regarded as very different in real weight from the reasoned opinion of the official." Ibid. at 322–323.
18. Ibid. at 318–319.
19. Ibid. at 319.
20. Ibid. at 322. Hand was referring to the Act of May 6, 1866, the Post Roads Act of 1866, and the Interstate Commerce Act. See ibid. at 319–321.
21. Ibid. at 322. The next quotation in the text also comes from this page.
22. Moreover, the citation to the Western Union case was a last-minute insertion that was not made until the June 2nd draft. See Jackson Papers, Box 176, June 2 Draft at 4 n.3 (handwritten edit).
23. 1 Op. O.L.C. 49 (1937) [hereinafter Bell Memo].
24. See Jackson Papers, Bell Memo, Box 92. Tom Corcoran, an influential lawyer in New Deal circles, gave Jackson the Bell Memo in 1940. See ibid. (including a covering note from "Mr. Corcoran's Office" in the Reconstruction Finance Corporation with Jackson's notation "Please file among personal things"). The Bell Memo was not made public until 2013.
25. Bell Memo at 64.
26. Chief Justice Marshall also took without attribution much of Alexander Hamilton's argument for the constitutionality of the National Bank. See M'Culloch v. Maryland, 17 U.S. (4 Wheat.) 316 (1819).
27. Neutrality Act of 1937, ch. 146, 50 Stat. 121.
28. See Bell Memo at 50–51; Ron Chernow, *Washington: A Life* (New York: Penguin, 2010), 691.
29. See Jonathan Gienapp, *The Second Founding: Fixing the Constitution in the Founding Era* (Cambridge, MA: Belknap, 2018.), 254–255; Jack N. Rakove, *Original Meanings: Politics and Ideas in the Making of the Constitution* (New York: Vintage, 1997), 356.
30. See Gienapp, *Second Founding*, 254–255; Rakove, *Original Meanings*, 356.
31. See Bell Memo at 52 (quoting Jefferson's Message to Congress on December 8, 1801, and his letter to John Breckenridge dated August 12, 1803).
32. See ibid. at 59 n.23 (quoting Taft's book on *The Chief Magistrate and His Powers* at 139–40); ibid. at n.22 (quoting TR's autobiography at 388–389).
33. See 299 U.S. 304 (1936); Bell Memo at 61–62. The Curtiss-Wright case stated that the President was "the sole organ of the federal government in the field of international relations" (299 U.S. at 320).
34. See Bell Memo at 68 (quoting Wilson's book on *Constitutional Government in the United States*); see also ibid. at 75 (quoting President Wilson's message to Congress of February 25, 1917).
35. The Bell Memo also said that presidential power depended, in part, on congressional authorization. See ibid. at 60. ("[M]ost decisions of the Court relating to matters in the field of foreign affairs, when carefully examined, involve both congressional and presidential action, and, therefore, involve some form of purported congressional delegation of power.

Such decisions are not pertinent here, since the question, so far from being one of congressional delegation of power, is one of what powers the President may exercise without authority from Congress.")

36. Ibid. at 64. The rest of the quotations in this paragraph of the text come from the same page of the Bell Memo.
37. Jackson did not name the Hamilton essays, but his citation to Hamilton in footnote 1 is identical to the Bell Memo's on the Pacificus essays. See ibid. at 50 n.1 (citing volume 7 of *The Works of Alexander Hamilton* at 76–117). The footnote's citation to Madison uses a different source than the memo, but both refer to the Helvidius essays. See ibid. at 50 n.3. On the Taft-Roosevelt debate, the citations in the memo and in the opinion are identical. See ibid. at 59 n.23; ibid. at n.22. Jackson added two other citations in footnote 1 to support the proposition that Taft himself held inconsistent views on presidential power. In fairness, Judge Pine's opinion in the District Court also cited the same contrasting statements from Taft and Roosevelt, so Jackson may have gotten the idea from there.
38. The Jefferson quotations appear at page 52 of the Bell Memo and in footnotes 5 and 10 of the Youngstown concurrence. I say that the choice of quotations is odd because, although Jackson explained that the Louisiana Purchase "had nothing to do with the separation of powers as between the President and Congress," he still quoted Jefferson's views about the Purchase. Likewise, Jefferson's quotation about the Barbary pirates and the extent to which Congress needed to authorize broader military action do not appear to be well-known otherwise.
39. The Bell Memo describes *Curtiss-Wright* this way: "It must be remembered, however, that the Curtiss-Wright case involved, not the question of the President's power to act without congressional authority, but the question of his right to act under and in accord with an act of Congress. In that case the constitutionality of the act under which the President had proceeded was assailed on the ground that it delegated legislative powers to the President. Much of the decision is dicta, and the ratio decidendi is contained in the following language." Ibid. at 62. The memo then quoted from the decision and added italics to the final sentence of the quote. See ibid. Here is Justice Jackson's version: "*United States v. Curtiss-Wright Corp.*, 299 U.S. 304, involved, not the question of the President's power to act without congressional authority, but the question of his right to act under and in accord with an Act of Congress. The constitutionality of the Act under which the President had proceeded was assailed on the ground that it delegated legislative powers to the President. Much of the Court's opinion is *dictum*, but the *ratio decidendi* is contained in the following language." He then used the same quotation from the case that the Bell Memo used and supplied italics for the same final sentence. The Bell Memo's conclusion was: "It is apparent, therefore, that the case leaves much of the controverted question still unsettled. It places internal and external affairs in separate categories, and holds that the strict rule applied by the court to congressional delegations of power to the President in connection with internal affairs does not apply to such delegations of power in connection with external affairs. It intimates that the President might act in external affairs without congressional authority, but it leaves undecided the question whether the Congress can enact a statute in derogation of the President's power in this field." Bell Memo at 62. Jackson condensed this passage and made one significant change to the final phrase: "That case does not solve the present controversy. It recognized internal and external affairs as being in separate categories, and held that the strict limitation upon congressional delegations of power to the President over internal affairs does not apply with respect to delegations of power in external affairs. It was intimated that the President might act in external affairs without congressional authority, but not that he might act contrary to an Act of Congress."
40. Jackson used a shorter version of the Bell Memo's quotation from Wilson's book, a passage taken from President Wilson's congressional message.
41. Newspaper research reveals that Bell left the Justice Department in 1939 to serve as the legal adviser to the Governor of the Philippines. He then returned to private practice, but was named general counsel to the Surplus Property Administration in 1946 before (apparently) retiring. I was unable to locate his papers or any living descendants.
42. For example, Jackson could have thanked Bell in an article or a lecture. But none of Jackson's posthumous unpublished works or private correspondence after *Youngstown* mention Bell. The Justice could also have decided against lifting quotations from the memo given that no attribution was possible in an opinion.
43. Robert H. Jackson, "Wartime Security and Liberty Under Law," *Buffalo Law Review* 1 (1951), 103–117.

44. See ibid. at 107–108.
45. See ibid. at 107 n.12 and 108 n.13; Clinton Rossiter, *Constitutional Dictatorship: Crisis Government in the Modern Democracies* (Princeton, NJ: Princeton University Press, 1948).
46. For example, in the Buffalo speech Justice Jackson said, "The French, taught by their history, provided for a different kind of emergency government, known as the 'state of siege.' Unlike the German emergency dictatorship, it can be invoked, not by action of the Executive, but as a parliamentary measure. And, unlike the German, it is not regarded as a suspension or abrogation of law but, with characteristic French logic, is made a legal institution, governed by legal principles and terminable by parliamentary authority." "Wartime Security," at 108. In the Youngstown concurrence, he made the same point this way: "The French Republic provided for a very different kind of emergency government known as the 'state of siege.' It differed from the German emergency dictatorship, particularly in that emergency powers could not be assumed at will by the Executive but could only be granted as a parliamentary measure. And it did not, as in Germany, result in a suspension or abrogation of law but was a legal institution governed by special legal rules and terminable by parliamentary authority."
47. Jackson Papers, Box 176, May 22 Draft at 24. Jackson subsequently crossed out much of this language in ink.
48. Here I am quoting a handwritten edit by Jackson rather than typed text.
49. See Jackson Papers, Box 176, May 29 Draft at 22 n.25.
50. See Robert H. Jackson, "A Presidential Legal Opinion," *Harvard Law Review* 66 (1953), 1353–1361.
51. In one draft, Jackson wrote of the legislative veto: "It thereby enabled a simple majority to terminate the Lend-Lease powers, whereas if the President could avail himself of the veto he could require a two-thirds majority to override him and terminate the powers." Jackson Papers, Box 176, May 22 Draft at 22 n.25. In the Harvard article, he wrote this: "It enabled a bare majority of a quorum in each of the two Houses to terminate his powers. But for the provision, they could not be cut off before the fixed date of expiration except by passing a repealing Act, which would be subject to veto. He could thus preserve his powers, unless two-thirds of each House voted to override his veto." Jackson, "Presidential Legal Opinion," 1355.
52. White, "Justice Jackson's Draft Opinions," 1132–1133.

Chapter 5

1. A similar tension exists in Attorney General Jackson's renowned speech on the appropriate role of federal prosecutors. See Robert H. Jackson, "The Federal Prosecutor," at https://www.justice.gov/sites/default/files/ag/legacy/2011/09/16/04-01-1940; see also Morrison v. Olson, 487 U.S. 654, 727–728 (1988) (Scalia, J., dissenting) (describing this as "a memorable speech to United States Attorneys"). On the one hand, Jackson stressed that personal character was vital: "The qualities of a good prosecutor are as elusive and as impossible to define as those which mark a gentleman. And those who need to be told would not understand it anyway." ("The Federal Prosecutor," at 7.) On the other hand, he said that "the prosecutor should have, as nearly as possible, a detached and impartial view of all groups in his community." (Ibid. at 4.) Thus, personal character is vital, but in the service of impersonal neutrality.
2. One example of the difficulty in striking this balance is that the opinion styles itself as a concurrence in the "opinion of the Court." Even a casual reader can see, though, that Jackson was concurring only in the Court's judgment. He set forth a different approach and implicitly criticized the Court's analysis as unduly formal. But Jackson may have thought that the law was best served by having an institutional opinion, and thus set himself aside (if only fictionally) by joining the Court's opinion as well as its judgment.
3. Joseph A. Loftus, "Black Gives Ruling: President Cannot Make Law in Good or Bad Times," *The New York Times*, June 3, 1952, at 23. The next quotation in the text also comes from this article.
4. Justice Jackson did receive at least one letter urging him to recuse. See the Robert H. Jackson papers, Library of Congress, Manuscript Division, Box 176 (including a letter dated May 12, 1952, from three citizens asking Jackson "to disqualify yourself in the forthcoming vote on the interpretation of presidential powers").
5. Jackson Papers, Box 176, May 7 Draft. The next set of quotations in the text come from the same draft, though there is no clear pagination here.

6. This custom no longer exists, as modern Justices are drawn almost entirely from the federal bench. In Jackson's day, though, politicians and senior executive officials were often sent directly to the Supreme Court.
7. Jackson Papers, Box 176, May 8 Draft at 5.
8. Jackson may also have thought twice about discussing recusal issues because of the messy controversy that followed his public criticism of Justice Black for not recusing from a case argued by Black's former law partner. See Brad Snyder, *Democratic Justice: Felix Frankfurter, the Supreme Court, and the Making of the Liberal Establishment* (New York: Norton, 2022), 476–478 (describing the *Jewell Ridge* incident in 1946).
9. Given the final 6–3 vote, Jackson's recusal would not have produced a tie. But he could not have known that before oral argument, when he made his decision to participate.
10. See Akhil Reed Amar, *The Law of the Land: A Grand Tour of Our Constitutional Republic* (New York: Basic Books, 2015), 75 ("Jackson's *Youngstown* concurrence repeatedly called attention to his own past professional life"); William R. Casto, *Advising the President: Attorney General Robert H. Jackson and Franklin D. Roosevelt* (Lawrence: University Press of Kansas, 2018), 93 (calling the concurrence "overtly autobiographical"); see also Sanford Levinson, "The Rhetoric of the Judicial Opinion," in *Law's Stories: Narrative and Rhetoric in the Law*, ed. Peter Brooks and Paul Gewirtz (New Haven, CT: Yale University Press, 1996), 203 ("I would, incidentally, be extraordinarily disappointed to find out that Jackson did not write the opinion himself, that the signature does not, at least in this case, attest to the authorship. It is vitally important that the voice really is that of Robert Jackson, not a clerk who has been told to mimic his master's voice").
11. Patricia L. Bellia, "The Story of the Steel Seizure Case," in *Presidential Power Stories*, ed. Christopher H. Schroeder and Curtis A. Bradley (New York: Foundation Press, 2009), 279.
12. Judges may make decisions based on their personal experience without saying so, but that is a different issue.
13. See Planned Parenthood of Southeastern Pa. v. Casey, 505 U.S. 833, 943 (1992) (Blackmun, J., concurring in the judgment in part and dissenting in part) ("I am 83 years old. I cannot remain on this Court forever, and when I do step down, the confirmation process for my successor may well focus on the issue before us today"), overruled by Dobbs v. Jackson Women's Health Org., 597 U.S. 215 (2022).
14. West Virginia State Board of Education v. Barnette, 319 U.S. 624, 646 (1943) (Frankfurter, J., dissenting).
15. For a related example, see Lawrence v. Texas, 539 U.S. 558, 605 (2003) (Thomas, J., dissenting) (declaring that a state law criminalizing same-sex sodomy was constitutional but "uncommonly silly. If I were member of the Texas legislature, I would vote to repeal it"). Justice Thomas got the "uncommonly silly" line from Justice Potter Stewart's dissent in Griswold v. Connecticut, which made a similar point about Connecticut's bar on using contraceptives. See Griswold v. Connecticut, 381 U.S. 479, 527 (Stewart, J., dissenting) (1965). Justice Stewart's personal condemnation in that case, though, was joined by Justice Black.
16. See Noah Feldman, *Scorpions: The Battles and Triumphs of FDR's Great Supreme Court Justices* (New York: Twelve, 2010), 229–31; Snyder, *Democratic Justice*, 424–425.
17. For instance, in a 2005 case involving the Twenty-First Amendment (the repeal of Prohibition), Justice John Paul Stevens remarked in dissent that his "recollection" of the historical context of the amendment's ratification in 1933 supported his view of how the provision should be read. But Justice Stevens was recollecting events that occurred more than seventy years earlier, which raises questions about the reliability of his memory. Moreover, it is unclear why his personal recollections were entitled to any more weight than those of any other octogenarian in determining the Amendment's meaning.
18. 347 U.S. 483 (1954).
19. David M. O'Brian, *Justice Robert H. Jackson's Unpublished Opinion in* Brown v. Board (Lawrence: University Press of Kansas, 2017), 123.
20. Ibid. at 131.
21. The first significant appearance of this line is in the Massachusetts Constitution of 1780. See Mass. Const. of 1780, art. XXX.
22. Max Weber, the famed German sociologist, made this point long ago in distinguishing among charismatic, traditional, and bureaucratic authority. See Weber, *The Theory of Social and Economic Organization*, trans. A. M. Henderson and Talcott Parsons (London: Free Press, 1947), 328.

23. See, e.g., Ogden v. Saunders, 25 U.S. (12 Wheat.) 213, 261 (1827) (opinion of Washington, J.) ("I have always thought that the power to pass such a [bankruptcy] law was exclusively vested by the constitution in the legislature of the United States. But it becomes me to believe that this opinion was, and is incorrect, since it stands condemned by a majority of this Court, solemnly pronounced").
24. Cf. Moragne v. States Marine Lines, Inc., 398 U.S. 375, 403 (1970) ("Very weighty considerations underlie the principle that courts should not lightly overrule past decisions. Among these are . . . the necessity of maintaining public faith in the judiciary as a source of impersonal and reasoned judgments").
25. Antony's funeral oration comes in act 3, scene 2, of *Julius Caesar*. Examples of judicial fibbing about personal views for rhetorical effect are hard to prove without a judge's private correspondence or earlier work, such as we have to some extent for Jackson.
26. I first gleaned this insight from an essay by Sandy Levinson, "Rhetoric of the Judicial Opinion," 203 ("What leads me to call the [concurring] opinion great is precisely the interplay of persona and analysis that is revealed—or, I suppose, constructed—by the rhetoric of the opinion").
27. Jackson Papers. Box 176, May 7 Draft. The next quote also comes from this draft, though again there is no pagination.
28. See ibid. ("The seizure of the North American plant, as the accounts of the time will indicate, took place when a line of workmen with their dinner pails was outside trying to go to work and a Communist-led picket line was standing at the gate preventing their entrance").
29. See Jackson Papers, Box 176, May 8 Draft at 1.
30. See Bellia, "Steel Seizure Case," 277 (stating that the concurrence "began as an *insider*'s critique of the government's position and that Justice Jackson gradually—but never completely—depersonalized the opinion").
31. See Jackson Papers, Box 176, May 22 Draft (typed insertion without pagination). The next quotation in the text comes from another typed fragment from the same draft. One wonders if the dig at unofficial advisers referred to the rumor that Chief Justice Vinson informally advised Truman that the steel seizure was lawful.
32. Justice Douglas's conference notes from Youngstown state that Jackson said, "wisdom in use of the power in the past has been in keeping it out of the courts." The William O. Douglas papers, Library of Congress, Manuscript Division, Box 221.
33. The citations discussed in the text appear in footnotes 14 and 16 of the final opinion.
34. In one draft, Jackson described his destroyer opinion as "frequently criticized as pushing the powers of the President to extreme limits." Jackson Papers, Box 176, May 8 Draft at 2.
35. See Bellia, "Steel Seizure Case," 275–276 ("The message was clear: that the advice that President Truman had legal authority to seize the mills would never have been given or followed in President Roosevelt's time").
36. Granted, President Truman did not make Jackson the Chief Justice when that position was vacant in 1946, and there is nothing to suggest that Jackson thought highly of Truman. That said, the Youngstown concurrence does not express antipathy toward Truman.
37. Nomination of John G. Roberts, Jr., to be Chief Justice of the United States: Hearing Before the S. Judiciary Comm., 109th Cong. 153 (2005). Justice Kavanaugh made a similar comment at his own confirmation hearing. See Nomination of Brett M. Kavanaugh to be an Associate Justice of the Supreme Court of the United States: Hearing Before the S. Judiciary Comm., 115th Cong. 119 (2018).
38. Noah Feldman, *Scorpions: The Battles and Triumphs of FDR's Great Supreme Court Justices* (New York: Twelve, 2010), 363. Professor Feldman argues that Justice Jackson "made several rather weak attempts in his opinion to distinguish the two situations." Ibid. at 366. I do not agree that the factual distinctions between the North American Aviation seizure and the steel seizure were weak. More important, the concurrence does not say that Jackson was changing his mind or doing so because he was a judge.
39. See 89 Cong. Rec. 3992 (1943) (reprinting in full the attorney general's statement of June 10, 1941). The next paragraph in the concurrence described the North American Aviation seizure, which clarified that the "press statement" was for that case.
40. For the classic biography of Coke, see Catherine Drinker Bowen, *The Lion and the Throne: The Life and Times of Sir Edward Coke* (Boston: Little Brown, 1957).
41. See Jackson Papers, Box 176, May 22 Draft at 30; Bellia, "Steel Seizure Case," 281–282. Coke was one of the royal officials who gave "tactful" advice to the Tudor Queen, which suggested another parallel with Jackson and FDR.

42. One other worthwhile example is that Justice Jackson said that "an interval of detached reflection may temper teachings of that [executive] experience." Again, this indirectly suggests a change in his views due to his different role.
43. See McGrath v. Kristinsen, 340 U.S. 162, 176 (1950) (Jackson, J., concurring) ("I concur in the judgment and opinion of the Court. But since it is contrary to an opinion which, as Attorney General, I rendered in 1940, I owe some word of explanation"). The next quotation in the text also comes from this page of the opinion.
44. Ibid. at 178 (Jackson, J., concurring); see ibid. (quoting Baron Bramwell's statement that the "matter [in a case] does not appear to me now as it appears to have appeared to me then"); ibid. (quoting Justice Story's comment in a case that his "own error, however, can furnish no ground for its being adopted by this Court"). The next textual quotation also comes from this page.
45. David McCullough's biography of Truman says that Attorney General Clark "advised him that a President, faced with a calamitous strike, had the 'inherent' power to prevent a paralysis of the national economy." McCullough, *Truman* (New York: Simon & Schuster, 1992), 896–897. I cannot verify this claim.
46. Jackson Papers, Box 176 (newspaper clipping).
47. Youngstown Sheet & Steel Tube Co. v. Sawyer, 343 U.S. 579, 662 (1952) (Clark, J., concurring in the judgment). In other words, Justice Clark also denied that he changed his position, though he never expressly said that.
48. Jackson noted that Justice Clark's statement was not cited by the briefs, but the Chief Justice did cite the statement in his dissent. See ibid. at 699 and n.76 (Vinson, C. J., dissenting).
49. The concurrence never mentions the Justice's work at Nuremberg. But a reader of the opinion cannot help but think about that experience with executive power run amok, especially when Jackson discusses Hitler.

Chapter 6

1. By contrast, many Supreme Court opinions refer to Darwin's concept of evolution. See, e.g., United States v. Windsor, 570 U.S. 744, 769 (2013) (stating that the legalization of same-sex marriage reflected the "evolving understanding of the meaning of equality"); Trop v. Dulles, 356 U.S. 86, 101 (1958) (stating that the Eighth Amendment "must draw its meaning from the evolving standards of decency that mark the progress of a maturing society").
2. The analogy to Einstein's theory is not perfect in that the theory of relativity contains at least one absolute—the speed of light.
3. Cf. Sanford Levinson, "The Rhetoric of the Judicial Opinion," in *Law's Stories: Narrative and Rhetoric in the Law*, ed. Peter Brooks and Paul Gewirtz (New Haven, CT: Yale University Press, 1996), 202–203 (stating that Jackson was "well aware of the limitations of ordinary legal materials in providing answers to the difficult problems presented by President Truman's attempt, from his perspective, to protect the interests of those Americans (and others) risking their lives on the Korean Peninsula in what many (including Chief Justice Vinson in dissent) viewed as the first battle of World War III").
4. See, e.g., Woods v. Cloyd W. Miller Co., 333 U.S. 138, 146 (1948) (Jackson, J., concurring) ("No one will question that [the war] power is the most dangerous one to free government in the whole catalogue of powers. It usually is invoked in haste and excitement when calm legislative consideration of constitutional limitation is difficult. It is executed in a time of patriotic fervor that makes moderation unpopular. And, worst of all, it is interpreted by judges under the influence of the same passions and pressures").
5. See Phillip Bobbitt, "*Youngstown:* Pages from the Book of Disquietude," *Constitutional Commentary* 19 (2002), 8 ("[M]uch of the Jackson opinion is directed toward fending off other approaches to the constitutional decision at hand").
6. See Noah Feldman, *Scorpions: The Battles and Triumphs of FDR's Great Supreme Court Justices* (New York: Twelve, 2010), 364 ("*Doctrine* is not usually a dirty word to judges; it is, after all, the stuff of judicial decisions").
7. Cf. Bobbitt, "Book of Disquietude," 9 (stating that Jackson also disparaged doctrine in Youngstown by stating that "court decisions are indecisive because of the judicial practice of dealing with the largest questions in the most narrow way").
8. Robert H. Jackson, *The Struggle for Judicial Supremacy: A Study of a Crisis in American Power Politics* (New York: Knopf, 1941), 291–292.

9. Ibid. at 295. The next quotation in the text also comes from this page.
10. The best discussion of fictions in the law is Lon L. Fuller, *Legal Fictions* (Stanford, CA: Stanford University Press, 1967).
11. A constitutional example is that King Charles III leads the British government, which everyone knows is not the case but is useful for the sake of legitimacy and tradition.
12. Jackson, *Struggle for Judicial Supremacy*, 294–295.
13. See, e.g., Brown v. Allen, 344 U.S. 443, 540 (1953) (Jackson, J., concurring) ("We are not final because we are infallible, but we are infallible only because we are final").
14. See Feldman, *Scorpions*, 364 ("No more pithy dismissal of originalism appears in the *U.S. Reports*"). While the line about Pharaoh's dreams is a staple in academic literature, the Supreme Court has quoted this only once. See Clinton v. Jones, 520 U.S. 681, 696–697 (1997).
15. The Biblical version can be found at Genesis 41: 1–57.
16. Scripture was part of our constitutional discourse in the past because the Bible was widely read. One famous example is Abraham Lincoln's Second Inaugural Address (March 4, 1865), which quotes Psalm 19: 9–10 ("[A]s was said three thousand years ago, so still it must be said 'the judgments of the Lord are true and righteous altogether'").
17. See Martin S. Flaherty, "The Future and Past of U.S. Foreign Relations Law," *Law and Contemporary Problems* 67, no. 4 (2004), 172 ("Jackson merely assumed history was invariably inconclusive").
18. 325 U.S. 1, 20 (1945); see Carlton F. W. Larson, *On Treason: A Citizen's Guide to the Law* (New York: HarperCollins, 2020), 167–170 (discussing the case more generally). Justice Jackson's unpublished draft in *Brown* was also skeptical about the utility of history (in that case, the history of the Fourteenth Amendment's ratification). See David M. O'Brian, *Justice Robert H. Jackson's Unpublished Opinion in* Brown v. Board: *Conflict, Compromise, and Constitutional Interpretation* (Lawrence: University Press of Kansas, 2017), 125.
19. The relevance (or lack thereof) of post-ratification history in constitutional interpretation is addressed by many of the opinions in a recent Second Amendment case. See United States v. Rahimi, 602 U.S. 680 (2024).
20. For the classic articulation of this view, see Walter Bagehot, *The English Constitution* (1873; reprint, New York: Cosimo Classics, 2007), 1–5.
21. Robert H. Jackson, "Founders Day Address" (Oct. 12, 1937), at 11: https://www.roberthjackson.org/wp-content/uploads/2015/01/Founders_Day_address_at_University_of_North_Carolina.pdf. For a thoughtful elaboration on the idea that constitutional law is more administrative than doctrinal, see Andrew Coan, *Rationing the Constitution: How Judicial Capacity Shapes Supreme Court Decision-Making* (Cambridge, MA: Harvard University Press, 2019).
22. The classic work on structural interpretation is Charles L. Black, Jr., *Structure and Relationship in Constitutional Law* (Baton Rouge: Louisiana State University Press, 1969).
23. Written constitutionalism sits uneasily alongside the common law. Britain did not have and still does not have a codified constitution in its common-law system. The idea of a code that sits at the apex of the legal system is central to civil-law systems (Justinian's Code is an obvious example), but those systems call for a different judicial approach.
24. See Bobbitt, "Book of Disquietude," 9 ("Structural arguments are deceptively simple. They typically depend on three or four steps; an uncontroversial statement derived from an explicit provision about the structure of government (e.g., 'We have states'); an inference from this structure when it is augmented with the premise that relationships should be so construed as to give the structure its best chance of success ('There must be one thing that states can do that is not determined by the federal government'); a practical assertion about how this inference manifests itself ('Controlling a state's budget is a power such that if it were in the hands of the federal government states would as a practical matter cease to exist qua states.'; [and] a conclusion that addresses the case at hand")).
25. See M'Culloch, 17 U.S. (4 Wheat.) 316, 358 (1819); Akhil Reed Amar, *America's Unwritten Constitution: The Precedents and Principles We Live By* (New York: Basic Books, 2012), 25–27.
26. See M'Culloch, 17 U.S. (4 Wheat.) at 391. A crucial assumption here was that the Bank of the United States, which was privately owned, was a federal institution because of its role in holding the Treasury's deposits and regulating the currency.
27. See Abraham Lincoln, First Inaugural Address (Mar. 4, 1861), in James D. Richardson, ed., *A Compilation of the Messages and Papers of the Presidents*, vol. 7, 3210 ("If a minority in such

case will secede rather than acquiesce, they make a precedent which in turn will divide and ruin them, for a minority of their own will secede from them whenever a majority refuses to be controlled by such minority").

28. Ibid. ("If the minority will not acquiesce, the majority must, or the Government must cease. There is no other alternative, for continuing the Government is acquiescence on one side or the other.")
29. Jackson, *Struggle for Judicial Supremacy*, 312–13. Jackson was attentive to other structural features such as the link between the Equal Protection and Due Process clauses of the Fourteenth Amendment. See Railway Express Agency v. New York, 336 U.S. 106, 112 (1949) (Jackson, J., concurring) ("The framers of the Constitution knew, and we should not forget today, that there is no more effective practical guaranty against arbitrary and unreasonable government than to require that the principles of law which officials would impose upon a minority must be imposed generally").
30. Robert H. Jackson, *The Supreme Court in the American System of Government* (Cambridge, MA: Harvard University Press, 1955), 62.
31. See Boumediene v. Bush, 553 U.S. 723, 743 (2008); Loving v. United States, 517 U.S. 748, 756 (1996); Metropolitan Washington Airports Auth. v. Citizens for Abatement of Aircraft Noise, Inc., 501 U.S. 252, 276 n.22 (1991); United States v. Munoz-Flores, 495 U.S. 385, 394 (1990); Mistretta v. United States, 481 U.S. 361, 381 (1989); Bowsher v. Synar, 478 U.S. 714, 721 (1986); idem. at 760 (White, J., dissenting); Buckley v. Valeo, 424 U.S. 1, 122 (1976) (per curiam); see also Blakely v. Washington, 542 U.S. 296, 326 (2004) (Kennedy, J., dissenting); Clinton v. City of New York, 524 U.S. 417, 472 (1998) (Breyer, J., dissenting); Patricia Bellia, "Executive Power in *Youngstown*'s Shadow," *Constitutional Commentary* 19 (2002), 107–109. The Office of Legal Counsel (OLC) also quotes this line with some frequency. See, e.g., "The Constitutional Separation of Powers Between the President and Congress," 20 Op. O.L.C. 124, 126–27 (1996); "Authority for the Continuance of Government Functions During a Temporary Lapse in Appropriations," 5 Op. O.L.C. 1, 6 (1981); "Scope of Congressional Oversight and Investigative Power with Respect to the Executive Branch," 9 Op. O.L.C. 60, 62 (1985).
32. Arguably there is an additional structural premise in the concurrence. See Bobbitt, "Book of Disquietude," 10 ("The Constitution provides for an Executive Power").
33. A helpful way of thinking about these categories is that they turn in part on whether Congress acts first. See Matthew Steilen, "Life and Afterlife in the *Steel Seizure Case*," *Buffalo Law Review* 70, no. 2 (2022), 895. If so (either to authorize or prohibit executive action), then Congress is owed deference. If the President acts first, then the analysis becomes more complicated.
34. See Jack M. Balkin, "The New Originalism and the Uses of History," *Fordham Law Review* 82 (2013), 666–68; Bobbitt, "Book of Disquietude," 10.
35. This reading is questionable, as the Reichstag did pass legislation in 1933 giving Hitler sweeping authority. See "Hitler Cabinet Gets Power to Rule as a Dictatorship: Reichstag Quits Sine Die," *The New York Times*, March 24, 1933, at 1 (describing the Enabling Act of 1933). On the other hand, this law passed only after President von Hindenburg declared an emergency following the Reichstag Fire, so the legislation was enacted under exceptional circumstances. See Kim Lane Scheppele, "Constitutional Coups and Judicial Review: How Transnational Institutions Can Strengthen Peak Court at Times of Crisis (with Special Reference to Hungary)," *Transnational Law and Contemporary Problems* 23 (2014), 55–56.
36. In recent decades, Justice Stephen Breyer was willing to use this method. See Printz v. United States 521 U.S. 898, 976–77 (1997) (Breyer, J., dissenting) (looking at European constitutions to construe American federalism).
37. The idea that a President's most important skill is his "power to persuade" is a major theme in Richard E. Neustadt's widely taught book *Presidential Power: The Politics of Leadership* (New York: Wiley, 1960).
38. For a splendid discussion of how practice informs constitutional construction, see Curtis A. Bradley, *Historical Gloss and Foreign Affairs: Constitutional Authority in Practice* (Cambridge, MA: Harvard University Press, 2024).
39. United States v. Western Union Telegraph Co., 272 F. 311, 319 (S.D.N.Y 1921).
40. Consistent with his theory of constitutional modalities, Professor Bobbitt argues that the concurrence also rejects the prudential and ethical methods of interpretation. See Bobbitt, "Book of Disquietude," 9 (citing Jackson's rejection of inherent executive emergency powers on the ground that they "would tend to kindle emergencies" and rested solely on "the customs and claims of preceding administrations").

41. Marbury v. Madison and M'Culloch cite no decisions, and both use structural reasoning. The Youngstown concurrence does cite cases, but only in footnotes that do not distract the reader. Another difference is that Chief Justice Marshall used other materials, including a close reading of the text, to support his constitutional conclusions. Justice Jackson's opinion is unusual in its almost exclusive use of structural arguments.
42. Of course, Jackson did not present his framework as an entirely abstract discussion.
43. A structural analysis can be persuasive about a constitutional right. For one example from Jackson, see Edwards v. California, 314 U.S. 160, 185–86 (1941) (Jackson, J., concurring) ("Rich or penniless, [appellant's] citizenship under the Constitution pledges his strength to the defense of California as a part of the United States, and his right to migrate to any part of the land he must defend is something she must respect under the same instrument").
44. In one draft, Jackson explained that he was trying to arrive "at an estimate of presidential power for purposes of this case," a probabilistic formulation that many lawyers might find imprecise but that many scientists would understand. See Robert H. Jackson papers, Library of Congress, Manuscript Division, Box 176, May 7 draft at Ex. Insert 4.
45. Professor Michael W. McConnell takes this position in his book *The President Who Would Not Be King: Executive Power Under the Constitution* (Princeton, NJ: Princeton University Press, 2020), 279–280 (arguing that Jackson's concurrence "essentially ignores Article II's structure").
46. Justice Douglas's concurrence focused on the takings issue. See Youngstown, 343 U.S. at 631–32 (1952) (Douglas, J., concurring). Jackson alluded to the issue in one draft. See Jackson Papers, Box 176, May 8 Draft at 3 ("[I]f the presidential seizure in the form now attempted is constitutional, that, too, would subject the United States to liability for the payment of just compensation.").
47. See Laurence H. Tribe, "Transcending the *Youngstown* Triptych: A Multidimensional Reappraisal of Separation of Powers Doctrine," *Yale Law Journal Forum* 126 (2016), 86 (describing the Youngstown concurrence as two-dimensional); ibid. at 100–106 (lamenting the absence of individual rights from the Youngstown framework).
48. Jackson Papers, Box 176, May 8 Draft at 3. He also said in a later draft, "It is of the essence of constitutional government that official powers are thus permeated with individual rights." Jackson Papers, Box 176, May 29 Draft at 14.
49. See Tribe, "Multidimensional Reappraisal," 99–100; see also Elizabeth Bahr and Josh Blackman, "Youngstown's Fourth Tier: Is There a Zone of Insight Beyond the Zone of Twilight?" *University of Memphis Law Review* 40 (2010), 541–602 (discussing how Youngstown might be understood to resolve conflicts between the executive branch and the courts).
50. See Tribe, "Multidimensional Reappraisal," 96–99. In other words, a leading threat to separation of powers could be Congress's eagerness to delegate power to the President that Congress can lawfully delegate but should not. Jackson was more concerned about congressional abdication, as Chapter 12 will explain.
51. Levinson, "Rhetoric of the Judicial Opinion," 203.
52. See Jacobellis v. Ohio, 378 U.S. 184, 197 (1964) (Stewart, J., concurring) (stating that the case was not about obscenity because "I know it when I see it, and the motion picture involved in this case is not that").
53. On the transformation of Jackson's rough categories into rigid ones, see Michael J. Turner, "Fade to Black: The Formalization of Jackson's Youngstown Taxonomy by Hamdan and Medellin," *American University Law Review* 58 (2009), 665–98.
54. See Memorandum from Jay S. Bybee, Assistant Attorney General, Office of Legal Counsel, to Alberto R. Gonzales, Counsel to the President, Aug. 1, 2002; see also Edward T. Swaine, "The Political Economy of Youngstown," *Southern California Law Review* 83, no. 2 (2010), 267 (stating that the Torture Memo's authors "were lambasted for neglecting Justice Jackson's concurrence").

Chapter 7

1. See Michael McConnell, *The President Who Would Not Be King: Executive Power Under the Constitution* (Princeton, NJ: Princeton University Press, 2020), 280 (explaining that Jackson's first category "is overcomplicated but largely correct"). The Office of Counsel opined in 2012 that Category One of *Youngstown* may not apply to actions taken by just one house of Congress. See "Recess Appointments amid Pro Forma Senate Sessions," 36 Op. O.L.C. 15, 44–45 n.27 (2012).

2. See Patricia L. Bellia, "The Story of the Steel Seizure Case," in *Presidential Power Stories*, ed. Christopher H. Schroeder and Curtis A. Bradley (New York: Foundation Press, 2009), 273 ("Justice Jackson's concurrence provides limited guidance on how courts should construe specific statutes. In a case raising such an issue, a substantive question is intertwined with an institutional one. The substantive question is whether the statute authorizes the challenged conduct, and the institutional question relates to who is in the best position—courts or the Executive—to interpret the statute, or, put another way, whether the courts owe the Executive's interpretation of the statute any deference"). Jackson did read the statutes pertaining to the steel seizure as barring executive action, but he did not dwell on that issue.
3. See Neal Katyal, "*Hamdan v. Rumsfeld*: The Legal Academy Goes to Practice," *Harvard Law Review* 120 (2006), 99 ("Under *Youngstown*, whether a given case falls within a particular zone depends on statutory construction. But the Court can toggle between categories depending on its stinginess or generosity with any given statute and how it reads legislative silence"); see also McConnell, *The President Who Would Not Be King*, 283 ("A clever lawyer can often describe a given action as falling into two or even all three of the categories").
4. See Selective Service Act of 1940, 54 Stat. 885, 892, § 9 (stating, in pertinent part, that the President was authorized to seize plants "who shall refuse to manufacture the kind, quantity, or quality of arms or ammunition, or the parts thereof, or any necessary supplies or equipment, as ordered by the Secretary of War"). This provision was no longer in force by 1952 and thus could not have authorized President Truman's seizure.
5. See Memorandum from CGN, "Presidential Seizure Power," May 8, 1952, in the Robert H. Jackson papers, Library of Congress, Manuscript Division, Box 176, at 2 ("Perhaps one could argue that North American 'refused' through its agents, the striking employees, to comply with the vast defense orders given the company, thereby bringing the seizure within the 1940 Act. I have gathered, however, from press reports of the seizure, that that was not what was actually contemplated at the time").
6. Nomination of Samuel A. Alito, Jr., to be an Associate Justice of the Supreme Court of the United States: Hearing Before the S. Judiciary Comm., 109th Cong. 4 (2006) (statement of Chairman Specter).
7. See Foreign Intelligence Surveillance Act, Pub L. 95-511, 92 Stat. 1783 (1978). For background on the program, see Neal Katyal and Richard Caplan, "The Surprisingly Stronger Case for the Legality of the NSA Surveillance Program: The FDR Precedent," *Stanford Law Review* 60 (2008), 1029–1034. Katyal and Caplan also discuss Jackson's role in FDR's surveillance program, though they conclude that the Roosevelt Administration's actions was not an adequate precedent for the Bush Administration's program. See ibid. at 1027–1028.
8. See Authorization for Use of Military Force, Pub. L. 107-40, 115 Stat. 224 (2001); "Legal Authorities Supporting the Activities of the National Security Agency Described by the President," 30 Op. O.L.C. 12–21 (2006). The Bush Administration made other statutory and constitutional arguments in defense of the NSA program.
9. Dames & Moore v. Regan, 453 U.S. 654, 674 (1981).
10. See McConnell, *The President Who Would Not Be King*, 326–27 (stating that Jackson "simply disregards the question" of non-delegation); cf. Eric A. Posner and Adrian Vermeule, "Inside or Outside the System?" *University of Chicago Law Review* 80, no. 4 (2013), 1743 (stating that "the President wields the full combined power of the legislative and executive branches" under Category One). One notable exception is William R. Casto, *Advising the President: Attorney General Robert H. Jackson and Franklin D. Roosevelt* (Lawrence: University Press of Kansas, 2018), 94.
11. See A.L.A. Schechter Poultry Company v. United States, 295 U.S. 495 (1935); Panama Refining Company v. Ryan, 293 U.S. 389 (1935). Both cases used the nondelegation doctrine to invalidate provisions of the National Industrial Recovery Act, though Schechter Poultry also held that part of the Act exceeded Congress's authority under the Commerce Clause.
12. The scholarly literature on nondelegation is too vast to summarize adequately. For a relatively recent judicial discussion, see Gundy v. United States, 588 U.S. 128, 149–179 (2019) (Gorsuch, J., dissenting).
13. This section of the text draws on a brief article of mine. See Gerard N. Magliocca, "Robert Jackson's Non-Delegation Doctrine," *Green Bag 2d* 25 (2022), 95–107.
14. The second sentence of Category One contains an error. Professor McConnell rightly criticizes Justice Jackson's sloppiness in saying that the President may be said "to personify the

federal sovereignty" when Congress delegates authority to him. See McConnell, *The President Who Would Not Be King*, 280 ("In this country sovereignty rests in the people, not the government. The idea that that king-in-Parliament embodies national sovereignty is a British notion that should not be imported into American jurisprudence"). In his early drafts, Jackson was more sensitive to this point. See Jackson Papers, Box 176, May 8 Draft at 4 ("I find little help in determining any concrete issue from the concept of sovereignty or the powers that it implies. Wherever this mystical sovereignty resides under our system of government and whatever it implies, the President is not a sovereign"). I do not know why he changed this passage.

15. Dames & Moore v. Regan, 453 U.S. at 674, removed the word "usually" from the quotation in its restatement of Category One. Whether that was a mistake or was done on purpose is unclear.
16. See Jackson Papers, Box 176, May 7 Draft at 1; ibid. at May 8 Draft at 1–2.
17. Remember from Chapter 3 that this footnote was largely taken from the Bell Memo. Footnote 2 cited United States v. Curtiss-Wright, 299 U.S. 304 (1936), which rejected a nondelegation challenge to a Joint Resolution of Congress authorizing the President to impose an arms embargo on Bolivia. This is one reason why Jackson (or, more accurately, the Bell Memo) drew a distinction between foreign and internal affairs.
18. See Brief for the United States, Currin v. Wallace, 306 U.S. 1 (No. 275), 1938 WL 63794 [hereinafter Jackson Brief]. There are limits to what this brief can tell us about *Youngstown*. For example, the brief was written over a decade earlier, and lawyers do change their minds, though in 1941 Jackson cited his brief with approval. See Robert H. Jackson, *The Struggle for Judicial Supremacy: A Study of a Crisis in American Power Politics* (New York: Knopf, 1941), 95, n.9. Jackson was also an advocate in Currin rather than a judge. Nevertheless, the Currin brief is consistent with what Justice Jackson said in the concurrence.
19. 306 U.S. 1 (1939).
20. See ibid. at 15–18.
21. See Jackson Brief at 46–47; ibid. at 45 ("The invocation of a vagrant and uncanalized judicial doctrine to prevent vagrant and uncanalized legislation leaves both legislators and litigants confused"). The merits of these arguments about the nondelegation doctrine need not be resolved in order to understand Category One.
22. See ibid. at 46–47. This statement is true, though Panama Refining said that Congress could not transfer its authority "to the President or other officer or to an administrative body" (295 U.S. at 430). Distinguished scholars who later became Supreme Court Justices later echoed Jackson's point. See, e.g., Elena Kagan, "Presidential Administration," *Harvard Law Review* 114, no. 8 (2001), 2365 (stating that the nondelegation doctrine "might well distrust presidential action but only when this action derives from a direct delegation to the President"); cf. Amy Coney Barrett, "Suspension and Delegation," *Cornell Law Review* 99 (2014), 251–326 (raising constitutional concerns about congressional delegation of habeas corpus suspension authority to the President).
23. See Jackson Brief at 44–45, 47–65. A more detailed discussion of Jackson's arguments can be found in Magliocca, "Robert Jackson's Non-Delegation Doctrine," 99–102.
24. See Jackson Brief at 47; cf. Vikram David Amar, "Indirect Effects of Direct Election: A Structural Examination of the Seventeenth Amendment," *Vanderbilt Law Review* 49, no. 6 (1996), 1384 ("Broad delegations to the President are thus the most structurally problematic; the President's dual role as recipient of delegated authority and participant in decisions about its retrieval creates the very real potential that lawmaking power is ceded in such a way that Congress's ultimate power to make laws is diminished"). Jackson did not renew his arguments in another brief. When he addressed the doctrine in an opinion for the Court, he distinguished the nondelegation cases in a different way. See Fahey v. Malonee, 332 U.S. 245, 249 (1947) (stating that Panama Refining and Schechter Poultry "dealt with delegation of a power to make federal crimes of acts that had never been such before and to devise novel rules of law in a field in which there had been no settled law or custom").
25. See Jackson Brief at 47; Robert H. Jackson, *The Supreme Court in the American System of Government* (Cambridge, MA: Harvard University Press, 1955), 63 ("In the cases striking down the [National Industrial Recovery Act], the Court refused to sanction the congressional practice of delegating power to make codes for industry that would be the equivalent of new laws").

26. Many laws grant power directly to the President; see Shalev Roisman, "Presidential Law," *Minnesota Law Review* 105 (2021), 1281–1288 (compiling these statutes). One widely used example is the Antiquities Act, which gives the President broad discretion to set aside federal lands as national monuments or parks. See Antiquities Act of 1906, Pub. L. 59-209, 34 Stat. 225. This law was the authority for the creation of the Grand Canyon National Park. See Cameron v. United States, 252 U.S. 450 (1920) (upholding the President's authority under the Act to make the Grand Canyon a national monument).
27. I do not mean to suggest that Category One applies only when Congress gives power directly to the President. If Congress gives power to an executive agency, this also comes with a strong presumption of constitutionality. My point is that Jackson's nondelegation discussion occurred in relation only to direct presidential delegations, which tracks the logic of the Currin brief that only those legislative delegations present a constitutional question.
28. An example from the Bell Memo that Jackson used in footnote 10 of the concurrence involved President Jefferson's Message to Congress about the Barbary pirates, in which the President suggested that Congress grant him authority to engage in offensive operations.
29. Attorney General Jackson participated in the FDR examples discussed in footnote 16 and said more about them than in an earlier draft. See Jackson Papers, Box 176, May 8 Draft at 4.
30. Franklin D. Roosevelt, "First Inaugural Address" (March 4, 1933), in *The Public Papers and Addresses of Franklin D. Roosevelt*, ed. Samuel I. Rosenman (New York: Harper, 1950), vol. 2, 15.
31. "The President's Compliance with the 'Timely Notification' Requirement of Section 501(b) of the National Security Act," 10 Op. O.LC. 159, 162, n.8 (1986).
32. There is also the possibility that Congress will grant a request under more restrictive terms than the President wants, which raises a problem if the President goes beyond them.
33. The credit for the insights in this textual paragraph belongs to Edward T. Swaine, "The Political Economy of *Youngstown*," *Southern California Law Review* 83, no. 2 (2010), 339.
34. Justice Black's opinion in Youngstown used Congress's rejection of seizure authority in the Taft-Hartley Act debate to draw an inference against presidential authority. See Youngstown Sheet & Tube Co. v. Sawyer, 343 U.S. 579, 586 (1952).
35. One example would be a major commitment of American forces abroad, as occurred during the two conflicts with Iraq. A president may not want to take such a dramatic step without congressional support, since the fight may not go well.
36. The Court's recent cases on the "major questions" doctrine makes this strategy more problematic, in that they are skeptical about reading statutes to give the executive broad authority that was never previously exercised under those statutes. See Biden v. Nebraska, 600 U.S. 477 (2023) (holding that the Secretary of Education lacked general authority under federal law to forgive student debt).
37. Tracking down the original source for this quote is nearly impossible. Perhaps the quote is apocryphal, though I cannot say for certain.
38. Napoleon did play an important (if unintended) role in strengthening the Constitution by agreeing to the Louisiana Purchase, which doubled the size of the United States. Jackson mentioned that agreement earlier in the concurrence, which may explain why he thought of Napoleon. In a draft, he also invoked Hitler and Oliver Cromwell to make the same point about power and inaction. See Jackson Papers, Box 176, May 22 Draft at 29 ("The autopsy of the Hitler regime at Nurnberg leaves a firm conviction that dictatorship in Germany was not due to the strength, ability, or other qualities of the man or clique that headed it, but came about by the weakness, decay, and disintegration of the Reichstag"); ibid. ("It was even so in England when Cromwell broke up the Long Parliament with imperious words: 'You have sat too long here for any good you have been doing. Depart I say and let us have done with you. In the name of God, go!'").
39. Robert Caro, *Master of the Senate*: *The Years of Lyndon Johnson* (New York: Knopf, 2002), 1035.
40. Jackson Papers, Box 176, May 22 Draft at 28.
41. Jackson's use of Napoleon may also have been an allusion to the risk of dictatorship presented by a broad reading of executive power or the merger of civilian and military authority.
42. A contrary view, also reasonable, is that Congress delegates too much power to the President by statute rather than letting power slip through its fingers by inaction.
43. See INS v. Chadha, 462 U.S. 919 (1983). Chadha is discussed in Chapter 11.

44. There are other formal tools that Congress can use to control delegations of power, such as sunset provisions. But time limits are a blunt instrument that cannot respond to new events.
45. Another possibility is retroactive legislative approval if public opinion approves executive action. See United States v. Western Union Telegraph Co., 272 F. 311, 315–316 (S.D.N.Y 1921) (discussing that possibility in the British parliamentary context). Retroactive authorization allows Congress to convert a Category Two or Three case into a Category One case before the courts get involved.
46. To answer an obvious question, Rod Serling did not get the name of his legendary television series from Justice Jackson's opinion. The phrase was around long before 1952, as the Bell Memo shows, and Serling never said that there was any connection with *Youngstown*.

Chapter 8

1. If the President has the power to act pursuant to Article II, then congressional silence is irrelevant. Accordingly, this chapter discusses Category Two only in the context of cases where the President lacks Article II authority.
2. Michael W. McConnell, *The President Who Would Not Be King: Executive Power Under the Constitution* (Princeton, NJ: Princeton University Press, 2020), 281.
3. See, e.g., Daniel Abebe and Aziz Z. Huq, "Foreign Affairs Federalism: A Revisionist Approach," *Vanderbilt Law Review* 66 (2006), 733; Edward T. Swaine, "The Political Economy of *Youngstown*," *Southern California Law Review* 83, no. 2 (2010), 281; Laurence H. Tribe, "Transcending the *Youngstown* Triptych: A Multidimensional Reappraisal of Separation of Powers Doctrine," *Yale Law Journal Forum* 126 (2016), 91.
4. Michael Coenen and Scott M. Sullivan, "The Elusive Zone of Twilight," *Boston College Law Review* 62, no. 3 (2021), 746. The two points are related. The difficulty of deciding Category Two cases makes courts less willing to do so. See ibid. at 746–747.
5. The leading modern case on political questions is Rucho v. Common Cause, 588 U.S. 684 (2019) (holding that partisan gerrymandering claims may not be considered by federal courts). Just to be clear, my position is that Category Two cases should be non-justiciable only if there is no alleged invasion of an individual right or another legal principle (such as federalism).
6. See United States v. Western Union Tel. Co., 272 F. 311, 317 (S.D.N.Y. 1921).
7. Professor Laura A. Cisneros was the first scholar to make this argument, and I build on her work in this chapter. See Cisneros, "Youngstown Sheet to Boumediene: A Story of Judicial Ethos and the (Un)Fastidious Use of Language," *West Virginia Law Review* 115 (2012), 594.
8. There is an analogy here to Jackson's dissent in Korematsu. Sometimes courts should allow a government action to go ahead without a decision rather than affirming the legality of that action with a decision. The former avoids creating a judicial precedent that can expand and that reduces the possibility of a negotiated settlement. Moreover, courts may feel undue pressure to cave in to presidential demands in the zone of twilight, just as they do in wartime.
9. For a rare counterexample, see Goodwin v. United States, 10 F. Cas. 625, 626 (C.C.D. Pa. 1811) (No. 5,554) (Washington, J.) ("After the closest examination of the point on which the controversy hangs, we can truly say, that our mind rather inclines to the opinion which we shall deliver, than that we feel a full confidence in its correctness").
10. There is a tradition of judges concurring in an opinion "dubitante," as a way of saying that they might reconsider their view in a future case. But no majority opinion is ever dubitante.
11. One clarification is that, in Jackson's early drafts, what we call Category Two was described as Category Three and vice versa.
12. The Robert H. Jackson papers, Library of Congress, Manuscript Division, Box 176. I have edited this note for clarity from the handwritten text.
13. In other handwritten notes, Jackson wrote "Gravitation of power to President" and again included "Airport." See Jackson Papers, Box 176 (undated).
14. Granted, one could say that a national airport concerns national security. Jackson did suggest that this was one of Roosevelt's motives but did not rely on that point in Youngstown. See Jackson, *That Man: An Insider's Portrait of Franklin D. Roosevelt*, ed. John Q. Barrett (New York: Oxford University Press, 2003), 47–48.
15. Western Telegraph, 272 F. at 316–317.
16. Ibid. at 318–19.
17. See, e.g., Harold Hongju Koh, *The National Security Constitution: Sharing Power After the Iran-Contra Affair* (New Haven, CT: Yale University Press, 1990); Roy E. Brownell II,

"The Coexistence of *United States v. Curtiss-Wright* and *Youngstown Sheet & Tube v. Sawyer* in National Security Jurisprudence," *Journal of Law & Politics* 16 (2000), 1–111.

18. Jackson Papers, Box 176, May 8 Draft at 6. The next quotation in the text comes from the same page of the draft.
19. See Jackson Papers, Box 176, May 22 Draft at 2–3.
20. See Jackson Papers, Box 176, May 29 Draft at 4 n.3.
21. See U.S. Const., art. I, § 9, cl. 2 ("The Privilege of the Writ of Habeas Corpus shall not be suspended, unless when in Cases of Rebellion or invasion the public Safety may require it").
22. For an excellent discussion of this question, see Amanda L. Tyler, *Habeas Corpus in Wartime: From the Tower of London to Guantanamo Bay* (New York: Oxford University Press, 2017), 159–167. The basic argument is that the Suspension Clause is in Article I, not Article II. Moreover, the purpose of habeas corpus is to ensure that the executive detentions are lawful, which would be dramatically undercut if the President can at his discretion suspend the writ. See Amy Coney Barrett, "Suspension and Delegation," *Cornell Law Review* 99 (2014), 251–326.
23. 17 F. Cas. 144 (C.C.D. Md. 1861) (No. 9,487) (Taney, C.J.). The report in Merryman is unclear about whether Taney was acting as a Circuit Justice or issuing an in-chambers opinion as a Supreme Court Justice. See Seth Barrett Tillman, "*Ex Parte Merryman*: Myth, History, and Scholarship," *Military Law Review* 224 (2016), 504–505.
24. See ibid. at 152 (concluding that the opinion would be transmitted to the President so that he could "determine what measures he will take to cause the civil process of the United States to be respected and enforced").
25. See ibid. (stating that the court is "resisted by a force too strong for me to overcome"); cf. Jackson, *Struggle for Judicial Supremacy*, 326 (stating that the answer to Taney's opinion, "if any, was drowned out by the measured tread of marching feet").
26. See Habeas Corpus Suspension Act, 12 Stat. 755 (1863); Tyler, *Habeas Corpus in Wartime*, 169–170. Footnote 3 said that "Congress eventually ratified" Lincoln's suspension in the Act, but "ratified" might mean either "authorized" (in the Category One sense), or "acknowledged the legality of" (which could describe Category Two or Category Three).
27. Jackson, *Struggle for Judicial Supremacy*, 326–327.
28. 272 U.S. 52 (1926) (holding that the President possessed unilateral authority to fire a federal postmaster notwithstanding an Act of Congress to the contrary).
29. 295 U.S. 602 (1935) (holding that the President could not fire a member of the Federal Trade Commission without cause, given that a federal statute supplied a "for cause" standard).
30. The Court's most recent discussion of Myers and Humphrey's Executor was in Seila Law LLC v. Consumer Financial Protection Bureau, 591 U.S. 197, 214–218 (2020). Litigation inviting the Court to overrule Humphrey's Executor is pending as this book goes to press.
31. The citation of Myers and Humphrey's Executor in footnote 3 may have been a proofreading error made under time pressure. One reason to think so is that footnote 4 contains a more detailed discussion of those cases. Why, then, was there a separate citation of them in the prior note? If the citation in footnote 3 was an error, then William H. Rehnquist, who was one of Justice Jackson's law clerks during Youngstown, might be partly to blame.
32. Jackson discussed Myers and Humphrey's Executor in *The Struggle for Judicial Supremacy* (pp. 107–109), and tried to reconcile them in an opinion as the acting attorney general (when he was solicitor general), "*In Re* Power to Remove Members of the Tennessee Valley Authority," 39 Op. A.G. 145 (1938).
33. 320 U.S. 81 (1943).
34. See Hirabayashi, 320 U.S. at 91–92. Adding to the confusion, Justice Jackson compared Hirabayashi to "the case at bar," which meant Youngstown itself. But he went on to conclude that Youngstown was not a Category Two case.
35. See *Ex Parte* Vallandigham, 68 U.S. (1 Wall.) 243 (1864) and *Ex Parte* Milligan, 71 U.S. (4 Wall.) 2 (1866).
36. See Vallandigham, 68 U.S. (1 Wall.) at 248–54; Gerard N. Magliocca, *American Founding Son: John Bingham and the Invention of the Fourteenth Amendment* (New York: NYU Press, 2013), 83–84 (discussing one of Vallandigham's antiwar speeches in Congress).
37. See Milligan, 71 U.S. (4 Wall.) at 130–131; Tyler, *Habeas Corpus in Wartime*, 171–174.
38. Congress neither authorized nor prohibited the use of military commissions during the Civil War. Milligan held that civilians could never be tried by a military commission when the civil

courts were open, but four dissenting Justices concluded that Congress could authorize the President to do so. See Milligan, 71 U.S. (4 Wall.) at 136 (Chase, C.J., dissenting).

39. Jackson Papers, "Memorandum: Ex Parte Quirin," Box 124. Perhaps Jackson was saying that the judicial precedents cancel each other in the same way that the historical materials do. Put another way, there was no pattern to Category Two cases other than inconsistency. If so, then maybe the best response was for courts to stay out.
40. Coenen and Sullivan advance a theory for deciding Category Two cases that is different from mine and does not treat them as political questions. See Coenen and Sullivan, "Elusive Zone of Twilight," 747. There are also nonjudicial examples. See "The Constitutional Separation of Powers Between the President and Congress," 20 Op. O.L.C. 124, 164 (1996) ("The President's take care authority to make temporary appointments rests in the twilight area where the President may act so long as Congress is silent, but may not act in the face of congressional prohibition," citing the concurrence and quoting a prior OLC Memo).
41. See Coenen and Sullivan, "Elusive Zone of Twilight," 746, 774–784. No Supreme Court case expressly uses a Category Two analysis, although Dames & Moore v. Regan does so in all but name, as chapter 14 will explain.
42. See ibid. at 784–788. One example is Massachusetts v. Laird, a circuit case about the Vietnam War that will be discussed in chapter 13.
43. The classic discussion of these problems remains Carl von Clausewitz, *On War*, ed. and trans. Michael Howard and Peter Paret (Princeton, NJ: Princeton University Press, 1984). Indeed, Jackson's choice of language here suggests that he ended up thinking that courts should not act in Category Two cases.
44. See, e.g., McConnell, *The President Who Would Not Be King*, 281 ("Does congressional silence limit the President to his independent—meaning residual and prerogative—powers? Or does it 'enable' or 'invite' something more? The passage says both").
45. See Coenen and Sullivan, "Elusive Zone of Twilight," 762–65; see also Contractors Ass'n of Eastern PA. v. Secretary of Labor, 442 F.2d 159, 171 (3d Cir. 1971) (upholding presidential authority to require federal contractors to use affirmative action in hiring).
46. See Coenen and Sullivan, "Elusive Zone of Twilight," 765–67; see also Barquero v. United States, 18 F.3d 1311, 1313–16 (5th Cir. 1994) (upholding presidential authority to enter into an executive agreement with Mexico to share certain tax information in part based on past similar practice with some other countries and the absence of congressional disapproval).
47. Youngstown Sheet & Tube Co. v. Sawyer, 343 U.S. 579, 610 (1952) (Frankfurter, J., concurring).
48. See Coenen and Sullivan, "Elusive Zone of Twilight," 768–70; see also Indigenous Environmental Network v. Trump, 428 F. Supp. 3d 296 (D. Mont. 2019) (holding that the President lacked authority to grant a permit to construct a portion of the Keystone Pipeline on the ground that discussion in Congress, including a relevant provision that was vetoed by a different President, counseled against unilateral presidential authority).
49. See Coenen and Sullivan, "Elusive Zone of Twilight," 770–74; Chas. T. Main Int'l, Inc. v. Khuzestan Water & Power Auth., 651 F.2d 800, 814 (1st Cir.) (upholding the President's authority to nullify legal claims against Iran), affirmed by Dames & Moore v. Regan, 453 U.S. 654 (1981).
50. In his fine book on the original understanding of the presidency, Michael McConnell offers another solution. He says that there is no zone of twilight. See McConnell, *The President Who Would Not Be King*, 281–282. Instead, every executive action is based on (1) a power delegated by Congress, (2) a prerogative power conferred by Article II, or (3) a power derived from the Vesting Clause of Article II that Congress may withdraw. See ibid. at 284. Chapter 9 discusses the Vesting Clause in more detail. See U.S. Const., art. II, § 1 ("The executive Power shall be vested in a President of the United States of America"). I am unpersuaded that all executive actions can be categorized in this way. First, there is good reason to think that the Framers and the state ratifying conventions understood that they were delegating many details of executive power to George Washington's wise discretion as the first President. See, e.g., Akhil Reed Amar, *America's Unwritten Constitution: The Precedents and Principles We Live By* (New York: Basic Books, 2012), 307–332. Thus, a zone of twilight was anticipated when the Constitution was designed. Second, some presidential practices do not fit within Professor McConnell's framework. These could be criticized as unlawful, but the better reading is that such examples instead confirm Justice Jackson's observation that Article II was a sketch rather than a blueprint. See generally Jonathan Gienapp, *The Second Creation: Fixing the Constitution in the Founding Era*

(Cambridge, MA: Belknap Press, 2018) (emphasizing that much of the Constitution's meaning was constructed during the Washington Administration). That said, I agree with Professor McConnell that the courts should not rule on the merits in a Category Two case. The difference is that he thinks that is because there are no such cases, whereas I think that there are some but that they should be deemed non-justiciable.

51. For example, Jackson served alongside Hugo Black (a former Senator), Tom Clark (another former attorney general), and many others who had held high government positions before joining the Court. By contrast, none of the current Justices (save for Elena Kagan, who served for one year as solicitor general) can say the same.
52. Since courts have broad discretion to interpret statutes in the Youngstown framework, they might steer cases into Category Two to avoid ruling on a separation-of-powers claim in a world where those claims are nonjusticiable. In that scenario, though, Congress can respond with a statute that clarifies the law. Moreover, the political tug-of-war between the President and Congress would continue and would eventually result in some agreement.
53. For a comprehensive discussion of foreign-affairs examples, see Curtis A. Bradley, *Historical Gloss and Foreign Affairs: Constitutional Authority in Practice* (Cambridge, MA: Harvard University Press, 2024).
54. See Jacob E. Cooke, ed., *The Federalist* (Hanover, NH: Wesleyan University Press, 1961), 349 ("[T]he great security against a gradual concentration of the several powers in the same department, consists in giving to those who administer each department, the necessary constitutional means, and personal motives, to resist encroachments of the others"). States present a more complicated problem. They have more power than individuals and have equal representation in the Senate, but they lack the authority of Congress or the White House. The Supreme Court does sometimes decide constitutional cases that pit the states against the national government in order to defend the states from federal encroachment. See, e.g., Printz v. United States, 521 U.S. 898 (1997) (stating the anti-commandeering principle).
55. To take a recent example, the periodic standoff over raising the debt ceiling has led to calls for courts to get involved under Section 4 of the Fourteenth Amendment ("The validity of the public debt of the United States . . . shall not be questioned"). The Youngstown analysis is complicated here given that the debt ceiling is an Act of Congress that prohibits the Treasury from borrowing money beyond a certain point (Category Three), but many Acts of Congress also require the Treasury to spend money (Category One). Maybe this congressional cacophony should just be treated as Category Two silence. In the end, Congress and the President make a deal, as they always do in debt-ceiling fights, and the courts do not get involved. While political negotiation is messy and creates some uncertainty, it is far from clear that judicial intervention in complex budgetary or financial matters would be better, especially given the lack of precedent.
56. See Patricia L. Bellia, "The Story of the Steel Seizure Case," in *Presidential Power Stories*, ed. Christopher H. Schroeder and Curtis A. Bradley (New York: Foundation Press, 2009), 273–274.
57. There is more federal statutory law now than there was in 1952, and thus the zone of twilight is smaller than what Justice Jackson may have imagined.
58. "The President's Power in the Field of Foreign Relations," 1 Op. O.L.C. 49, 64 (1937). This is in the Bell Memo, discussed in chapter 4.
59. Richard Nixon is an obvious example.
60. One counterargument is that courts should defer rather than abdicate in Category Two cases. See Michael Stokes Paulsen, "Youngstown Goes to War," *Constitutional Commentary* 19, no. 1 (2002), 230–231 (commenting on the zone of twilight that "courts should not lightly invalidate, on separation of powers grounds involving congressional versus presidential power, presidential action that Congress concedes to be within the president's domain"). The problem is that it is unclear when courts should not defer. In an extreme case, courts may use their statutory-interpretation discretion to sort the issue into Category One or Three. There is no need for an emergency justiciability exception in Category Two.

Chapter 9

1. For an excellent overview of these issues, see David J. Barron and Martin S. Lederman, "The Commander in Chief at the Lowest Ebb—Framing the Problem, Doctrine, and Original Understanding," *Harvard Law Review* 121, no. 3 (2008), 689–804.

2. See Defense Production Act of 1950, Pub. L. 81-774, 64 Stat. 799; Selective Service Act of 1948, Pub. L. 80-759, 62 Stat. 625; Taft-Hartley Act, Pub. L. 80–101, 61 Stat. 136 (1947). This approach was suggested to the Justice in the bench memo from his clerk George Niebank. See Memorandum from CGN, "Presidential Seizure Power," May 8, 1952, in the Robert H. Jackson papers, Library of Congress, Manuscript Division, Box 176, at 4 ("If there are statutory alternatives, might it be said that, as a matter of law, there can be no such necessity as to authorize or excuse seizure by Executive Order alone? I should think that an entirely reasonable, sensible, and workable solution").
3. Congress sometimes relies on the Youngstown concurrence to restrict executive authority to the Article II core. The Iran-Contra Affair is one example. There Congress prohibited military aid to opponents of the Nicaraguan government. See House Select Comm. to Investigate Covert Arms Transactions with Iran and Senate Select Comm. on Secret Military Assistance to Iran and the Nicaraguan Opposition, *Report of the Congressional Comms. Investigating the Iran-Contra Affair*, 100th Cong., 1st Sess., S. Rept. 216, H. Rept. 433, 471–72 (1987) (discussing the Youngstown concurrence and its application to that scandal). The Reagan Administration defied Congress and secretly gave military aid until the covert operation was exposed. Likewise, the 1978 House Conference Report on FISA (Foreign Intelligence Surveillance Act) explained that the "intent of the conferees is to apply the standard set forth in Justice Jackson's concurring opinion" and limit the President to whatever Article II authority he might have to conduct wiretapping plus what FISA confers. H.R. Conf. Rep. No. 95-1720, at 35, reprinted in 1978 U.S.C.C.A.N. 4048, 4064; see S. Rep. No. 95-604, at 64, reprinted in 1978 U.S.C.C.A.N. 3996 (same); see also Foreign Intelligence Surveillance Act, Pub. L. 95-511, 92 Stat. 1783 (1978). The National Emergencies Act was also enacted to establish that the President could not invoke emergency powers on his own. See Frank Church, "Ending Emergency Government," *American Bar Association Journal* 63, no. 2 (1977), 199; National Emergencies Act, Pub. L. No. 94-112, 90 Stat. 1255 (1976). An interesting thought experiment is whether Congress could enact a general statute stating that all powers not delegated to the President or exclusively in his possession may not be exercised by him. In other words, can Congress eliminate the zone of twilight in one law? A statute giving the President all legislative powers would run into constitutional objections on nondelegation grounds. But the same is not true for a law that prohibits the President from exercising any (or most) legislative powers, as that would not be delegating anything.
4. Cf. Michael McConnell, *The President Who Would Not Be King: Executive Power Under the Constitution* (Princeton, NJ: Princeton University Press, 2020), 283 ("The word 'will' points to what Congress *wants*, when all that should matter is what Congress has *enacted*").
5. See Youngstown Sheet and Tube Co. v. Sawyer, 343 U.S. 579, 701–703 (1952) (Vinson, C.J., dissenting).
6. See McConnell, *The President Who Would Not Be King*, 283 ("The concurrence lends legitimacy to the notion that Congress's failure to enact a measure authorizing presidential action can be interpreted as expressing disapproval"). Footnote 8 concurred with the "analysis, history, and application" of the Taft-Hartley Act in the opinion of the Court and in the concurrences of Justice Frankfurter and Justice Burton. All three opinions relied on Congress's rejection of executive seizure authority in the Taft-Hartley debate, as Jackson must have also done.
7. Jackson Papers, Box 176, May 8 Draft at 2.
8. See Youngstown, 343 U.S. at 670–672 (Vinson, C.J., dissenting).
9. President Truman's action could be defended on the ground that Congress expressed no view on the steel seizure itself, but that is not quite correct. The Senate did reject a supplemental appropriation providing money to the Commerce Department to run the mills. See C. P. Trussell, "Senate Bars Fund for Steel Seizure, Defying President," *New York Times* (Apr. 22, 1952), at 1. But that had no meaningful impact because the firms were paying for the operations. See Maeva Marcus, *Truman and the Steel Seizure Case: The Limits of Presidential Power* (Durham, NC: Duke University Press, 1994), 99.
10. Kristen E. Eichensehr, "The *Youngstown* Canon: Vetoed Bills and the Separation of Powers," *Duke Law Journal* 70 (2021), 1247–48.
11. Harry S. Truman, Veto of the Taft-Hartley Labor Bill (June 20, 1947), in 1947 *Harry S. Truman, Containing the Public Messages, Speeches, and Statements of the President* (Washington, DC: Government Printing Office, 1961–1966), 288–298.

12. Chapter 11 notes than an exception might be warranted for vetoes of attempts to repeal declarations of national emergencies.
13. 295 U.S. 602 (1935); 272 U.S. 52 (1926).
14. I will not attempt to reconcile those decisions here. Chapter 8 pointed out that Justice Jackson also (confusingly) cited the same cases for Category Two.
15. See Jackson Papers, Box 176, May 8 Draft at 2 ("The struggle of Andrew Johnson with Congress over the Tenure of Office Act is an historic example of a contest between the two branches to control the same subject matter"); Gerard N. Magliocca, *American Founding Son: John Bingham and the Invention of the Fourteenth Amendment* (New York: NYU Press, 2013), 138, 148–150. Myers declared (in dictum) that the Act was unconstitutional.
16. See Jackson Papers, Box 176, May 7 Draft at 2. A diagonal line through the typewritten passage indicates a deletion.
17. From a structural perspective, the presidential veto is fascinating because the power is granted in Article I rather than Article II. The inference could therefore be drawn that this makes the veto power concurrent, though perhaps only in the sense that Congress may override a veto with a two-thirds vote of each House.
18. Jackson Papers, Box 176, May 8 Draft at 3.
19. See ibid., May 22 Draft at 4.
20. 603 U.S. 593, 607–609 (2024).
21. Chapter 14 discusses Trump v. United States at greater length.
22. Dennis J. Hutchinson, *The Man Who Once Was Whizzer White: A Portrait of Justice Byron R. White* (New York: Free Press, 1998), 363.
23. See U.S. Const., art II, § 2, cl. 1; McConnell, *The President Who Would Not Be King*, 280 ("The third paragraph is misleading because it disregards the existence of prerogative powers, such as those listed in Article II, Section 2. . . . Either the Constitution gives the President the claimed prerogative power or it does not").
24. See, e.g., Patricia L. Bellia, "Executive Power in *Youngstown*'s Shadow," *Constitutional Commentary* 19 (2002), 93 ("[T]he notion that presidential powers 'fluctuate' is misleading. The Constitution either grants the President a particular power or it does not").
25. Jackson added that the principle that the President possesses only delegated powers was not open to question "at least in the courts." This was a nod to his argument in Korematsu that the elected branches or the military might be required in dire circumstances to take actions that the courts could not accept but should not review.
26. U.S. Const., art. II, § 1, cl. 1.
27. Jackson added that some of the enumerated items were "trifling," though it is unclear which parts of Article II he was referring to.
28. In his first draft, Jackson wrote: "The argument that the President possesses all power that is not expressly taken from him by the Constitution is a complete legal and historical perversion which may have been entertained by some political figures but, as far as I know, has never had the endorsement of any responsible legal officer of the Government." Jackson Papers, Box 176, May 7 Draft, Sovereignty Insert at 3.
29. See Jackson Papers, Box 176, May 8 Draft at 6. The final version was toned down: "[I]f we seek instruction from our own times, we can match it only from the executive powers in those governments we disparagingly describe as totalitarian."
30. Jackson Papers, Box 176, May 7 Draft at Sovereignty Insert at 3.
31. See Akhil Reed Amar, *The Law of the Land: A Grand Tour of Our Constitutional Republic* (New York: Basic Books, 2015), 74 ("Jackson did not shine at textual analysis in this opinion. At one point, he botched a key clause—the opening sentence of Article II, vesting executive power in the president—and needlessly undercut his own conclusions"); ibid. at 322 n.21 (explaining this point); McConnell, *The President Who Would Not Be King*, 258 ("Justice Jackson was right to reject the argument for unlimited executive power, but not right to reject the substantive reading of the Vesting Clause").
32. My discussion of the Vesting Clause draws mainly from Julian Davis Mortenson, "The Executive Power Clause," *University of Pennsylvania Law Review* 168 (2020), 1269–1367.
33. U.S. Const., art. I, § 1.
34. But see Richard Primus, "Herein of 'Herein Granted': Why Article I's Vesting Clause Does Not Support the Doctrine of Enumerated Powers," *Constitutional Commentary* 35, no. 3 (2020), 301–44 (raising objections to attributing that meaning to "herein granted" for Article I and Article II).

35. See U.S. Const., art. II, § 2, cl. 2; ibid. § 3. The Commander-in-Chief Clause confers foreign-policy power in some instances, but that does not solve the enumeration shortfall.
36. McConnell, *The President Who Would Not Be King*, 236. A similar argument applies to domestic policy, though I need not go into detail on that point.
37. Hamilton made the claim in one of his 1793 Pacificus essays defending President Washington's Neutrality Proclamation. See Jonathan Gienapp, *The Second Creation: Fixing the Constitution in the Founding Era* (Cambridge, MA: Belknap Press, 2018), 254–255. Footnote 1 in the concurrence dismissed this essay as part of the historical sources that "cancel each other."
38. See U.S. Const., art. II, § 2, cl. 1.
39. Jackson Papers, Box 176, May 8 Draft at 4.
40. Jackson Papers, Box 176, May 22 Draft at 7. By then, Jackson had abandoned his earlier position that the Vesting Clause conferred some executive power in favor of his final view that the text merely stated that the enumerated powers belonged to the President. In the final opinion, Jackson also moved the line about "no beginning or no end" to reject the doctrine of inherent emergency powers.
41. See Mortenson, "Executive Power Clause," 1274–1279 (summarizing three schools of thought on the scope of the Vesting Clause and then endorsing the view that the provision gives the President the power to execute the law); see also McConnell, *The President Who Would Not Be King*, 257–258 ("[T]he Solicitor General led Justice Jackson astray in *Youngstown* when he invoked the Vesting Clause in support of an executive order seizing militarily-significant private property without statutory authority. No plausible reading of the term 'executive power' could support that result").
42. See Youngstown, 343 U.S. at 610–611 (Frankfurter, J., concurring).
43. The application of this idea in Youngstown would hinge on the idea—emphasized by Justice Douglas in his concurrence—that the seizure was a constitutional taking and that takings authority must come from the legislature.
44. See U.S. Const., art. II, § 3. The best recent article on the Take Care Clause is Ethan J. Leib, Jed Handelsman Shugerman, and Andrew Kent, "Faithful Execution and Article II," *Harvard Law Review* 132 (2019), 2111–2192.
45. See McConnell, *The President Who Would Not Be King*, 288–289 ("In taking care that the law be faithfully executed, the President is limited not only to the goals of the statutes but to the means").
46. Attorney General Jackson cited the Take Care Clause as a justification for the North American Aviation seizure, but also claimed that some unspecified statutes supported the President's action.
47. Youngstown, 343 U.S. 701 (Vinson, C.J., dissenting) (quotation marks omitted). The Chief Justice quoted President Benjamin Harrison for the "central idea" point.
48. Ibid. at 709 (Vinson, C.J., dissenting); see ibid. at 703 ("[T]he single Presidential purpose disclosed on this record is to faithfully execute the laws by acting in an emergency to maintain the status quo, thereby preventing collapse of the legislative programs until Congress could act. The President's action served the same purposes as a judicial stay entered to maintain the status quo in order to preserve the jurisdiction of a court").
49. Ibid. at 688 (Vinson, C.J., dissenting) (quoting TR's autobiography).

Chapter 10

1. Youngstown Sheet & Tube Co. v. Sawyer, 343 U.S. 579, 591 (1952) (reproducing the text of Executive Order No. 10340).
2. U.S. Const., art. II, § 2, c. 1. For a recent wide-ranging discussion of the clause, see Saikrishna Bangalore Prakesh, "Deciphering the Commander-in-Chief Clause," *Yale Law Journal* 133 (2023), 1–98.
3. See; Michael Stokes Paulsen, "Youngstown Goes to War," *Constitutional Commentary* 19, no. 1 (2002), 216; see also Amanda L. Tyler, "Judicial Review in Times of Emergency: From the Founding Through the COVID-19 Pandemic," *Virginia Law Review* 109, no. 3 (2023), 521 (stating that one possible explanation for the Court's refusal to defer to the President in *Youngstown* was "that with the onset of the Cold War, many Court members understood war to take on a new and boundless dimension such that the Court itself should evolve too. Justice Jackson's opinion suggests that this concern weighed heavily on his mind. (Perhaps his time in Nuremberg also influenced his thinking.)").

4. See Garry Wills, *Bomb Power: The Modern Presidency and the National Security State* (New York: Penguin Press, 2010).
5. Ibid. at 3.
6. Harry S. Truman, "Radio and Television Address to the American People on the Need for Government Operation of Steel Mills" (Apr. 8, 1952), in 1952–53 *Harry S. Truman, Containing the Public Messages, Speeches, and Statements of the President* (Washington, DC: Government Printing Office, 1961–1966), 246 [hereinafter Truman Papers]. Atomic energy was a euphemism for atomic bombs, as there were no nuclear power plants at the time. Proof of this comes from the fact that Truman's discussion was sandwiched by a reference to bombs "going directly to our soldiers" and "engines for the Air Force planes."
7. See Brief for Petitioners in Youngstown, 343 U.S. at 41–43.
8. *Yes, Prime Minister*, episode 1, "The Grand Design," aired on Jan. 6, 1986, on BBC 1.
9. See Select Draft Law Cases, 245 U.S. 366 (1918) (affirming the constitutionality of federal conscription); see also Jacobson v. Massachusetts, 197 U.S. 11, 29 (1905) (upholding a state compulsory-vaccination law in part because a person "may be compelled, by force if need be, against his will and without regard to his personal wishes or his pecuniary interests, or even his religious or political convictions, to take his place in the ranks of the army of his country, and risk the chance of being shot down in its defense").
10. Buck v. Bell, 274 U.S. 200, 207 (1927).
11. See Youngstown, 343 U.S. at 709 (Vinson, C.J., dissenting).
12. The literature on the Cuban Missile Crisis is vast. For one perspective, see Evan Thomas, *Robert Kennedy: His Life* (New York: Simon & Schuster, 2000), 209–229.
13. See Atomic Energy Act of 1946, Pub. L. 79-585, 60 Stat. 755; Wills, *Bomb Power*, 31.
14. National Security Act of 1947, Pub. L. 80-2534, 61 Stat. 495; see Harold Hongju Koh, *The National Security Constitution* (New Haven, CT: Yale University Press, 1990), 100 ("Together with Justice Jackson's concurring opinion in *Youngstown*, that framework statute would help to shape the National Security Constitution into its current form").
15. See National Security Act of 1947, §§ 102, 202. Congress can waive this requirement with respect to the Secretary of Defense, and did so in 1950 so that George Marshall could serve in that role during the Korean War.
16. See Maeva Marcus, *Truman and the Steel Seizure Case: The Limits of Presidential Power* (Durham, NC: Duke University Press, 1994), 1–2; David McCullough, *Truman* (New York: Simon & Schuster, 1992), 789. One possible explanation for that omission was that doing so might weaken the nuclear deterrent by implying that congressional authorization was required to use the ultimate weapon. See Wills, *Bomb Power*, 105–108.
17. Chapter 2 recounts the exchange between the solicitor general and Justice Jackson at oral argument.
18. See Mary L. Dudziak, "The Gloss of War: Revisiting the Korean War's Legacy," *Michigan Law Review* 122 (2023), 194.
19. The Robert H. Jackson papers, Library of Congress, Manuscript Division, Box 176, May 22 Draft at 9.
20. See Jackson Papers, June 2 Draft at 9. The Justice also added that "a state of war may exist without a formal declaration."
21. Footnote 10, which was largely copied from the Bell Memo, noted how much things had changed since President Jefferson's cautious approach to the unilateral use of force during the undeclared war against the Barbary pirates. But Jackson did not embrace Jefferson's view.
22. Americans now commonly refer to the "Korean War," even though there was no formal war declaration. See Dudziak, "Gloss of War," 195 (citing subsequent Supreme Court cases that described the conflict as the "Korean War"); ibid. at 196–203 (discussing subsequent executive practice).
23. See, e.g., Authorization for Use of Military Force, Pub. L. 107-40, 115 Stat. 224 (2001) (authorizing use of force against anyone involved in the September 11, 2001, terrorist attacks).
24. A war declaration constitutes a Category One authorization from Congress. For an early discussion of this issue, see Brown v. United States, 12 U.S. (8 Cranch) 110 (1814) (Marshall, C.J.).
25. "Legal Authorities Supporting the Activities of the National Security Agency Described by the President," 30 Op. O.L.C. 1, 40 (2006).
26. Jackson Papers, Box 176, May 8 draft (unpaginated).

27. U.S. Const., art I, § 8, cl. 12 & 13. The examples discussed in the concurrence are not the only ones. For a comprehensive discussion, see Michael W. McConnell, *The President Who Would Not Be King: Executive Power Under the Constitution* (Princeton, NJ: Princeton University Press, 2020), 188–212.
28. See An Act Declaring the Rights and Liberties of the Subject and Settling the Succession of the Crown, 1689, 1 W. and M., Sess. 2, ch. 2 (condemning King James II for "levying money for and to the use of the Crown by pretense of prerogative for other time and in other manner than the same was granted by Parliament" and "raising and keeping a standing army within the kingdom in time of peace without consent of Parliament").
29. See, e.g., William Howard Taft, "Veto Message" (Aug. 15, 1912), in *A Compilation of the Messages and Papers of the Presidents*, ed. James D. Richardson (New York: Bureau of National Literature, 1922), vol. 16, 7752 (stating that the veto involved "one of the great supply bills necessary for the maintenance of the government").
30. See U.S. Const., amend. III ("No Soldiers shall, in time of peace be quartered in any house, without the consent of the Owner, nor in time of war, but in a manner to be prescribed by law"). Today the Third Amendment is read more often as a privacy guarantee rather than as a statement about the relationship between civil and military power. See Griswold v. Connecticut, 381 U.S. 479, 484 (1965).
31. In an early draft, Jackson played with the idea that the President could requisition beef for his troops, "but it would be a different question whether he could requisition farms and impress farm labor and cowboys into service to assure future supplies of beef." Jackson Papers, Box 176, May 8 draft at 2. At oral argument, Justice Frankfurter passed Jackson a note asking, "[T]ell me whether the President could commandeer men to run the seized plants." The note is in Justice Jackson's Youngstown case file. I thank Brad Snyder for confirming that the unsigned note was from Justice Frankfurter.
32. U.S. Const., art I, § 8, cl. 14. The quotation marks in Jackson's opinion are incorrect, but I have not changed them in the text.
33. U.S. Const., art I, § 8, cl. 14.
34. The concurrence cited the First Ku Klux Klan Act and the Civil Rights Act of 1866 in footnote 12, but the Military Reconstruction Acts more generally involved robust congressional direction to the President about using the military within the former Confederacy after the Civil War.
35. Posse Comitatus Act, Pub. L. 45-263, 20 Stat. 152 (1878).
36. Jackson Papers, Box 176, May 8 draft at 3.
37. See, e.g., "Authority to Use United States Military Forces in Somalia," 16 Op. O.L.C. 6, 10 (1992); "Extraterritorial Effect of the Posse Comitatus Act," 13 O.L.C. 321, 334 (1989); "The President and the War Power: South Vietnam and the Cambodian Sanctuaries," 1 Op. O.L.C. 321, 325 (1970). Justice Jackson used the phrase "widest latitude of interpretation" twice in the concurrence. The other use of that language came in his formulation of Category 1, where he said that the President's actions would receive "the widest latitude of judicial interpretation." When the Supreme Court stayed a District Court opinion blocking the US Navy from taking adverse actions against personnel who refused to receive the COVID-19 vaccine, Justice Kavanaugh concurred with a quote of Justice Jackson's "outside world" language. See Austin v. U.S. Navy Seals 1–26, 142 S. Ct. 301 (2022) (Kavanaugh, J., concurring).
38. "Training of British Flying Students in the United States," 40 Op. Att'y Gen. 58, 62 (1941). By contrast, Jackson said that when the military "is turned inward, not because of rebellion but because of a lawful economic struggle between industry and labor, it should have no such indulgence."
39. War Powers Act, Pub. L. 93-148, 87 Stat. 555 (1973).
40. Presidents sometimes invoke their position as commander in chief as a persuasive rhetorical device ("Your Commander in Chief needs your vote").
41. See Declaration of Independence, para. 2 (U.S. 1776).
42. See Massachusetts Const. of 1780, art. XVII.
43. Ex Parte Milligan, 71 U.S. (4 Wall.) 2, 124–25 (1866).
44. For a broad overview of that dispute, see McCullough, *Truman*, 814–817, 823–824, 832–834; see also Robert Caro, *Master of the Senate: The Years of Lyndon Johnson* (New York: Knopf, 2002), 367–382 (chronicling the Senate hearings into MacArthur's dismissal).
45. McCullough, *Truman*, 836.

46. Harry S. Truman, *Memoirs*, vol 2: *Years of Trial and Hope* (1955; New York: Simon and Schuster, 1992), 441–442.
47. Harry S. Truman, "Statement and Order by the President on Relieving General MacArthur of His Commands" (April 11, 1951), in 1951 Truman Papers, 222–223.
48. See Caro, *Master of the Senate*, 368–370; McCulloch, *Truman*, 844–846.
49. General MacArthur's removal can be seen as the culmination of the post–World War II effort to ensure civilian control over atomic weapons and the military establishment. MacArthur was out of the country running Japan during this entire period. Thus, one can understand why he did not appreciate this point or why in his mind the line between civil and military authority might have been blurred.
50. See, e.g., John H. Fenton, "Eisenhower Defeats Taft, Kefauver Wins over Truman in New Hampshire's Primary," *New York Times* (March 12, 1952), at 1.
51. See Dwight D. Eisenhower, "Farewell Address," reprinted in part in *Lend Me Your Ears: Great Speeches in History*, 2nd ed., ed. William Safire (New York: Norton, 2004), 433.

Chapter 11

1. Letter from Thomas Jefferson to John B. Colvin (Sept. 20, 1810), in *The Life and Selected Writings of Thomas Jefferson*, ed. Adrienne Koch and William Peden (New York: Modern Library, 1993), 556.
2. This chapter uses the phrase "emergency powers," though Justice Jackson pointed out that terms such as "inherent," "implied," "incidental," "plenary," and "war" were used to describe such powers "often interchangeably and without fixed or ascertainable meanings."
3. Cf. Sanford Levinson, "The Rhetoric of the Judicial Opinion," in *Law's Stories: Narrative and Rhetoric in the Law*, ed. Peter Brooks and Paul Gewirtz (New Haven, CT: Yale University Press, 1996), 203 ("Jackson provides a magnificent, inspiring example of how a serious person wrestles with the difficult problem of preserving some notion of liberal democracy in a modern world full of horrendous threats and 'emergencies' calling for vigorous response").
4. As this book goes to press, the Trump Administration has many emergency requests pending in the Supreme Court.
5. For a perceptive analysis of emergency powers, see Amanda L. Tyler, "Judicial Review in Times of Emergency: From the Founding Through the COVID-19 Pandemic," *Virginia Law Review* 109, no. 3 (2023), 521; see also Bruce Ackerman, *Before the Next Attack: Preserving Civil Liberties in an Age of Terrorism* (New Haven, CT: Yale University Press, 2006).
6. Jackson invoked Hitler in other opinions. See American Communications Ass'n, C.I.O. v. Douds, 339 U.S. 382, 430 (1950); (Jackson, J., concurring and dissenting in part); Terminiello v. City of Chicago, 337 U.S. 1, 23 (1949) (Jackson, J., dissenting); West Virginia State Bd. of Educ. v. Barnette, 319 U.S. 624, 627 (1943).
7. 39 Op. Att'y Gen. 343, 348–364 (1939). This was not an opinion of the attorney general, as the attorney general could not issue a formal opinion upon congressional request. See ibid. at 344–48. Some of the emergency powers in the report could be invoked only if Congress formally declared war. Another set could be triggered only if Congress declared a national emergency. Other authorities could be used only if the President declared a national emergency.
8. A review of the list shows that only about one-quarter of the emergency laws were enacted before 1916.
9. The Robert H. Jackson papers, Library of Congress, Manuscript Division, May 22 Draft, at 28.
10. Terminiello, 337 U.S. 1, 37 (1949) (Jackson, J., dissenting).
11. One could argue that the Justices who joined Korematsu and Youngstown (namely, Justices Black, Frankfurter, and Douglas) did so because they saw World War II as a life-or-death struggle and the Korean War as something less important.
12. Lend-Lease Act, Pub. L. 77-11, 55 Stat. 32 (1941).
13. Jackson Papers, May 22 Draft, at 24. Jackson's terminology was imprecise in that he was describing a concurrent resolution rather than a joint resolution. A legislative veto can also come from only one house of Congress; see INS v. Chadha, 462 U.S. 919, 923 (1983). But Jackson did not mention this option.
14. Jackson Papers, May 22 draft, at 22.
15. See Jackson Papers, May 29 draft, at 20.

16. Frank Church, "Ending Emergency Government," *American Bar Association Journal* 63, no. 2 (1977), 199; see National Emergencies Act, Pub. L. No. 94-112, 90 Stat. 1255 (1976); see also Elizabeth Goitein, "The Alarming Scope of the President's Emergency Powers," *The Atlantic*, Jan./Feb. 2019, https://www.theatlantic.com/magazine/archive/2019/01/presidential-emergency powers/576418/ (providing a thoughtful overview of the Act and possible reforms).
17. The Act provides, among other things, that the President must declare a national emergency, must specify which emergency powers he seeks to use, must update Congress periodically on any emergency expenditures, and may not exercise the powers invoked beyond one year without formally reaffirming the existence of an emergency.
18. National Emergencies Act of 1976, § 202. This section of the NEA was repealed by Congress after the Chadha decision.
19. Church, "Emergency Government," at 199.
20. 462 U.S. 919 (1983).
21. See Chadha, 462 U.S. at 976 n.14 (citing Jackson's 1953 Harvard Law Review article). Perhaps Chadha would have come out differently if Justice Jackson's Youngstown concurrence had made the legislative veto a linchpin of its analysis. After all, Chadha ended by paraphrasing Justice Jackson's finale. See ibid. at 959 ("With all the obvious flaws of delay, untidiness, and potential for abuse, we have not yet found a better way to preserve freedom than by making the exercise of power subject to the carefully crafted restraints spelled out in the Constitution.").
22. See ibid. at 971 (White, J., dissenting).
23. Ibid. at 968 (White, J., dissenting).
24. See ibid. at 978 (White, J., dissenting) (quoting the concurrence's passage on "[t]he art of actual governing").
25. See 50 U.S.C. § 1622(a)(1) (2018); Kristen E. Eichensehr, "The *Youngstown* Canon: Vetoed Bills and the Separation of Powers," *Duke Law Journal* 70 (2021), 1296.
26. See, e.g., David B. Froomkin, "The Nondelegation Doctrine and the Structure of the Executive," *Yale Journal on Regulation* 41 (2024), 102.
27. See, e.g., David Landau, "Rethinking the Federal Emergency Powers Regime," *Ohio State Law Journal* 84 (2023), 603–676.
28. See ibid. at 622–624; see generally Goitein, "Alarming Scope."
29. See Brief for the United States, Currin v. Wallace, 306 U.S. 1 (No. 275), 1938 WL 63,794, 46–47 (stating that in the Supreme Court's non-delegation cases "[t]he executive was there endowed with nonexecutive functions. The legislative power was there delegated to the President . . .").
30. See Amy Coney Barrett, "Suspension and Delegation," *Cornell Law Review* 99 (2014), 251–326. Professor Barrett became Justice Barrett in 2020. Professor Barrett did not discuss Youngstown in her article and was writing at a point when Chadha ruled out the possibility of using a legislative veto to constrain contingent suspension authority.
31. See U.S. Const., art. I, § 9, cl. 2; Barrett, "Suspension and Delegation," 299.
32. For example, the Suspension Clause is in Article I, not Article II. Recall from Chapter 8 that Jackson discussed Lincoln's suspension as a zone-of-twilight case because the Civil War debate about his action was not clearly resolved.
33. See Barrett, "Suspension and Delegation," 302–8; see also William Blackstone, *Commentaries on the Laws of England* (1765–1769; Chicago: University of Chicago Press, 1979), vol. 1, 132 (stating that "it is not left to the executive power to determine when the danger of the state is so great, as to render [suspension of the writ] expedient").
34. See Barrett, "Suspension and Delegation," 309–310.
35. Ibid. at 317.
36. See Sierra Club v. Trump, 929 F.3d 670, 707 (9th Cir. 2019) (quoting Justice Jackson's concurrence at length as a justification for construing the National Emergencies Act narrowly and denying preliminary relief); cf. Eichensehr, "The *Youngstown* Canon," 1245–1320 (arguing that courts should consider vetoed congressional resolutions seeking to terminate emergencies to interpret the scope of the President's delegated authority narrowly). This also is the one circumstance where courts should adopt Professor Eichensehr's proposal (discussed in Chapter 9) to consider vetoed congressional bills that if enacted would have repealed an emergency declaration when interpreting the President's authority for the same declaration.
37. Slaughter-House Cases, 83 U.S. (16 Wall.) 36, 71 (1873) (describing the Civil War).

38. In 2023, Justice Neil Gorsuch criticized the curtailment of civil liberties during the pandemic and called on Congress to reconsider the National Emergencies Act. See Arizona v. Mayorkas, 143 S. Ct. 1312 (2023) (dismissing the case as moot); ibid. at 1314–1316 (statement of Gorsuch, J.).
39. See *In re* Certified Questions, 958 N.W.2d 1 (2020). The Court was answering questions certified by a federal district court in Michigan.
40. Ibid. at 21; see ibid. at 6 (noting the Emergency Powers of the Governor Act of 1945).
41. Ibid. at 24. The statute gave the Governor emergency power to "promulgate reasonable orders, rules, and regulations as he or she considers necessary to protect life and property." Ibid.
42. See Cameron v. Beshear, 628 S.W. 3d 61, 73 (Ky. 2021); ibid. at 74 n. 17 (citing the Jackson concurrence to refute the Governor's assertion that his state commander-in-chief power gave him unilateral power to take emergency pandemic measures).
43. See ibid. at 67.
44. See Desrosiers v. Governor, 486 Mass. 369 (2020).
45. See ibid. at 384; see also ibid. at 381 (laying out Justice Jackson's three categories).
46. Ibid. at 384. The court added that the state legislature was enacting pandemic measures in conjunction with the governor's actions. See ibid.
47. The Massachusetts opinion did not say expressly that Justice Jackson's concurrence should be read in conjunction with the legislative veto. For a more wooden approach to Jackson's analysis, see Casey v. Lamont, 258 A.3d 647, 664 (Conn. 2021) (upholding the exercise of delegated executive emergency authority during the pandemic with a basic citation to the definition of Category One).
48. See Grisham v. Romero, 483 P.3d 545, 564–65 (N.M. 2021) (Thomson, J., specially concurring).
49. See ibid. at 559.
50. Ibid. at 563; see ibid. at 564 (quoting Justice Jackson's discussion of inherent powers and other vague terminology for that authority).
51. Ibid. at 564. The next quotation in the text comes from the same page of the opinion.

Chapter 12

1. Bruce Ackerman's scholarship is the best in explaining how the presidency evolved into a form very different from the Framers' expectations. See Ackerman, *The Failure of the Founding Fathers: Jefferson, Marshall, and the Rise of Presidential Democracy* (Cambridge, MA: Harvard University Press, 2005).
2. See Rudyard Kipling, "The Old Issue," in *The Collected Poems of Rudyard Kipling*, ed. R. T. Jones (Ware, UK: Wordsworth, 1994), 307–8. The poem was first published in 1899.
3. Walter Bagehot, *The English Constitution* (1873; reprint, New York: Cosimo Classics, 2007), 1. *The English Constitution* is my favorite book on constitutions. It is now better known to Americans because of its central role in an episode from season 1 of *The Crown*, the Netflix series on Queen Elizabeth II.
4. See Patrick Schmidt, "'The Dilemma to a Free People': Justice Robert Jackson, Walter Bagehot, and the Creation of a Conservative Jurisprudence," *Law and History Review* 20, no. 3 (2002), 517–539 (discussing Jackson's notes on Bagehot and their connection to his dissent in Terminiello v. City of Chicago).
5. See John Milton Cooper, Jr., *Woodrow Wilson: A Biography* (New York: Knopf, 2009), 30 (describing Wilson's discovery of Bagehot).
6. See ibid. at 47–49 (quoting Wilson's view that he wanted to "treat the American Constitution as Mr. Bagehot . . . has treated the English Constitution"); see also Wilson, *Congressional Government: A Study in American Politics* (1885; reprint, with a Preface by Walter Lippmann, New York: Meridian, 1956).
7. See Cooper, *Woodrow Wilson*, 201–202, 214. Wilson abandoned press conferences in 1915 (see ibid. at 204), but Roosevelt made them a regular event. See Jackson, *That Man: An Insider's Portrait of Franklin D. Roosevelt*, ed. John Q. Barrett (New York: Oxford University Press, 2003), 160–161 ("Press conferences were a means of communication that he utilized effectively, albeit one of dubious value"). In his posthumously published Godkin Lectures, Justice Jackson also recognized that "a senatorial coalition may break the foreign policy of even an able and strong President like Wilson." Jackson, *The Supreme Court in the American System of Government* (Cambridge, MA: Harvard University Press, 1955), 63.

8. Jackson's book on his work in the Justice Department tells that story well. See *The Struggle for Judicial Supremacy: A Study of a Crisis in American Power Politics* (New York: Knopf, 1941).
9. *That Man*, 159. Jackson described FDR's prose with words that apply to the Justice's best opinions: "[H]e eliminated all long, unfamiliar foreign or technical words and brought the thought into simple, plain words, of Anglo-Saxon origin if possible. He knew the forcefulness of plain Bible English with the American people." Ibid. at 160. Jackson had firsthand knowledge of FDR's writing process because he sometimes helped draft presidential speeches. See ibid.
10. Ibid. at 163.
11. See Jacob E. Cooke, ed., *The Federalist* (Hanover, NH: Wesleyan University Press, 1961), 471–480.
12. One OLC opinion quoted this line to defend the view that a sitting president is not subject to criminal prosecution. See "A Sitting President's Amenability to Indictment and Criminal Prosecution," 24 O.L.C. 222, 247 (2000).
13. Jackson, *American System of Government*, 64.
14. Another aspect of this influence that was unknown to the Framers in 1787 but familiar to Jackson was the President's ability to claim a "mandate" from the voters after winning a landslide victory.
15. Winston S. Churchill, "Chateau Laurier" (Jan. 14, 1952), in *Winston S. Churchill: His Complete Speeches, 1897–1963* (New York: Bowker, 1974), vol. 8, 8223.
16. Constitutional monarchs and ceremonial presidents also possess some reserve executive powers, but that authority is not relevant to Justice Jackson's use of the term.
17. For example, Section 68 of the Australian Constitution states: "The command in chief of the naval and forces of the Commonwealth is vested in the Governor-General as the Queen's representative." Today the Governor-General represents King Charles III.
18. See, e.g., Gerard N. Magliocca, "'Not a Lawyer's Contract': Reflections on FDR's Constitution Day Address," *Journal of American Constitutional History* 1, Winter (2023), 43–82 (describing how Roosevelt used a speech marking the 150th anniversary of the Constitution's proposal to defend the New Deal).
19. See, e.g., Anne O'Hare McCormick, "The Predestined Leader of the Free World," *New York Times* (Nov. 9, 1952), at SM7 ("This is the role to which the President-elect is called"). This phrase was not used to describe the President before World War II.
20. A darker possibility is that Jackson's experience at Nuremberg forced him to think more carefully about how political parties can undermine the law.
21. Jackson, *That Man* at 17.
22. Ibid. at 46. The next quotation comes from the same page of the memoir.
23. Ibid. at 23.
24. For example, FDR tried and failed in 1938 to defeat leading Dixiecrats in the Senate because they were lukewarm supporters of the New Deal. See Susan Dunn, *Roosevelt's Purge: How FDR Fought to Change the Democratic Party* (Cambridge, MA: Harvard University Press, 2010).
25. Daryl J. Levinson and Richard H. Pildes, "Separation of Parties, Not Powers," *Harvard Law Review* 119, no. 8 (2006), 2315. This statement dates from 2006 but is still true today.
26. This is the central theme of the Levinson and Pildes article. In Justice Jackson's day, the issue was more complex because both parties were more ideologically diverse.
27. Jackson, *American System of Government*, 63–64.
28. The only case that has quoted this line was the D.C. Circuit's opinion rejecting Donald Trump's claim of immunity from criminal prosecution. See United States v. Trump, 91 F.4th 1173, 1199 (D.C. Cir. 2024), vacated and remanded by Trump v. United States, 603 U.S. 593 (2024). The criminal immunity issue is more complicated, though, because that can be seen as a limitation on presidential power (in other words, the power of the President to prosecute one of his predecessors).
29. See Clinton Rossiter, *The Supreme Court and the Commander in Chief* (Ithaca, NY: Cornell University Press, 1951), 126–132.
30. See ibid. at 131–32.
31. Ibid. at 126–27. Rossiter also argued that no court is likely to brand the President as unreasonable when assessing an executive action. See ibid. at 131.
32. Ibid. at 131. Rossiter also discussed the atomic bomb on the first page of his book. See ibid. at 1 and n.1 (citing his article on "Constitutional Dictatorship in the Atomic Age").

33. One irony is that Woodrow Wilson's scholarship in the 1880s concluded that the Constitution's "real power" was concentrated in congressional committees. Under that understanding, the President should win close cases. Jackson's opinion can be understood as a response to Wilson's book on *Congressional Government* by pointing out that in the 1950s real power was concentrated in the executive more akin to "Presidential Government."
34. See, e.g., I.N.S. v. Chadha, 462 U.S. 919 (1983); see also Nixon v. Fitzgerald, 457 U.S. 731 (1982) (holding that ex-Presidents may not be held civilly liable for their official actions). To be fair, some post-Watergate cases rejected broad claims of presidential power, although without citing the relevant tiebreaker language from Justice Jackson's opinion.
35. For example, most of the current Justices (as of 2025) served in the executive branch. Chief Justice Roberts worked in the Justice Department before entering private practice. Justice Thomas was the head of the Equal Employment Opportunity Commission. Justice Alito was a US Attorney. Justice Kagan served as solicitor general. Justice Gorsuch worked in the Justice Department. And Justice Kavanaugh served in the White House under President George W. Bush. None of the current Justices served in Congress.
36. See the Robert H. Jackson papers, Library of Congress, Manuscript Division, Box 133, "Draft Opinion: Ex Parte Endo" (stating that failure to reject the idea that freedom could be denied by prejudice would betray "Ancient rights, unnoticed as the breath we draw, / Leave to live by no man's leave, underneath the law").
37. Chapter 1 discussed this reference and noted where video of Justice Jackson's opening statement can be found. Jackson also quoted Kipling in his summation. See Jackson, "Closing Address to the Nuremberg Tribunal," at https://avalon.law.yale.edu/imt/07-26-46.asp ("I must, as Kipling put it, 'splash at a ten-league canvas with brushes of comet's hair'").
38. "The Old Issue" was published shortly after the outbreak of the Boer War and was ostensibly about that conflict. But the poem says almost nothing about the war.
39. See John Q. Barrett, "Heard July 5th on the National Mall: An Impending Supreme Court Justice's Independence Day Speech," at 1, 7, at https://thejacksonlist.com/wp content/uploads/2019/08/20190705-Jackson-List-July-5-National-Mall.pdf ("As Kipling has said, 'Though all we knew depart, / The old Commandments stand:— / 'In courage keep your heart, / In strength lift up your hand'").
40. See David M. O'Brian, *Justice Robert H. Jackson's Unpublished Opinion in* Brown v. Board: *Conflict, Compromise, and Constitutional Interpretation* (Lawrence: University Press of Kansas, 2017), at 7 (stating that this line came from "The Winners").
41. See Michelson v. United States, 335 U.S. 469, 478 n.13 (1948) ("The law apparently ignores the existence of such human ciphers as Kipling's Tomlinson, of whom no ill is reported but no good can be recalled").
42. "The Old Issue," at 307; see A. E. Dick Howard, ed., *Magna Carta: Text and Commentary* (Charlottesville: University of Virginia Press, 1998), 7–8 [hereinafter *Magna Carta*].
43. "The Old Issue," at 307. See William Safire, ed., *Lend Me Your Ears: Great Speeches in History*, 2nd ed. (New York: Norton, 2004), 397–400, for an edited version of Charles I's speech from the Whitehall scaffold before his beheading.
44. "The Old Issue," at 307. "Ell by all" is a poetic expression that means "little by little."
45. This portion of "The Old Issue" appears as an epigraph to this book.
46. Ibid. at 308.
47. See An Act Declaring the Rights and Liberties of the Subject and Settling the Succession of the Crown, 1689, 1 W. and M., Sess. 2, ch. 2 ("That levying money for or to the use of the Crown by pretense of prerogative, without grant of Parliament, for longer time, or in other manner than the same is or shall be granted, is illegal").
48. See ibid. ("That the subjects which are Protestants may have arms for their defense suitable to their conditions and as allowed by law"); see also U.S. Const., amend. II ("A well regulated Militia, being necessary to the security of a free State, the right of the people to keep and bear Arms, shall not be infringed").
49. See, e.g., Steve Pincus, *1688: The First Modern Revolution* (New Haven, CT: Yale University Press, 2009); Lois G. Schwoerer, *The Declaration of Rights, 1689* (Baltimore: Johns Hopkins University Press, 1981).
50. "The Old Issue," at 308.
51. Ibid.; see *Magna Carta* at 15 (describing this guarantee).
52. "The Old Issue," at 308. The next quotation in the text also comes from this page.
53. Jackson Papers, Box 176, May 22nd Draft, at 32.

Chapter 13

1. Edward S. Corwin, "The Steel Seizure Case: A Judicial Brick Without Straw," *Columbia Law Review* 53, no. 1 (1953), 63.
2. Louis L. Jaffe, "Mr. Justice Jackson," *Harvard Law Review* 68, no. 6 (1955), 989 n.199.
3. See Schlesinger, *The Imperial Presidency* (Boston: Houghton Mifflin, 1973; reprinted with a new epilogue, 1989). Schlesinger quoted Justice Jackson's opinion, as is discussed later in this chapter.
4. The only significant judicial reference to Jackson's Youngstown concurrence prior to 1968 was in a dissent by Judge David Bazelon. See Briehl v. Dulles, 248 F.2d 561, 588, 594–595 (D.C. Cir. 1957) (Bazelon, J., dissenting) (arguing that the Secretary of State lacked the power to deny passports to alleged communists), reversed by Kent v. Dulles, 357 U.S. 116 (1958). In 1968, Justice William O. Douglas cited the concurrence in a dissent from the denial of a petition for a writ of certiorari asking the Supreme Court to declare unconstitutional the draft for the Vietnam War. See Holmes v. United States, 391 U.S. 936, 944 n.6 (1968) (Douglas, J., dissenting from denial of certiorari). Scholarly citations to the concurrence in this period were only occasional.
5. See Earl Warren, "The Bill of Rights and the Military," *New York University Law Review* 37 (1962), 199. The Madison Lecture at NYU is one of the most prestigious legal lecture series.
6. See, e.g., John A. Farrell, *Richard Nixon: The Life* (New York: Doubleday, 2017), 372 ("Nixon was the first first-term president since Zachary Taylor, in 1849, to take office with both houses of Congress in the hands of the opposition party").
7. See New York Times Co. v. United States, 403 U.S. 713, 731–739 (White, J., concurring) (1971) (concluding that the President was implicitly prohibited by Acts of Congress from obtaining a prior restraint on publication); Walter Isaacson, *Kissinger: A Biography* (New York: Simon & Schuster, 1992), 171–179; Note, "Impoundment of Funds," *Harvard Law Review* 86 (1973), 1505–1535.
8. One internal feature may also be necessary for judicial glory. Classic opinions, like classic literature, draw strength from ambiguity. Both can have a broader appeal if they have a protean quality that accommodates many perspectives. Professor Neal Katyal wrote that Justice Jackson's "framework has become the gold standard, perhaps because its all-things-to-all-people quality can provide arguments favoring any branch of government under many circumstances." Katyal, "*Hamdan v. Rumsfeld*: The Legal Academy Goes to Practice," *Harvard Law Review* 120 (2006), 99.
9. For a fine discussion of how certain dissents become canonical because they aid a court in overruling precedent, see Richard A. Primus, "Canon, Anti-Canon, and Judicial Dissent," *Duke Law Journal* 48 (1998), 243–303.
10. For example, the Supreme Court's plurality opinion in Perry v. United States is a subtle discussion of the constitutional questions raised by the decision to abandon the gold standard in 1933 that included the only judicial analysis of Section Four of the Fourteenth Amendment. See Perry v. United States, 294 U.S. 330 (1935) (opinion of Hughes, C.J.). No similar currency crisis has occurred, though, so the opinion remains obscure.
11. See Richard A. Posner, *Cardozo: A Study in Reputation* (Chicago: University of Chicago Press, 1990), 42 ("Cardozo's name on an opinion has a halo effect"). Justice Frankfurter's Youngstown concurrence, for instance, suffers from the handicap that his modern reputation is not strong.
12. Infamous opinions can be written by obscure judges. See Plessy v. Ferguson, 163 U.S. 537 (1896) (upholding racial segregation). Plessy was written by Justice Henry Billings Brown, who today is known (if at all) only for this opinion.
13. Since Jackson's mantra was "He who travels fastest travels alone," it should not be surprising that he sometimes fell into the latter category.
14. See Plessy, 163 U.S. at 552–564 (Harlan, J., dissenting). Justice Harlan wrote other influential (or prophetic) lone dissents. See Maxwell v. Dow, 176 U.S. 581, 605–617 (1900) (Harlan, J., dissenting) (arguing that the first eight amendments applied to the states); United States v. E. C. Knight, 156 U.S. 1, 18–46 (1895) (Harlan, J., dissenting) (articulating a broad view of the commerce power); Civil Rights Cases, 109 U.S. 3, 33–62 (1883) (Harlan, J., dissenting) (rejecting the Court's view that Congress lacked the power to enact the Civil Rights Act of 1875).
15. See Lochner v. New York, 198 U.S. 45, 74–76 (1905) (Holmes, J., dissenting).
16. See Korematsu v. United States, 323 U.S. 214, 242–248 (1944) (Jackson, J., dissenting).
17. 442 F.2d 159 (3d Cir. 1971); see ibid. at 163–164.

18. Ibid. at 167–168.
19. Ibid. at 168.
20. See ibid. at 168–171; see also ibid. at 171 ("If such action has not been authorized by Congress (Justice Jackson's first category), at the least it falls within the second category. . . . Particularly is this so when Congress, aware of Presidential action with respect to federally assisted construction projects since June of 1963, has continued to make appropriations for such projects").
21. See ibid. at 171–175.
22. 451 F.2d 26 (1st Cir. 1971); see Maeva Marcus, *Truman and the Steel Seizure Case: The Limits of Presidential Power* (Durham, NC: Duke University Press, 1994), 235–236 (discussing the District Court's disposition of the case).
23. Laird, 451 F.2d at 33.
24. Ibid. at 34. The next two quotations in the text also come from this page.
25. Ibid. at 34. Both Contractors and Laird could have reached the same result by following chapter 8's recommendation that Category Two cases should be deemed non-justiciable.
26. One example of the sea change in how scholars thought about the opinion comes from Professor Louis Henkin's well-respected book *Foreign Affairs and the United States Constitution*, 2nd ed. (New York: Clarendon Press, 1996). In the first edition, published in 1972, Professor Henkin said that "Mr. Justice Jackson provided a suggestive formula" in his *Youngstown* concurrence and quoted the three categories. The second edition was revised to say that Justice Jackson's opinion "has become a starting point for constitutional discussion of concurrent powers" (94).
27. A "third-rate burglary attempt" was the infamous initial description of Watergate by President Nixon's press secretary. See Tad Szulc, "Ex-G.O.P. Aide Linked to Political Raid," *New York Times*, June 20, 1972, at 24.
28. The literature on Richard Nixon and Watergate is immense; one of the better books is Evan Thomas, *Being Nixon: A Man Divided* (New York: Random House, 2015).
29. 120 Cong. Rec. 8967 (1974) (quoting the second article of impeachment).
30. See ibid. The same can be said about the accusations that President Nixon misused federal agencies such as the IRS to violate the constitutional rights of individuals. See ibid.
31. See United States v. Nixon, 418 U.S. 683 (1974).
32. See Marcus, *Steel Seizure*, 241. The President took the same position before the Supreme Court. See Brief for Respondent, United States v. Nixon, at 86 ("[T]he assertion of privilege by a President is necessarily absolute and unreviewable").
33. Caraley, Demetrios James, and Frances Penn, "Separation of Powers and Executive Privilege: The Watergate Briefs," *Political Science Quarterly* 88, no. 4 (1973), 620.
34. Ibid.
35. Ibid. at 621 n.9.
36. *In Re* Subpoena to Nixon, 360 F. Supp. 1, 9 (D.D.C. 1973). Judge Sirica did not specify that this language came from Justice Jackson's concurrence.
37. Nixon v. Sirica, 487 F.2d 700, 711 (D.C. Cir. 1973) (*en banc*); see ibid. at 715 (quoting the "workable government" point).
38. See, e.g., Akhil Reed Amar, *America's Unwritten Constitution: The Precedents and Principles We Live By* (New York: Basic Books, 2012), 376–377.
39. See Marcus, *Steel Seizure*, 245–246; Seth Stern and Stephen Wermiel, *Justice Brennan: Liberal Champion* (New York: Houghton Mifflin Harcourt, 2010), 379–380.
40. 418 U.S. 683 (1974).
41. One of the conversations disclosed was the "smoking gun" in which President Nixon instructed his chief of staff to order the CIA to tell the FBI to stop its Watergate investigation. This revelation destroyed Nixon's remaining support in Congress and compelled his resignation to avoid certain impeachment and conviction. See Farrell, *Nixon*, 478–479, 529–530.
42. See Nixon, 418 U.S. at 703–707. Justice Rehnquist was recused in Nixon. See ibid. at 716.
43. See ibid. at 702, 707–08, 713–715; see also Trump v. Vance, 591 U.S. 786, 793–797 (2020) (recounting the Burr trial and connecting that episode to the Nixon case and President Trump's claim that he could not be required to answer a criminal subpoena from a state court); Clinton v. Jones, 520 U.S. 681, 695, 699, 703–704 (1997) (responding to points about the Burr trial). The Burr trial was cited by the Supreme Court before Nixon but was not a focal point for analysis.

44. Nixon, 418 U.S. at 707. The Court's first citation to the concurrence came in a footnote in a case decided a month before Nixon. See Old Dominion Branch No. 496, Nat'l Ass'n of Letter Carriers, AFL-CIO v. Austin, 418 U.S. 264, 273 n.5 (1974).
45. Nixon, 418 U.S. at 707.
46. Nixon v. Administrator of Gen. Servs., 433 U.S. 425, 443 (1977).
47. Schlesinger, *Imperial Presidency*, 145.
48. See, e.g., David B. Frohnmeyer, "The Separation of Powers: An Essay on the Vitality of Separation of Powers," *Oregon Law Review* 52 (1973), 219 ("One much-quoted proposal for adjudicating the jurisdiction of the respective branches was articulated by Justice Jackson in the Steel Seizure Case"). Professor Frohnmeyer later served as Oregon's attorney general and as the president of the University of Oregon.
49. Eugene Rostow, "Great Cases Make Bad Law: The War Powers Act," *Texas Law Review* 50, no. 5 (1972), 849, 862–863; see idem. at 857 (referring again to "Justice Jackson's comment about Pharaoh's dream"). See also Norman I. Silber, *Outside In: The Oral History of Guido Calabresi* (New York: Oxford University Press, 2023), vol. 1, 239–240, and vol. 2, 5 (recounting Rostow's deanship).
50. See Matthew Steilen, "Life and Afterlife in the *Steel Seizure Case*," *Buffalo Law Review* 70, no. 2 (2022), 904–05; see also Gerald Gunther, ed., *Cases and Materials on Constitutional Law*, 9th ed. (New York: Foundation Press, 1975), 401–414.
51. Philip B. Kurland, "Justice Robert H. Jackson—Impact on Civil Rights and Civil Liberties: The David C. Baum Memorial Lecture," *University of Illinois Law Review* 1977, 567. Professor Kurland began but never completed a biography of Robert Jackson.
52. For instance, Maeva Marcus's 1977 book on Youngstown did not emphasize Justice Jackson's concurring opinion. And neither did Laurence Tribe's treatise during the 1970s. See Steilen, "Life and Afterlife," 905.
53. See Ethics in Government Act of 1978, Pub. L. 95–521, 92 Stat. 1824 (providing for an independent counsel); Presidential Recordings and Materials Preservation Act, Pub. L. 93–526, 88 Stat. 1695 (1974) (putting President Nixon's papers into federal custody); Congressional Budget and Impoundment Control Act of 1974, Pub. 93–344, 88 Stat. 297 (making clear that the President cannot exercise broad discretion to impound funds); War Powers Act, Pub. L. 93–148, 87 Stat. 555 (1973). The War Powers Act was enacted over President Nixon's veto. See John Hart Ely, "Suppose Congress Wanted a War Powers Act That Worked," *Columbia Law Review* 88, no. 7 (1988), 1389.
54. National Emergencies Act, Pub. L. No. 94–112, 90 Stat. 1255 (1976).
55. Foreign Intelligence Surveillance Act, Pub L. 95–511, 92 Stat. 1783 (1978).
56. 453 U.S. 654 (1981).

Chapter 14

1. See William H. Rehnquist, *The Supreme Court* (New York: Vintage, 2002), 7 (stating that he began his clerkship on February 1, 1952). John Q. Barrett, in a note to the author, points to evidence that Rehnquist misremembered his start date and actually began a week earlier on January 25.
2. Rehnquist's clerkship was complicated, especially with respect to his work on Brown v. Board of Education. For more on Rehnquist's clerkship and on his Brown memo that endorsed Plessy v. Ferguson, see David M. O'Brian, *Justice Robert H. Jackson's Unpublished Opinion in* Brown v. Board (Lawrence: University Press of Kansas, 2017), 56–77; Brad Snyder and John Q. Barrett, "Rehnquist's Missing Letter: A Former Law Clerk's 1955 Thoughts on Justice Jackson and *Brown*," *Boston College Law Review* 53 (2012), 631–660.
3. See Rehnquist, *Supreme Court*, 166–167.
4. See, e.g., William H. Rehnquist, "Constitutional Law and Public Opinion," *Suffolk University Law Review* 20 (1986), 751–769; Rehnquist, "Robert H. Jackson: A Perspective Twenty-Five Years Later," *Albany Law Review* 44 (1980), 533–41. An interview with the Chief Justice about Youngstown can be found at https://www.youtube.com/watch?v=I1M3OORPbJc.
5. 453 U.S. 654 (1981); 487 U.S. 654 (1988); Rehnquist stated that although Justice Jackson "gave both my fellow clerk and me courtesy opportunities to suggest changes and modifications in his concurring opinion, each of us had the good sense to decline the opportunity insofar as any but the most minor changes were concerned." See Rehnquist, "Robert H. Jackson," 538.
6. Trump v. United States, 603 U.S. 593 (2024).

7. See John A. Farrell, *Richard Nixon: The Life.* (New York: Doubleday, 2017), 363–365; "The President and the War Power: South Vietnam and the Cambodian Sanctuaries," 1 Op. O.L.C. 321 (1970). Senator Robert Dole quoted from Rehnquist's OLC opinion (albeit without attribution) during the congressional debate on the War Powers Act. See 119 Cong. Rec. 33,563 (1973) (statement of Sen. Dole).
8. See 1 Op. O.L.C. 321–38 (1970). A separate memo by Rehnquist contended that "Congress has clearly affirmed the President's authority to take all necessary measures to protect U.S. troops in Southeast Asia." "Presidential Authority to Permit Incursion into Communist Sanctuaries in the Cambodia-Vietnam Border Area," 1 Op. O.L.C. 313 (1970); see ibid. at 313–320 (laying out the history of congressional support for the Vietnam War).
9. "Rehnquist's Achilles Heel," *New York Times*, November 14, 1971, at E12. This letter was written by the co-chairs of the Lawyers Committee on American Policy Toward Vietnam, which opposed the war. The next quotation in the text also comes from that page.
10. Rehnquist was confirmed to the seat vacated by the retirement of Justice John Marshall Harlan II, who had filled the seat opened by Justice Jackson's death in 1954.
11. Rehnquist, "Robert H. Jackson," 539. The next quotation in the text comes from this page. Justice Rehnquist cited the concurrence for the first time in the same year as his Albany lecture. See Chrysler Corp. v. Brown, 441 U.S. 281, 306 n.37 (1979).
12. A search of Justice Rehnquist's papers revealed nothing of interest with respect to the drafting of Dames & Moore. See William H. Rehnquist Papers, Stanford University, Hoover Institute, Folder 80–2078.
13. See Dames & Moore v. Regan, 453 U.S. 654, 662 (1981); Kai Bird, *The Outlier: The Unfinished Presidency of Jimmy Carter* (New York: Crown, 2021), 490–500 (discussing the initial phase of the hostage crisis).
14. See Dames & Moore, 453 U.S. at 663–664.
15. See ibid. at 664–665.
16. See ibid. at 665–666.
17. See ibid. at 666–667; American Intern. Group, Inc. v. Islamic Republic of Iran, 657 F.2d 430, 434 (D.C. Cir. 1981). An attachment in this context was a judicially enforceable lien on, say, an Iranian bank account in the United States.
18. See American Intern. Group, 657 F.2d 430; Charles T. Main Intern. v. Khuzestan Water & Power Auth., 651 F.2d 800 (1st Cir. 1981).
19. See American Intern. Group, 657 F.2d at 439.
20. See Dames & Moore, 453 U.S. at 671–672 (quoting from the D.C. Circuit's opinion).
21. See ibid. at 670–71 (quoting from the First Circuit's opinion).
22. See American Intern. Group, 657 F.2d at 439.
23. Khuzestan, 651 F.2d at 812–813.
24. Ibid. at 814. The Court declined to recognize a general presidential power to suspend legal claims against a foreign power. See ibid.
25. See ibid. at 816 (Breyer, J., concurring).
26. Dames & Moore, 453 U.S. at 660.
27. Ibid. at 661.
28. See ibid. at 661–662.
29. Ibid. at 668.
30. Ibid. at 669. The next two quotes in the text also come from this page. It is unclear what Justice Rehnquist meant when he said "we have in the past found" the three categories useful. The Court had never cited or quoted the three Youngstown boxes. If "we" meant more than one Justice who joined Dames & Moore, then the statement could be correct.
31. See Dames & Moore, 453 U.S. at 669–674.
32. See ibid. at 674. The Court did not entertain a non-delegation challenge in Dames & Moore, perhaps because the case could be seen as involving foreign rather than domestic affairs.
33. Ibid. at 677.
34. Ibid. at 678. See ibid. at 678–679 ("At least this is so where there is no contrary indication of legislative intent and when, as here, there is a history of congressional acquiescence in conduct of the sort engaged in by the President").
35. The Court also reasoned that there was longstanding executive practice on settling claims with foreign powers such that Justice Frankfurter's test of an "unbroken practice" pursued with

congressional knowledge and acquiescence was satisfied. See ibid. at 686; see also Youngstown Sheet & Tube Co. v. Sawyer, 343 U.S. 579, 610–611 (1952) (Frankfurter, J., concurring).
36. See, e.g., Patricia Bellia, "Executive Power in *Youngstown*'s Shadow," *Constitutional Commentary* 19 (2002), 145 ("The conventional critique of the Court's decision in *Dames & Moore*... is that the Court softened the barriers between Justice Jackson's categories"); Laura A. Cisneros, "*Youngstown Sheet* to *Boumediene*: A Story of Judicial Ethos and the (Un)Fastidious," *West Virginia Law Review* 115 (2012), 614 (stating that Dames & Moore blurred the lines between the three categories).
37. See, e.g., Edward T. Swaine, "The Political Economy of Youngstown," *Southern California Law Review* 83, no. 2 (2010), 309; Laurence H. Tribe, "Transcending the *Youngstown* Triptych: A Multidimensional Reappraisal of Separation of Powers Doctrine," *Yale Law Journal Forum* 126 (2016), 93.
38. If the Court had followed Chapter 8's recommendation and declared that the executive orders raised "political questions" because they fell within Category Two, then the orders would not have been invalidated.
39. See Morrison v. Olson, 487 U.S. 654 (1988). These provisions are no longer in force.
40. See Morrison, 487 U.S. at 660–665.
41. Ibid. at 693–94 (citations omitted). Chief Justice Rehnquist's only other citation to the concurrence came in a dissent a decade later. See Minnesota v. Mille Lacs Band of Chippewa Indians, 526 U.S. 172, 215 (1999) (Rehnquist, C.J., dissenting) (quoting Category 1).
42. The Watergate special prosecutors could be fired by the President for any reason, and, indeed, Archibald Cox was fired by President Nixon.
43. See Seila Law LLC v. Consumer Financial Protection Bureau, 591 U.S. 197, 217–218 (2020) (reaffirming Morrison's holding).
44. Morrison, 487 U.S. at 709 (Scalia, J., dissenting).
45. Ibid. at 711 (Scalia, J., dissenting).
46. See Seila Law, 591 U.S. at 213 (holding that Congress could not insulate the CFPB Director from at-will presidential removal); Free Enterprise Fund v. Public Co. Accounting Oversight Bd., 561 U.S. 477, 484 (2010) (holding that multilevel for-cause protection for executive officials violates separation of powers); ibid. at 498 (rejecting arguments grounded in the Youngstown concurrence).
47. Morrison, 487 U.S. at 727 (Scalia, J., dissenting).
48. See ibid. at 727–728 (Scalia, J., dissenting); Robert H. Jackson, "The Federal Prosecutor," at https://www.justice.gov/sites/default/files/ag/legacy/2011/09/16/04-01-1940.
49. Morrison, 487 U.S. at 728 (Scalia, J., dissenting).
50. See ibid. at 728–729 (Scalia, J., dissenting); see ibid. at 729–734 (Scalia, J., dissenting) (offering other practical criticisms of the independent-counsel provisions).
51. Compare Myers v. United States, 272 U.S. 52 (1926) (upholding broad presidential authority to remove executive officials), with Humphrey's Executor v. United States, 295 U.S. 602 (1935) (upholding Congress's power to limit presidential removal authority).
52. Trump v. United States incorrectly implied that Justice Jackson placed the President's removal power only within Category Three. See Trump, 603 U.S. at 609 (citing footnote 4 of the concurrence but not footnote 3).
53. Jackson, *That Man: An Insider's Portrait of Franklin D. Roosevelt*, ed. John Q. Barrett (New York: Oxford University Press, 2003), 19.
54. The Rehnquist Papers say nothing on this question.
55. See Nomination of John G. Roberts, Jr. to be Chief Justice of the United States: Hearing Before the S. Judiciary Comm., 109th Cong. 153 (2005).
56. 552 U.S. 491 (2008).
57. Ibid. at 524.
58. See ibid. at 525–528.
59. See ibid. at 530–332. Justice Breyer's dissent instead concluded that Medellin was a Category Two case. See ibid. at 564 (Breyer, J., dissenting). For a robust criticism of this aspect of Medellin, see Michael J. Turner, "Fade to Black: The Formalization of Jackson's Youngstown Taxonomy by Hamdan and Medellin," *American University Law Review* 58, no. 3 (2009), 665–98.
60. 591 U.S. 848, 854 (2020).

61. See Trump, 603 U.S. at 605–606 and 641. Some might say that the Court focused unduly on the transient result of Trump's criminal prosecution at the expense of the principle that presidents are not above the law.
62. See ibid. at 638.
63. See ibid. at 608. The Chief Justice also replicated the concurrence's tripartite scheme by dividing presidential actions into three groups: (1) unofficial, (2) official and exclusive, and (3) official and shared with Congress. See ibid. at 606–10. Unofficial acts receive no immunity from criminal liability. See ibid. at 606.
64. See ibid. at 614–615.
65. For an excellent discussion of this topic, watch Professor Kate Shaw's 2024 Robert H. Jackson lecture at https://www.youtube.com/watch?v=KwtC3Si43QI.
66. See Zivotofsky ex rel. Zivotofsky v. Kerry, 576 U.S. 1, 62 (2015) (Roberts, C.J., dissenting). I thank Marty Lederman for first pointing this out in a blog post about Trump v. United States.
67. Trump, 603 U.S. at 638.
68. Gerald R. Ford, "Proclamation 4311, Granting a Pardon to Richard Nixon," Sept. 8, 1974, reprinted in *Gerald R. Ford: Containing the Public Messages, Speeches, and Statements of the President* (Washington, DC: Government Printing Office, 1977), vol. 1, 104.
69. See United States v. Trump, 91 F.4th 1173, 1194 (D.C. Cir. 2024) (internal citation omitted), vacated and remanded by Trump v. United States, 603 U.S. 593 (2024).
70. Trump, 603 U.S. at 609.
71. See U.S. Const., art II, § 4 ("The President, Vice President, and all civil Officers of the United States, shall be removed from Office on Impeachment for, and Conviction of, Treason, Bribery, or other high Crimes and Misdemeanors"); ibid. at art. I, § 3, cl. 7 (stating that a party convicted in an impeachment trial shall "be liable and subject to Indictment, Trial, Judgment and punishment, according to Law"); see Trump, 603 U.S. at 661–662 (Sotomayor, J, dissenting).
72. I say "dicta" because there was no treason or bribery allegation in the *Trump* case.
73. The statement can be read more narrowly to mean only crimes that are "malum in se" (in other words, actions like murder that are always and everywhere understood as crimes).
74. See Gerald Gunther, *Learned Hand: The Man and the Judge*, 2d ed. (New York: Oxford University Press, 2011), 470 (quoting Judge Hand's 1944 "Spirit of Liberty" speech).

Epilogue

1. Robert H. Jackson, *The Struggle for Judicial Supremacy: A Study of a Crisis in American Power Politics* (New York: Knopf, 1941), xv–xvi.
2. See, e.g., Agency for Int'l Dev. v. Alliance for Open Society Intern., Inc., 570 U.S. 205, 220 (2014) ("[W]e cannot improve upon what Justice Jackson wrote for the Court 70 years ago"); General Motors Corp. v. Tracy, 519 U.S. 278, 299 (1997) (quoting "Justice Jackson's now famous words" on the Commerce Clause); Texas v. Johnson, 491 U.S. 397, 415 (1989) ("Justice Jackson described one of our society's defining principles in words deserving of their frequent repetition"). When I met Justice Scalia and asked him who his favorite Justice was, his answer was Robert Jackson.
3. Chief Justice Rehnquist and Chief Justice Roberts cannot be described as originalists, though they might be called fellow travelers or sympathizers to that point of view. A more pragmatic (dare I say Jacksonian) view might be that Supreme Court nominees who praise the concurrence in a Senate confirmation hearing find that disparaging the opinion becomes more difficult after confirmation.
4. See Michael McConnell, *The President Who Would Not Be King: Executive Power Under the Constitution* (Princeton, NJ: Princeton University Press, 2020), 278; see also Georgia v. Public.Resource.Org, Inc., 590 U.S. 255, 288 n.6 (2020) (Thomas, J, dissenting) ("[S]ometimes a separate writing takes on canonical status, like Justice Jackson's concurrence regarding the executive power in *Youngstown*"). Perhaps it is just a matter of time before there is a reckoning for the contradiction between originalism and the Youngstown concurrence.
5. Consider the following hypothetical: When the Supreme Court decided two cases on affirmative action in 2023, one could have imagined Justice Elena Kagan writing an opinion that offered personal reflections on her tenure as dean of the Harvard Law School, where she surely dealt with the issue of racial preferences in admissions. Even if Justice Kagan had been inclined to do that, though, it might have been awkward in view of the fact that one of the cases involved undergraduate admissions at Harvard. Though this did not require her recusal, any discussion of her Harvard experience might have struck the wrong note.
6. This line comes from Kipling's poem "The Winners."

Bibliography

Manuscript Collections and Oral Histories

Robert H. Jackson papers, Library of Congress, Manuscript Division.

William O. Douglas papers, Library of Congress, Manuscript Division.

Reminiscences of Robert Houghwout Jackson (Harlan B. Phillips, ed., 1955), Columbia University.

Robert H. Jackson Archive, Robert H. Jackson Center, Jamestown, NY.

William H. Rehnquist papers, Hoover Institute, Stanford University.

Books and Law-Review Articles

Abebe, Daniel, and Aziz Z. Huq. "Foreign Affairs Federalism: A Revisionist Approach." *Vanderbilt Law Review* 66, no. 3 (2013): 723–794.

Ackerman, Bruce. *We the People*, vol. 2: *Transformations*. Cambridge, MA: Harvard University Press, 1998.

Ackerman, Bruce. *The Failure of the Founding Fathers: Jefferson, Marshall, and the Rise of Presidential Democracy*. Cambridge, MA: Harvard University Press, 2005.

Ackerman, Bruce. *Before the Next Attack: Preserving Civil Liberties in an Age of Terrorism*. New Haven, CT: Yale University Press, 2006.

Adler, David Gray. "The Steel Seizure Case and Inherent Presidential Power." *Constitutional Commentary* 19, no. 1 (2002): 155–213.

Amar, Akhil Reed. *America's Unwritten Constitution: The Precedents and Principles We Live By*. New York: Basic Books, 2012.

Amar, Akhil Reed. *The Law of the Land: A Grand Tour of Our Constitutional Republic*. New York: Basic Books, 2015.

Amar, Vikram David. "Indirect Effects of Direct Election: A Structural Examination of the Seventeenth Amendment." *Vanderbilt Law Review* 49, no. 6 (1996): 1347–1405.

Bagehot, Walter. *The English Constitution*. 1873; reprint, New York: Cosimo Classics, 2007.

Bahr, Elizabeth, and Josh Blackman. "Youngstown's Fourth Tier: Is There a Zone of Insight Beyond the Zone of Twilight?" *University of Memphis Law Review* 40 (2010): 541–602.

Balkin, Jack M. "The New Originalism and the Uses of History." *Fordham Law Review* 82 (2013): 641–719.

Barrett, Amy Coney. "Suspension and Delegation." *Cornell Law Review* 99 (2014): 251–326.

Barron, David J., and Martin S. Lederman. "The Commander in Chief at the Lowest Ebb—Framing The Problem, Doctrine, and Original Understanding." *Harvard Law Review* 121, no. 3 (2008): 689–804.

Bellia, Patricia L. "Executive Power in *Youngstown*'s Shadow." *Constitutional Commentary* 19 (2002): 87–154.
Bellia, Patricia L. "The Story of the Steel Seizure Case." In *Presidential Power Stories*, edited by Christopher H. Schroeder and Curtis A. Bradley, 233–285. New York: Foundation Press, 2009.
Bird, Kai. *The Outlier: The Unfinished Presidency of Jimmy Carter*. New York: Crown, 2021.
Black, Charles L., Jr. *Structure and Relationship in Constitutional Law*. Baton Rouge: Louisiana State University Press, 1969.
Blackstone, William. *Commentaries on the Laws of England*. 4 vols. 1765–1769; reprint, Chicago: University of Chicago Press, 1979.
Bobbitt, Philip. "*Youngstown*: Pages from the Book of Disquietude." *Constitutional Commentary* 19 (2002): 3–35.
Bowen, Catherine Drinker. *The Lion and the Throne: The Life and Times of Sir Edward Coke (1552–1634)*. Boston: Little, Brown, 1957.
Bradley, Curtis A. *Historical Gloss and Foreign Affairs: Constitutional Authority in Practice*. Cambridge, MA: Harvard University Press, 2024.
Brownell, Roy E., II. "The Coexistence of *United States v. Curtiss-Wright* and *Youngstown Sheet & Tube v. Sawyer* in National Security Jurisprudence." *Journal of Law & Politics* 16 (2000): 1–111.
Cannadine, David. *Mellon: An American Life*. New York: Knopf, 2006.
Caraley, Demetrios James, and Frances Penn. "Separation of Powers and Executive Privilege: The Watergate Briefs." *Political Science Quarterly* 88, no. 4 (1973): 582–654.
Caro, Robert. *Master of the Senate: The Years of Lyndon Johnson*. New York: Knopf, 2002.
Casto, William R. *Advising the President: Attorney General Robert H. Jackson and Franklin D. Roosevelt*. Lawrence: University Press of Kansas, 2018.
Chernow, Ron. *Washington: A Life*. New York: Penguin, 2010.
Church, Frank. "Ending Emergency Government." *American Bar Association Journal* 63, no. 2 (1977): 197–199.
Churchill, Winston S. *Winston S. Churchill: His Complete Speeches, 1897–1963*. 8 vols. Edited by Robert Rhodes James. New York: Bowker, 1974.
Cisneros, Laura A. "Youngstown Sheet to Boumediene: A Story of Judicial Ethos and the (Un)Fastidious Use of Language." *West Virginia Law Review* 115 (2012): 577–641.
Clausewitz, Carl Von. *On War*. Edited and translated by Michael Howard and Peter Paret. Princeton, NJ: Princeton University Press, 1984.
Coan, Andrew. *Rationing the Constitution: How Judicial Capacity Shapes Supreme Court Decision-Making*. Cambridge, MA: Harvard University Press, 2019.
Coenen, Michael, and Scott M. Sullivan. "The Elusive Zone of Twilight." *Boston College Law Review* 62, no. 3 (2021): 741–798.
Cooke, Jacob E., ed. *The Federalist*. Hanover, NH: Wesleyan University Press, 1961.
Cooper, John Milton, Jr. *Woodrow Wilson: A Biography*. New York: Knopf, 2009.
Corwin, Edward S. "The Steel Seizure Case: A Judicial Brick Without Straw." *Columbia Law Review* 53, no. 1 (1953): 53–66.

Devins, Neal, and Louis Fisher. "The Steel Seizure Case: One of a Kind?" *Constitutional Commentary* 19 (2002): 63–86.

Dudziak, Mary L. "The Gloss of War: Revisiting the Korean War's Legacy." *Michigan Law Review* 122 (2023): 149–205.

Dunn, Susan. *Roosevelt's Purge: How FDR Fought to Change the Democratic Party.* Cambridge, MA: Belknap Press, 2010.

Eichensehr, Kristen E. "The *Youngstown* Canon: Vetoed Bills and the Separation of Powers." *Duke Law Journal* 70 (2021): 1245–1320.

Ely, John Hart. "Suppose Congress Wanted a War Powers Act That Worked." *Columbia Law Review* 88, no. 7 (1988): 1379–1421.

Farrell, John A. *Richard Nixon: The Life.* New York: Doubleday, 2017.

Feldman, Noah. *Scorpions: The Battles and Triumphs of FDR's Great Supreme Court Justices.* New York: Twelve, 2010.

Flaherty, Martin S. "The Future and Past of U.S. Foreign Relations Law." *Law and Contemporary Problems* 67, no. 4 (2004): 169–193.

Ford, Gerald R. *Gerald R. Ford: Containing the Public Messages, Speeches, and Statements of the President.* 6 vols. Washington, DC: Government Printing Office, 1977.

Frohnmeyer, David B. "The Separation of Powers: An Essay on the Vitality of Separation of Powers." *Oregon Law Review* 52 (1973): 211–235.

Froomkin, David B. "The Nondelegation Doctrine and the Structure of the Executive." *Yale Journal on Regulation* 41 (2024): 60–108.

Fuller, Lon L. *Legal Fictions.* Stanford, CA: Stanford University Press, 1967.

Gage, Beverly. *G-Man: J. Edgar Hoover and the Making of the American Century.* New York: Viking, 2022.

Gerhart, Eugene C. *America's Advocate: Robert H. Jackson.* Indianapolis, IN: Bobbs-Merrill, 1958.

Gienapp, Jonathan. *The Second Creation: Fixing the American Constitution in the Founding Era.* Cambridge, MA: Belknap Press, 2018.

Goitein, Elizabeth. "The Alarming Scope of the President's Emergency Powers." *The Atlantic*, January-February 2019. https://www.theatlantic.com/magazine/archive/2019/01/presidential-emergencypowers/576418/.

Gunther, Gerald. *Cases and Materials on Constitutional Law.* 9th ed. New York: Foundation Press, 1975.

Gunther, Gerald. *Learned Hand: The Man and the Judge.* 2nd ed. New York: Oxford University Press, 2011.

Henkin, Louis. *Foreign Affairs and the US Constitution.* 2nd ed. New York: Clarendon Press, 1996.

Howard, A. E. Dick, ed. *Magna Carta: Text and Commentary.* Charlottesville: University of Virginia Press, 1965.

Hutchinson, Dennis J. *The Man Who Once Was Whizzer White: A Portrait of Justice Byron R. White.* New York: Free Press, 1998.

Hutchinson, Dennis J. "'The Achilles Heel' of the Constitution: Justice Jackson and the Japanese Exclusion Cases." *Supreme Court Review* 2002 (2002): 455–494.

"Impoundment of Funds." *Harvard Law Review* 86 (1973): 1505–1535.

Isaacson, Walter. *Kissinger: A Biography*. New York: Simon & Schuster, 1992.

Jackson, Robert H. "Founders Day Address," University of North Carolina (October 12, 1937). http//www.roberthjackson.org/wp-content/uploads/2015/01/Founders_Day_address_at_University_of_North_Carolina.pdf.

Jackson, Robert H. *The Struggle for Judicial Supremacy: A Study of a Crisis in American Power Politics*. New York: Knopf, 1941.

Jackson, Robert H. "Report to the President on the Prosecution of Axis War Criminals." *American Journal of International Law* 39 (1945): 178–190.

Jackson, Robert H. "Wartime Security and Liberty Under Law." *Buffalo Law Review* 1, no. 2 (1951): 103–117.

Jackson, Robert H. "A Presidential Legal Opinion." *Harvard Law Review* 66, no. 8 (1953): 1353–1361.

Jackson, Robert H. *The Supreme Court in the American System of Government*. Cambridge, MA: Harvard University Press, 1955.

Jackson, Robert H. *That Man: An Insider's Portrait of Franklin D. Roosevelt*. Edited and introduced by John Q. Barrett. New York: Oxford University Press, 2003.

Jaffe, Louis L. "Mr. Justice Jackson." *Harvard Law Review* 68, no. 6 (1955): 940–998.

Jefferson, Thomas. *The Life and Selected Writings of Thomas Jefferson*. Edited by Adrienne Koch and William Peden. New York: Modern Library, 1993.

Jenkins, Roy. *Churchill: A Biography*. New York: Plume, 2002.

Kagan, Elena. "Presidential Administration." *Harvard Law Review* 114, no. 8 (2001): 2245–2385.

Kalman, Laura. *FDR's Gambit: The Court Packing Fight and the Rise of Legal Liberalism*. New York: Oxford University Press, 2022.

Katyal, Neal. "*Hamdan v. Rumsfeld*: The Legal Academy Goes to Practice." *Harvard Law Review* 120 (2006): 65–123.

Katyal, Neal Kumar, and Richard Caplan. "The Surprisingly Stronger Case for the Legality of the NSA Surveillance Program: The FDR Precedent." *Stanford Law Review* 60 (2008): 1024–1077.

Kipling, Rudyard. *The Collected Poems of Rudyard Kipling*. Edited by R. T. Jones. Ware, UK: Wordsworth, 1994.

Koh, Harold Hongju. *The National Security Constitution: Sharing Power After the Iran-Contra Affair*. New Haven, CT: Yale University Press, 1990.

Kurland, Philip B. "Justice Robert H. Jackson—Impact on Civil Rights and Civil Liberties: The David C. Baum Memorial Lecture." *University of Illinois Law Review* 1977: 551–576.

Landau, David. "Rethinking the Federal Emergency Powers Regime." *Ohio State Law Journal* 84 (2023): 603–676.

Larson, Carlton F. W. *On Treason: A Citizen's Guide to the Law*. New York: HarperCollins, 2020.

Leib, Ethan J., Jed Handelsman Shugerman, and Andrew Kent. "Faithful Execution and Article II." *Harvard Law Review* 132 (2019): 2111–2192.

Levinson, Daryl J., and Richard H. Pildes. "Separation of Parties, Not Powers." *Harvard Law Review* 119, no. 8 (2006): 2311–2386.

Levinson, Sanford. "The Rhetoric of the Judicial Opinion." In *Law's Stories: Narrative and Rhetoric in the Law*, edited by Peter Brooks and Paul Gewirtz, 187–205. New Haven, CT: Yale University Press, 1996.

Levinson, Sanford. "Speaking in the Name of the Law: Some Reflections on Professional Responsibility and Judicial Accountability." *University of St. Thomas Law Journal* 1, no. 1 (2003): 447–463.

Magliocca, Gerard N. "The Gold Clause Cases and Constitutional Necessity." *Florida Law Review* 64, no. 5 (2012): 1243–1278.

Magliocca, Gerard N. *American Founding Son: John Bingham and the Invention of the Fourteenth Amendment*. New York: NYU Press, 2013.

Magliocca, Gerard. *Washington's Heir: The Life of Justice Bushrod Washington*. New York: Oxford University Press, 2022.

Magliocca, Gerard N. "Robert Jackson's Non-Delegation Doctrine." *Green Bag 2d* 25 (2022): 95–107.

Magliocca, Gerard N. "'Not a Lawyer's Contract': Reflections on FDR's Constitution Day Address." *Journal of American Constitutional History* 1, Winter (2023): 43–82.

Marcus, Maeva. *Truman and the Steel Seizure Case: The Limits of Presidential Power*. Durham, NC: Duke University Press, 1994.

Martin, George. *CCB: The Life and Century of Charles C. Burlingham, New York's First Citizen, 1858–1959*. New York: Hill and Wang, 2005.

McConnell, Michael W. *The President Who Would Not Be King: Executive Power Under the Constitution*. Princeton, NJ: Princeton University Press, 2020.

McCormick, Anne O'Hare. "The Predestined Leader of the Free World." *New York Times* (Nov. 9, 1952).

McCullough, David. *Truman*. New York: Simon & Schuster, 1992.

Meltzer, Bernard D. "Robert H. Jackson: Nuremberg's Architect and Advocate." *Albany Law Review* 68 (2004): 55–65.

Mortenson, Julian Davis. "The Executive Power Clause." *University of Pennsylvania Law Review* 168 (2020): 1269–1367.

Neustadt, Richard E. *Presidential Power: The Politics of Leadership*. New York: Wiley, 1960.

Newman, Roger K. *Hugo Black: A Biography*. New York: Pantheon, 1994.

Newton, Jim. *Justice For All: Earl Warren and the Nation He Made*. New York: Riverhead, 2006.

O'Brian, David M. *Justice Robert H. Jackson's Unpublished Opinion in* Brown v. Board: *Conflict, Compromise, and Constitutional Interpretation*. Lawrence: University Press of Kansas, 2017.

Paulsen, Michael Stokes. "Youngstown Goes to War." *Constitutional Commentary* 19, no. 1 (2002): 215–259.

Pincus, Steve. *1688: The First Modern Revolution*. New Haven, CT: Yale University Press, 2009.

Posner, Eric, and Adrian Vermeule. "Inside Or Outside the System?" *University of Chicago Law Review* 80, no. 4 (2013): 1743–1797.

Posner, Richard A. *Cardozo: A Study in Reputation.* Chicago: University of Chicago Press, 1990.

Prakesh, Saikrishna B. "Deciphering the Commander-in-Chief Clause." *Yale Law Journal* 133, no. 1 (2023): 1–98.

Primus, Richard A. "Canon, Anti-Canon, and Judicial Dissent." *Duke Law Journal* 48 (1998): 243–303.

Primus, Richard A. "Herein of 'Herein Granted': Why Article I's Vesting Clause Does Not Support the Doctrine of Enumerated Powers." *Constitutional Commentary* 35, no. 3 (2020): 301–344.

Rakove, Jack N. *Original Meanings: Politics and Ideas in the Making of the Constitution.* New York: Knopf, 1996.

Rehnquist, William H. "Robert H. Jackson: A Perspective Twenty-Five Years Later." *Albany Law Review* 44 (1980): 533–541.

Rehnquist, William H. "Constitutional Law and Public Opinion." *Suffolk University Law Review* 20 (1986): 751–769.

Rehnquist, William H. *The Supreme Court.* New York: Vintage, 2002.

Richardson, James D., ed. *A Compilation of the Messages and Papers of the Presidents.* 20 vols. New York: Bureau of National Literature, 1922.

Roisman, Shalev. "Presidential Law." *Minnesota Law Review* 105 (2021): 1269–1343.

Roosevelt, Franklin D. *The Public Papers and Addresses of Franklin D. Roosevelt.* Edited by Samuel L. Rosenman. 13 vols. New York: Harper and Brothers, 1950.

Rossiter, Clinton. *Constitutional Dictatorship: Crisis Government in the Modern Democracies.* Princeton, NJ: Princeton University Press, 1948.

Rossiter, Clinton. *The Supreme Court and the Commander in Chief.* Ithaca, NY: Cornell University Press, 1951.

Rostow, Eugene V. "Great Cases Make Bad Law: The War Powers Act." *Texas Law Review* 50, no. 5 (1972): 833–900.

Safire, William, ed. *Lend Me Your Ears: Great Speeches in History.* 2nd ed. New York: Norton, 2004.

Scheppele, Kim Lane. "Constitutional Coups and Judicial Review: How Transnational Institutions Can Strengthen Peak Court at Times of Crisis (with Special Reference to Hungary)." *Transnational Law and Contemporary Problems* 23 (2014): 51–117.

Schlesinger, Arthur M., Jr. *The Imperial Presidency.* Boston: Houghton Mifflin, 1973; reprinted with a new epilogue, 1989.

Schmidt, Patrick. "'The Dilemma to a Free People': Justice Robert Jackson, Walter Bagehot, and the Creation of a Conservative Jurisprudence." *Law and History Review* 20, no. 3 (2002): 517–539.

Schwoerer, Lois G. *The Declaration of Rights, 1689.* Baltimore: Johns Hopkins University Press, 1981.

Silber, Norman I. *Outside In: The Oral History of Guido Calabresi.* 2 vols. New York: Oxford University Press, 2023.

Skowronek, Stephen. *The Politics Presidents Make: Leadership from John Adams to Bill Clinton.* Cambridge, MA: Harvard University Press, 1997.

Snyder, Brad. *Democratic Justice: Felix Frankfurter, the Supreme Court, and the Making of the Liberal Establishment.* New York: Norton, 2022.

Snyder, Brad, and John Q. Barrett. "Rehnquist's Missing Letter: A Former Law Clerk's 1955 Thoughts on Justice Jackson and *Brown*." *Boston College Law Review* 53 (2012): 631–660.

Steilen, Matthew. "Life and Afterlife in the *Steel Seizure Case*." *Buffalo Law Review* 70, no. 2 (2022): 875–911.

Stern, Seth, and Stephen Wermiel. *Justice Brennan: Liberal Champion.* New York: Houghton Mifflin Harcourt, 2010.

Swaine, Edward T. "The Political Economy of *Youngstown*." *Southern California Law Review* 83, no. 2 (2010): 263–339.

Taylor, Telford. *The Anatomy of the Nuremberg Trials: A Personal Memoir.* New York: Knopf, 1992.

Thomas, Evan. *Robert Kennedy: His Life.* New York: Simon & Schuster, 2000.

Thomas, Evan. *Being Nixon: A Man Divided.* New York: Random House, 2015.

Tillman, Seth Barrett. "*Ex Parte Merryman*: Myth, History, and Scholarship." *Military Law Review* 224 (2016): 481–540.

Tribe, Laurence H. "Transcending the *Youngstown* Triptych: A Multidimensional Reappraisal of Separation of Powers Doctrine." *Yale Law Journal Forum* 126 (2016): 86–106.

Truman, Harry S. *Memoirs, Vol. 2: Years of Trial and Hope.* Garden City, NY: Doubleday, 1956.

Turner, Michael J. "Fade to Black: The Formalization of Jackson's Youngstown Taxonomy by Hamdan and Medellin." *American University Law Review* 58 (2009): 665–698.

Tyler, Amanda L. *Habeas Corpus in Wartime: From the Tower of London to Guantanamo Bay.* New York: Oxford University Press, 2017.

Tyler, Amanda L. "Judicial Review in Times of Emergency: From the Founding Through the COVID-19 Pandemic." *Virginia Law Review* 109, no. 3 (2023): 489–594.

Urofsky, Melvin I. *Louis D. Brandeis: A Life.* New York: Pantheon, 2009.

Vladeck, Stephen I. "Foreign Affairs Originalism in *Youngstown*'s Shadow." *Saint Louis University Law Journal* 53, no. 1 (2008): 29–38.

Warren, Earl. "The Bill of Rights and the Military." *New York University Law Review* 37 (1962): 181–203.

Weber, Max. *The Theory of Social and Economic Organization.* Translated by A. M. Henderson and Talcott Parsons. London: Free Press, 1947.

White, Adam J. "Justice Jackson's Draft Opinions in the Steel Seizure Cases." *Albany Law Review* 69, no. 4 (2006): 1107–1133.

Wills, Garry. *Bomb Power: The Modern Presidency and the National Security State.* New York: Penguin Press, 2010.

Wilson, Woodrow. *Congressional Government: A Study in American Politics.* 1885; reprint, with a Preface by Walter Lippmann, New York: Meridian, 1956.

Wright, Charles Alan. "My Favorite Opinion—The Second Flag-Salute Case." *Texas Law Review* 74 (1996): 1297–1300.

Cases and Statutes

Act Declaring the Rights and Liberties of the Subject and Settling the Succession of the Crown, 1689, 1 W. and M., Sess. 2, ch. 2.
Adamson v. California, 332 U.S. 46 (1947).
Agency for Int'l Dev. V. Alliance for Open Society Intern., Inc., 570 U.S. 205 (2014).
A.L.A. Schechter Poultry v. United States, 295 U.S. 495 (1935).
American Communications Ass'n, C.I.O. v. Douds, 339 U.S. 382 (1950).
American Ins. Ass'n v. Garamendi, 539 U.S. 396 (2003).
American Intern. Group, Inc. v. Islamic Republic of Iran, 657 F.2d 430 (D.C. Cir. 1981).
Antiquities Act of 1906, Pub. L. 59-209, 34 Stat. 225.
Arizona v. Mayorkas, 143 S. Ct. 1312 (2023).
Atomic Energy Act of 1946, Pub. L. 79-585, 60 Stat. 755.
Austin v. U.S. Navy Seals 1-16, 142 S. Ct. 1301 (2022).
Authorization For Use of Military Force, Pub. L. 107-40, 115 Stat. 224 (2001).
Barquero v. United States, 18 F.3d 1311 (5th Cir. 1994).
Biden v. Nebraska, 600 U.S. 477 (2023).
Blakely v. Washington, 542 U.S. 296 (2004).
Boumediene v. Bush, 553 U.S. 723 (2008).
Bowsher v. Synar, 478 U.S. 714 (1986).
Briehl v. Dulles, 248 F.2d 561 (D.C. Cir. 1957), *rev'd by* Kent v. Dulles, 357 U.S. 116 (1958).
Brown v. Allen, 344 U.S. 443 (1953).
Brown v. United States, 12 U.S. (8 Cranch) 110 (1814).
Buck v. Bell, 274 U.S. 200 (1927).
Buckley v. Valeo, 424 U.S. 1 (1976).
Cameron v. Beshear, 628 S.W. 3d 61 (Ky. 2021).
Cameron v. United States, 252 U.S. 450 (1920).
Casey v. Lamont, 338 Conn. 479 (2021).
Chas. T. Main Int'l, Inc. v. Khuzestan Water & Power Auth., 651 F.2d 800 (1st Cir. 1981).
Chrysler Corp. v. Brown, 441 U.S. 281 (1979).
Civil Rights Cases, 109 U.S. 3 (1883).
Clinton v. City of New York, 524 U.S. 417 (1998).
Clinton v. Jones, 520 U.S. 681 (1997).
Congressional Budget and Impoundment Control Act of 1974, Pub. 93-344, 88 Stat. 297.
Contractors Ass'n of Eastern PA. v. Secretary of Labor, 442 F.2d 159 (3d Cir. 1971).
Craig v. Harney, 331 U.S. 367 (1947).
Cramer v. United States, 325 U.S. 1 (1945).
Currin v. Wallace, 306 U.S. 1 (1939).
Dames & Moore v. Regan, 453 U.S. 654 (1981).
Defense Production Act of 1950, Pub. L. 81-774, 64 Stat. 799.
Dennis v. United States, 341 U.S. 494 (1950).
Desrosiers v. Governor, 486 Mass. 369 (2020).
Edwards v. California, 314 U.S. 160 (1941).
Ex Parte Endo, 323 U.S. 283 (1944).
Ex Parte Merryman, 17 F. Cas. 144 (C.C.D. Md. 1861) (No. 9,487).

Ex Parte Milligan, 71 U.S. (4 Wall.) 2 (1866).
Ex Parte Vallandigham, 68 U.S. (1 Wall.) 243 (1864).
Everson v. Board of Ed. of Ewing Tp., 330 U.S. 1 (1947).
Fahee v. Malonee, 332 U.S. 245 (1947).
Foreign Intelligence Surveillance Act, Pub L. 95-511, 92 Stat. 1783 (1978).
Free Enterprise Fund v. Public Co. Accounting Oversight Bd., 561 U.S. 477 (2010).
General Motors Corp. v. Tracy, 519 U.S. 278 (1997).
Georgia v. Public.Resource.Org., Inc., 590 U.S. 255 (2020).
Goodwin v. United States, 10 F. Cas. 625 (C.C.D. Pa. 1811) (No. 5,554).
Granholm v. Heald, 544 U.S. 460 (2005).
Grisham v. Romero, 483 P.3d 545 (N.M. 2021).
Griswold v. Connecticut, 381 U.S. 479 (1965).
Gundy v. United States, 588 U.S. 128 (2019).
Hamdan v. Rumsfeld, 548 U.S. 557 (2006).
Hirabayashi v. United States, 320 U.S. 81 (1943).
Holmes v. United States, 391 U.S. 936 (1968).
Humphrey's Executor v. United States, 295 U.S. 602 (1935).
Indigenous Environmental Network v. Trump, 428 F. Supp. 3d 296 (D. Mont. 2019).
In Re Certified Questions, 958 N.W. 2d 1, 506 Mich. 332 (2020).
In Re Debs, 158 U.S. 564 (1895).
In Re Subpoena to Nixon, 360 F. Supp. 1 (D.D.C. 1973).
INS v. Chadha, 462 U.S. 919 (1983).
Jacobellis v. Ohio, 378 U.S. 184 (1964).
Jacobson v. Massachusetts, 197 U.S. 11 (1905).
Korematsu v. United States, 323 U.S. 214 (1944).
Lawrence v. Texas, 539 U.S. 558, 605 (2003).
Lend–Lease Act, Pub. L. 77-11, 55 Stat. 32 (1941).
Lochner v. New York, 198 U.S. 45 (1905).
Loving v. United States, 517 U.S. 478 (1996).
Massachusetts v. Laird, 451 F.2d 26 (1st Cir. 1971).
Maxwell v. Dow, 176 U.S. 581 (1900).
McGrath v. Kristinsen, 340 U.S. 162 (1950).
M'Culloch v. Maryland, 17 U.S. (4 Wheat.) 316 (1819).
Medellín v. Texas, 552 U.S. 491 (2008).
Metropolitan Washington Airports Auth. v. Citizens for Abatement of Aircraft Noise, Inc., 501 U.S. 252 (1991).
Michelson v. United States, 335 U.S. 469 (1948).
Minnesota v. Mille Lacs Band of Chippewa Indians, 526 U.S. 172 (1999).
Mistretta v. United States, 488 U.S. 361 (1989).
Moragne v. States Marine Lines, Inc., 398 U.S. 375 (1970).
Morrison v. Olson, 487 U.S. 654 (1988).
Myers v. United States, 272 U.S. 52 (1926).
Nardone v. United States, 308 U.S. 338 (1939).
National Emergencies Act, Pub. L. No. 94-112, 90 Stat. 1255 (1976).

National Security Act of 1947, Pub. L. 80-2534, 61 Stat. 495.
Neutrality Act of 1937, ch. 146, 50 Stat. 121.
New York Times Co. v. United States, 403 U.S. 713 (1971).
Nixon v. Administration of Gen. Servs., 433 U.S. 425 (1977).
Nixon v. Fitzgerald, 457 U.S. 731 (1982).
Nixon v. Sirica, 487 F.2d 700 (D.C. Cir. 1973).
Ogden v. Saunders, 25 U.S. (12 Wheat.) 213 (1827).
Old Dominion Branch No. 496, Nat'l Ass'n of Letter Carriers, AFL-CIO v. Austin, 418 U.S. 264 (1974).
Panama Refining Company v. Ryan, 295 U.S. 388 (1935).
Perry v. United States, 294 U.S. 330 (1935).
Planned Parenthood of Southeastern Pa v. Casey, 505 U.S. 833, *overruled by* Dobbs v. Jackson Women's Health Ass'n, 597 U.S. 215 (2022).
Plessy v. Ferguson, 163 U.S. 537 (1896).
Posse Comitatus Act, Pub. L. 45-263, 20 Stat. 152 (1878).
Printz v. United States 521 U.S. 898 (1997).
Railway Express Agency v. New York, 336 U.S. 106 (1949).
Rucho v. Common Cause, 588 U.S. 684 (2019).
Seila Law LLC v. Consumer Financial Protection Bureau, 591 U.S. 197 (2020).
Select Draft Law Cases, 245 U.S. 366 (1918).
Selective Service Act of 1948, Pub. L. 80-759, 62 Stat. 625.
Shaughnessy v. United States *ex rel.* Mezei, 345 U.S. 206 (1953).
Slaughter-House Cases, 83 U.S. (16 Wall.) 36 (1873).
Taft-Hartley Act, Pub. L. 80-101, 61 Stat. 136 (1947).
Terminiello v. City of Chicago, 337 U.S. 1 (1949).
Texas v. Johnson, 491 U.S. 397 (1989).
Trop v. Dulles, 356 U.S. 86 (1958).
Trump v. Hawaii, 585 U.S. 667 (2018).
Trump v. Mazars USA, LLP, 591 U.S. 848 (2020).
Trump v. Vance, 591 U.S. 786 (2020).
United States v. Curtiss-Wright, 299 U.S. 304 (1936).
United States v. E. C. Knight, 156 U.S. 1 (1895).
United States v. Munoz-Flores, 495 U.S. 385 (1990).
United States v. Nixon, 418 U.S. 683 (1974).
United States v. Rahimi, 602 U.S. 680 (2024).
United States v. Trump, 91 F.4th 1173 (D.C. Cir. 2024), *vacated and remanded by* Trump v. United States, 603 U.S. 593 (2024)
United States v. Western Union Telegraph Co., 272 F. 311 (S.D.N.Y 1921).
United States v. Windsor, 570 U.S. 744, 769 (2013).
War Powers Act, Pub. L. 93-148, 87 Stat. 555 (1973).
Wellness Intern. Network, Ltd. v. Sharif, 575 U.S. 665 (2015).
West Virginia State Bd. of Educ. v. Barnette, 319 U.S. 624 (1943).
Wickard v. Filburn, 317 U.S. 111 (1942).
Wisconsin Legislature v. Palm, 391 Wisc. 2d 497 (2020).

Woods v. Cloyd W. Miller Co., 333 U.S. 138 (1948).
Youngstown Steel & Tube Co. v. Sawyer, 103 F. Supp. 569 (D.D.C. 1952), *affirmed by* Youngstown Sheet & Steel Tube Co. v. Sawyer, 343 U.S. 579.
Zitovsky *ex rel.* Zitovsky v. Clinton, 566 U.S. 189 (2012).
Zitovsky *ex rel.* Zitovsky v. Kerry, 576 U.S. 1 (2015).

Index

For the benefit of digital users, indexed terms that span two pages (e.g., 52–53) may, on occasion, appear on only one of those pages.

Tables, figures, and boxes are indicated by an italic *t*, *f*, or *b*.

www.ingramcontent.com/pod-product-compliance
Ingram Content Group UK Ltd.
Pitfield, Milton Keynes, MK11 3LW, UK
UKHW021137160926
475595UK00024B/187/J

9 780197 768532